In Search of My America is a searing account of the rigor and drama of pursuing a life of letters. Jid Lee's voice is gripping and honest, and her story is a forceful rendering of a range of passions -- intellectual and embodied -- grounded in the politics and pain of national belonging.

– Josephine Nock-Hee Park, author of *Apparitions of Asia: Modernist Form and Asian American Poetics*

***

An unsparing, brutally honest memoir about a Korean immigrant woman making her way through a world stacked against her. She tells the unadorned truth about her life in America, no matter how beautiful or ugly. She writes a book about how to become an American, how to embrace America's merits and reject its flaws.

One can see that her love for America is truthful because it has been repeatedly tested by the threat of hate. She maintains an intensity of focus attuned to the vitality of moments in frank, direct prose. It is a raw, unfiltered meditation on life robustly lived, regardless of the challenges that conspire against her.

– Joseph Jeon, author of *Racial Things, Racial Forms: Objecthood in Avant-Garde Asian American Poetry*

***

Jid Lee arrived in the United States at age 24, speaking little English, and rose to become a tenured professor in English at an American university. Her memoir, *In Search of My America*, is her story of how she made her dreams a reality, and her love for the "husband country" where she made her home. The tales it recounts relate a series of inconvenient but important truths for us as white Americans to absorb about the experience of Asian Americans, and the day-to-day unexamined assumptions and racial and gender stereotyping that they are forced to deal with in this country.

– Greg Robinson, author of *The Unsung Great: Stories of Extraordinary Japanese Americans*

***

American idealism always preaches a good game, but Lee discovers that it still refuses to acknowledge the systematic racial prejudice permanently baked into the culture. . . This starkly honest memoir is an insightful, and at times, painful journey of one very uncompromising woman.

– Bill Drucker, *Korean Quarterly*

Jid Lee is the author of *To Kill a Tiger: A Memoir of Korea,* winner of a ForeWord Book of the Year Award and an Indie Book Award in 2011. *To Kill a Tiger* has been and is being taught as a primary textbook at several universities and colleges in America. Lee graduated from Korea University with a BA in English in 1979, received her Master's in English from SUNY Albany in 1982 and her PhD in English from the University of Kansas in 1994. She is an associate professor of English at Middle Tennessee State University.

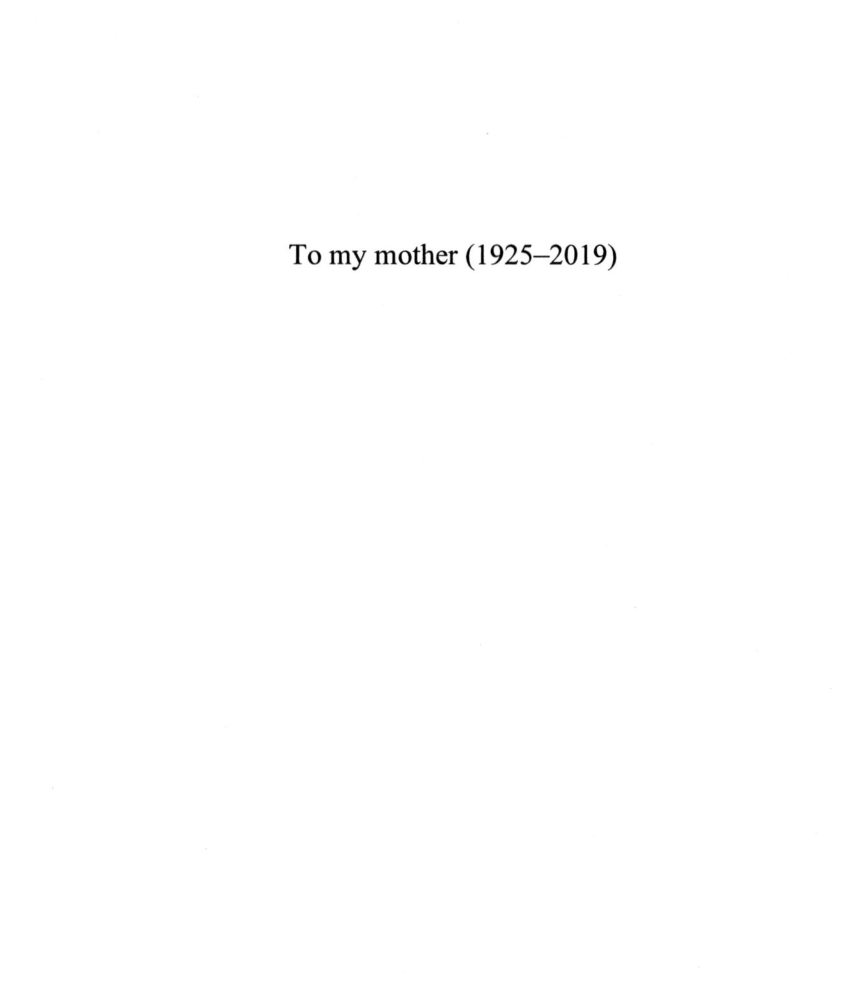

To my mother (1925–2019)

Jid Lee

In Search of My America

Austin Macauley Publishers™
London • Cambridge • New York • Sharjah

All of the events in this memoir are true to the best of the author's memory and the narrative sequence and content the author had to modify in order to be faithful to the integrity of the book. The views expressed in this memoir are solely those of the author.

Ordering Information
Quantity sales: Special discounts are available on quantity purchases by corporations, associations, and others. For details, contact the publisher at the address below.

Publisher's Cataloging-in-Publication data
Lee, Jid
In Search of My America

ISBN 9798886935608 (Paperback)
ISBN 9798886935615 (ePub e-book)

Library of Congress Control Number: 2023918626

www.austinmacauley.com/us

First Published 2024
Austin Macauley Publishers LLC
40 Wall Street, 33rd Floor, Suite 3302
New York, NY 10005
USA

mail-usa@austinmacauley.com
+1 (646) 5125767

My agent, Ken Atchity, saved my life by picking up the book, and his co-partner, Yasemin Isil, helped him to save my life by finding Austin Macauley. My friends at Austin Macauley, Kage Amani and Jessica Bosak, graciously followed suit. My friends, Barry Lamb, Inhwa Lee, Sylvie Grignard, Duane Coon, Kathy Kirkman, Michele Balliet, Guy and Becky Goff, Mr. and Mrs. Yangsoo Kim, Kirsten West, Candie Moonshower, Tony Khim, Peggy Swann, and Steve Severn, inspired me. Finally, I owe much to my cat, Jisan.

Table of Contents

Preface: The Banality of Racism

In Search of My America is much more than an exploration of race relations. It is a record of my life in America and how I lived with myself and others in a foreign country. It is about the mask I had to wear and how the mask inevitably became part of my true face. Far from a book with politically correct statements, it is about the human condition that forces us to engage in a delicate dance of deception and honesty. With honesty, I describe a range of issues, including my process of Americanization, my loneliness as an expatriate, my endeavors to reconcile the conflicting demands of human sexuality and intellect, my efforts to observe myself from an objective perspective, and my attempts to build bridges between different worlds. I weave a giant piece of embroidery with all these components, and to have them shine against a colorful background, I set them against a series of tales I created from Korean myths, folklore, and legends. In the end, *In Search of My America* is about the complexities of human nature.

In Search of My America is about issues, not settling personal scores. I expose the individuals who were—and still are—dear to me only to tell the truth: that racism is a force deeply ingrained in one's subconscious. From what I have observed, I can with a high degree of confidence declare that racism is not a nefarious, deliberately committed evil as we are trained to believe. Having personally experienced racism in the hands of some incredibly conscientious individuals who devoted their entire lives to promoting racial justice, I am convinced that racism has the power to rise to the surface at any given moment. It is a force that even the most extraordinary minds aren't entirely free from. For instance, FDR, one of the greatest leaders of the modern world, interred 120,000 Japanese Americans during World War II. Because people recognize the ubiquitous presence of racism, history has not and probably will not downgrade his achievements because of this racist act.

Hannah Arendt coined the term, the "banality of evil," to describe the amorphous and ambiguous nature of evil. I would like to propose the phrase, the "banality of racism," to explain the all-pervasive impact of racism that invades the innermost recesses of the human mind. When unchecked and unchallenged, this underlying force spreads like a virus. It becomes a plague that can infect anyone and everyone. Individual differences, which we Americans love to emphasize and which I do not at all underestimate, determine who is most and least susceptible. Those with a strong immune system of high moral standards have a lower risk factor, while those with a weaker immune system become infected to a severe degree.

I am proud of my former mentors and friends in Kansas who, through their own honest self-analyses, grew to understand the banality of racism. Recognizing how deeply infected they were by the evil, they immediately changed their ways. In the atonements they made for those individuals they interacted with, I could see how fast and far they traveled in a short time. In their progress, I see hope for the United States. Unless we—all of us Americans—acknowledge the truth that racism is like the air we breathe, that it is invisible and all permeating, we will merely continue to recite what sounds politically correct without addressing the issue at its core.

I do not use the three words that matter to me the most—honesty, forgiveness, and love—lightly. Because I know and admit that I, too, may be guilty of the banality of racism, and because I, too, would wish to be forgiven if I made the same mistake of showing it, I must practice what I preach. If my theory comes without practice, I would have no right to hope I would be forgiven and loved by those whom I forgive and love. Having also used the laughable cliché, "I'm not prejudiced, but…" I now prefer to say, "I *am* prejudiced and therefore I am human." Being able to make confessions such as this brings us closer to the goal of creating a country with less paranoia about racism. It would lead us one step toward building a nation in which the word *race* would stop carrying such a terrifying dimension. Because we define racism as some sort of nefarious evil, not as an ingrained human force, we end up condemning it to the extent that we deny our very humanness.

Nothing would be further from my intentions than condoning racism. It is precisely because I refuse to condone racism that I ask that we confront it as part of what lies within us. What I call the banality of racism is what lives in our subconscious most of the time rather than in the realm of our consciousness that we can plainly see. In order to construct a country that transcends racism, we need to bring what is in our subconscious into our conscious, accept it, and try to change it. When we can make our subconscious conscious, it will be easier for us to be honest, to forgive and love ourselves and others. It will be easier for us to practice what we preach. We will become more fully human, less terrified by the word *race*, less repressed by the need to hide our banality of racism.

Because we define racism as an irrational non-human force, we are forced to hide behind a thin transparent mask through which we can see our true faces when we are fully honest. It is this unnatural definition of racism that partly made it possible for Donald Trump, the outspoken bigot who has been trying to normalize racism, to be elected president of the United States. Instead of treating racism as a natural product of our humanness, and instead of understanding the banality of racism, many of my fellow Americans are bent on denouncing racism as if it were an "inhuman" evil. By eliminating the "human" dimension from the issue of racism, we make the error of defining racism as the monopoly of evil people deprived of humanity, and by doing that, we silently ostracize our fellow Americans who make the honest mistake of showing their racism. We brand them as being evil because they don't bother to repress their racism by putting on the mask we put on. By self-righteously assuming that we are free from what lies in their conscious and subconscious, we create the deplorable us-them division, and by doing so, we end up increasing the degree of their anger and frustration. We drive them to feel they are a breed far less educated and advanced than we, which drives them further into hiding. No wonder they began to come out in droves when Donald Trump so fearlessly manifested what lies lurking in their very "human" minds! The dam we—and they—built together broke, and naturally, they feel validated and emboldened. Once we face the fact that we, too, might be as repressed as they are, having to maintain the tenuous mask, the mask that makes us *seem* un-racist, we will be able to realize that the biggest and probably only difference between them and us is that they show their true faces and that we don't.

Unless we can make our subconscious conscious, we would hardly be better than they. Unless we can be as honest and brave as my former mentors and friends in Kansas, who admitted the banality of racism in themselves and tried to make atonements for those they had wronged, we will continue to walk on the treadmill of self-ignorance and denial. We will do nothing but ask the same old question that has been asked a million times: "Does evil come from the inside or the outside?" We wouldn't be able to accept the simple answer Shakespeare gave us in *Macbeth*: The witches come from within Macbeth, meaning the evil in the story is manifested from within himself, as well as his wife.

When I claim to love my former mentors and friends in Kansas, I mean it. To me, the only true love is love that conquered the threat of hate, and having conquered the threat of hate toward them, I can safely say I love them. Likewise, I can say without hypocrisy that I came to love this country truthfully, having survived the seduction of hate. I can sincerely call it *my* country because my love for it has been tested – because it is not an untested love that one buys without question. What we call American exceptionalism is the American ability to accept and apply our fellow citizens' fearless criticism of our country, and being one of these fearless citizens, I must be an American practicing the theory of American exceptionalism. Having left Korea, my motherland, to live in America, I call America my husband country. As I wouldn't spare harsh words to criticize my motherland for her own good, I don't hesitate to criticize my husband country because I want to help make it better. I don't mince my words to tell the defects of the American social system because I want to help improve it. I don't shy away from suggesting solutions to the problems because I want to help fix them. Whenever a fellow American says, "We created a system that's better than any other country's," I retort with my usual patriotism, "Our standard should be higher than that. If we're satisfied with being better than other countries, that means our standard is fairly low." As I criticize America because I am a patriotic American, I criticize my former mentors and friends in Kansas because I am a lover of Kansas. Kansas, after all, is the home where the dreams of my America were formed.

I know it is unthinkable for anyone to admit they are racist. It is the same for me as well. But when it becomes thinkable because we recognize and acknowledge the banality of racism within us, we'll be able to construct a more open, honest country where the word *race* will no longer carry such an inhuman dimension.

In an attempt to acknowledge the banality of racism within myself, and in an effort to eliminate it from within myself, I have written Chapter One of this memoir, "I Can See My Face without a Mirror." As is painfully obvious, I am unable to see my face without a mirror. Even as I try to see it without a mirror, I find myself endlessly interrupted by the memory of my reflection. I project what I see when I look in the mirror into my imagination, describing the features in my visual memory as if my memory were born of a sense unrelated to my eyes. The effort to figure out what I receive from the touch of my fingers doesn't yield anything different from what my eyes perceive. Nevertheless, I try, hoping that my effort to transcend my visual preconceptions will eventually bring me to a mental state in which I can at least stay aware that my eyes are capable of deceiving me. As vain as it may be, such an effort helps me question the visual preconceptions I carry with myself. It encourages me to keep in mind how important it is to go beyond the color of one's skin – to go beyond what my eyes tell me about a person, consciously and subconsciously. I am convinced that I would be more able to see the person in my mind's eye, regardless of their race seen by my physical eyes.

Author's Note on Authenticity

Although most of the large events in the book are true, I altered the chronology and contents of some incidents to accommodate narrative flow. Since I had to depend on my memory, which at times is inevitably faulty, there might be discrepancies between what actually happened and what I remember, between the actual words exchanged with the people and the words I remember. My retrospective reinterpretations of the incidents and events, therefore, might be different from those of the individuals described in the book, and this is why I had to change their names. To fill the gap, I also had to invent some fictional details.

In most of the large events, I am almost—although not entirely—certain that my memory is reliable, but in the speculations, I offer about the individuals I worked and lived with closely, I do not claim accuracy. The details of the emotional and intellectual lives of the individuals I came into contact with are largely products of my own observation.

Chapter 1
I Can See My Face without a Mirror

I touch my face in the mirror of my mind. With closed eyes, I sit and face a blank wall, my legs folded on the floor. Lifting my jaw slightly, I pinch my chin and spread my fingers along my cheek, sloping up toward my earlobe. The outline of the cheek, caught in the fully stretched fingers, is round, without prominence. Good! According to Asian face reading, a person with a sharp, prominent chin will have many hardships and pain and, worst of all, a life looked down upon by society. Women with such a jaw let their passion override their reason and eventually destroy themselves. I know a Korean woman whose jaw was as pointed as the sheath of a dagger. She ended up as the concubine of an old rich entrepreneur who bought her a secret house in the heart of downtown Seoul. She was eventually found out by the man's wife and dragged out of a tryst into a dark alley on one cold night and kicked around like a piece of trash by the wife's hired muscle. Her face was slashed in long, deep strokes by their Swiss knives, her mouth muzzled by torn cotton tights and her hands cuffed by ropes behind her back. When she was found the next morning, her eyes were wide-open in terror and shame, gazing blankly into the air.

I face the white wall and imagine her eyes. With closed eyes, I touch the soft, silky skin on my cheeks and let my fingers slide over it like long, thin skeins of nylon thread. My little fingers go over the low hills of my nose and push them down like a sponge. A typical Mongolian nose! My nostrils are so small that the tip of a finger can cover them entirely and the bridge of my nose is so low that I can grab the whole of it in one pinch. I let out another sigh of relief. A tiny nose means I am not likely to have a rough life. My husband, if I marry, won't die young or abandon me with a hoard of children. Nor will I be a lonely career woman who works her life away with no husband or children.

I open my eyes and see the dark scratches my books have made on the wall. After thirty-eight years in America, I should be used to working at a desk with a chair, but I prefer to sit on the floor, at a low table that comes up to right below my chest. The books leaning on the wall are my best and only friends, and they make frequent trips from their spots to my hands and mind. According to my nose bridge, I am meant to have an easy life with a kind, well-providing husband and happy, smiling children. But all I have is books, plants, a computer, a car to get to the lake on the edge of town, and two long-haired black-and-white cats. I'm living a life reserved for a woman with a nose shaped like the Empire State Building.

Laughing, I close my eyes and my fingers locate the source of my stubborn character. From what I have heard, a woman with such high cheekbones is an anomaly. She does not seek happiness but something else that most people cannot understand. I do not want to be happy. I long for immortality. I prefer to remain in history.

I grope for more signs of anomalies in my face, but the only thing that comes to my fingers is fat round cheeks with almost no grooves. I remember how they made me feel self-conscious when I first came to America. Compared to the angular cubic contours of the white Americans surrounding me, my facial outline looked like a pancake. In a crowd of white Americans, I still feel a strange sense of being different that makes me want to disappear. But I don't want to change my face. I think I might be destined to look different anywhere in this world. Even in Korea, the high cheekbones made me stand out from most other women.

I stop and look at my upturned eyes. As a child, I would look in the mirror and try to curve the ends of the eyes upward even more by pulling my hair up to the top of my head and binding it over and over again with a thick, long rubber band. I had heard that warriors of ancient China bunched their long hair up to their apex to make their eyes go up and look awe-inspiring. They believed long, thin, ascending eyes were the mark of a conqueror. When my mother took me to a barber and had him cut my hair like a boy's, I pulled my eyes up instead with my hands.

My fingers pass my short, chubby eyelashes and over the long, thin brows to reach my narrow, small, and square forehead. I can almost feel the rough areas over and under the brows, where the parts I had shaved off pop out like little stubs in a cornfield. Long, thick, slanting brows paired with thin upturned eyes give the look of a great leader. In addition to compassion and rigor, such a person has the shrewd and sometimes wicked tactics of a Machiavellian prince. But I am now plucking out half of the hair because having discovered beauty and grace, I want brows shaped like crescent moons. In an Asian aesthetic, they, together with white teeth, are a must for a beautiful face.

But the decision to have crescent-shaped brows was planted in me a long time ago. When I was fifteen, a fruit peddler came to our house and asked my mother to buy her leftovers for half price.

"If I talk my mother into buying everything you have left, will you sell it for less than half price?" I asked the peddler. I was an avid peach eater because one of my aunts once had told me that they make a woman's skin soft.

"Is this your daughter?" the peddler asked Mother.

"Yes. She came out to haggle for me," Mother said with a laughing look in her eyes.

"She is pretty!" The peach seller gazed at me, her mouth open. "She's going to have everything she wants, including money, fame, a loving husband, and a long, healthy life. There won't be a trace of a knife on her body, either." (Koreans believe that not having surgery in one's lifetime is a privilege.) "But…" she hesitated, watching the pride in Mother's eyes freezing into anxiety, "she can kill. She has four knives in her head – one short of five that makes a murderer, two short of six that makes a serial killer."

Mother gasped. The peddler explained in haste, "No, no, she's not going to be a murderer. The four knives in her head symbolize the cutting, decisive boldness she carries in herself. She'll use them to tear down trees, rocks, and hills to build houses and roads. She'll remove the barriers in her way, not the people."

"But won't people be on the road? Couldn't she destroy someone by mistake?" Mother was still uneasy.

"That's why she'll have to be careful," the peddler warned. "She'll have to tread carefully."

Suddenly, I felt an impulse to dispel their seriousness, to prove how silly their worries were. Laughing, I asked, "Who on earth do I kill?"

"You kill in spite of yourself." The peddler looked at me as she would look at a child who was unaware she was carrying explosives. "You don't know who you are hurting. You're so preoccupied with paving the road that you don't see who's underneath your feet."

"But you said I am pretty. Can a pretty woman kill?" I was flattered. Raised in a culture where being feminine was synonymous to being inferior, I had always thought that power was the monopoly of the masculine.

"When a pretty woman has four knives in her head, she is doomed to suffer. You will be haunted with pain forever."

"Why?" I asked, still laughing.

"Because a pretty face and four knives are like oil and water." She turned to Mother. "But she *can* change her personality, although it'll be a lot of work."

"I don't want to," I declared flatly. "I want to show off my knives. I'm going to polish them every day."

"Then, you'll have to give up using your pretty face. Get rid of the oil from the water," Mother interrupted. She always taught her children how not to be greedy, but at that moment, I thought I saw a glimmer of awe and hope in her face. Her eyes were revealing the pride her words didn't dare show.

"No way! I'm going to let both of them work."

"Pain will kill you then." The peddler shook her head.

That night, I ate nine of the dozen peaches Mother had bought from the peddler. I chewed the peels, too, until they were ground like rice porridge in my mouth, reciting what one of my uncles had said to me, "Men like thrifty women, and thrifty women don't take peels off their fruit." Then, with nine peach seeds in a straight line on my desk, I quietly recited over and over, "Logic, logic is the key! And metaphysics!" I was planning to sharpen the four knives in my head by having imaginary conversations with Less Big Brother. As the second oldest son in my family, he was right beneath Big Brother and just above me in birth order, and he loved to harass me with his notion that women didn't know how to think logically and metaphysically. How glad I was, punching him out in my mind, aiming the blades of my knives at his speechless tongue! How happy I was, brushing my hair endlessly—my long, thick, wild, and rich hair that resisted a brush so strongly but yielded to it so obediently once it was groomed—rubbing my palm against my cheeks softened by the peaches! The next day, I had to come home early from school because of a stomachache, but for four knives and a pretty face, I could pay any price.

Gathering my hair in bent fingers over the right shoulder, I now long for someone else's hands—a man's—to caress it. I see myself lying face down, with his fingers under my hair, his lips on my forehead, and his arm across my back. I am reading *The New York Review of Books* to make my knives shine, but he is kissing me on the back of my neck, which is as white as a baby's thigh because my long hair shields it from the sun. In the crisp morning air, I tell him how I dream of remaining in history by using my knives and how many peaches I have eaten to make my skin soft and full of sheen, and he tells me, folding his leg over mine, gliding his toes on my calves, that he wishes to help me realize my dreams and to make my lips moist with his kisses. Then we agree to spend our Sunday mornings pursuing a union of work and love. We promise to strive for immortality by exercising our high minds and to revel in the present by exploring the joys of the senses.

I press my temples and follow the outline of my forehead. The top portion is definitely smaller than the bottom, and this means I have a narrow, short front.

"JFK had a great face, but he had a narrow forehead. He was out of luck," Father would say, watching the president on television. A face shaped like a heart, with the upper half wider than the lower half, brings luck. But I have a triangular face. Am I going to be assassinated? Will the four knives in my head cut innocent people down and my energy, like drops of oil in water, mix terribly with the trees, rocks, and hills I tear down? No, nothing like that will ever happen because I have a dream. I have a dream of making oil and water blend.

I pinch my earlobes. I won't have much money because thin earlobes don't bring riches. But the contours of my ears, tapering into a soft end like an abalone shell, predict the dexterous magic of an alchemist who can transmute incompatible metals into one whole piece. I will use the four knives in my head to gain exquisite joy as I mince and measure the infinitesimal weight of each separate atom in the metal, uniting, separating, diluting, thinning, and thickening them. I will make all of the hostile elements fuse into one another. My four knives will live on in history.

My eyes will help. "Look at her eyes! They show distant places and unknown worlds. They scare me," my neighbors used to tell my parents. "She's going to suffer. A girl with such radiance…should have been a boy." My neighbors didn't *see* me. Only I knew that the four knives shining in my mind were a girl's – even better, a pretty girl's. Only I realized I didn't want to relinquish my pain because I couldn't give up my dream.

I have a dream. I see my face without a mirror.

What follows is what I have done to live this dream of mine. It is an account of my adult life as I saw it in my mind's mirror, the pictures I have painted in my soul of all the strokes I made in my adopted country, the United States. It is a highly subjective account—as subjective as a memoir is supposed to be—an exploration of what happens in the innermost sanctum of a mind.

Chapter 2
Even the Moon Looks Bigger in America

Living in a dorm, I had to eat three meals a day at a cafeteria, where giant plates of fattening foods put me through a month-long episode of diarrhea. My digestive organs were used to steamed rice and kimchi, so white bread and ground meat came as a shock. *This is why I'll never fully be an American*, I thought. "Father was right. 'If you immigrate to another country after a certain age, your diet will deny you. You may speak the language perfectly and be culturally assimilated, but you won't be able to live without the food you're used to. Your stomach will refuse what your head is ready to accept.'"

As my stomach rejected what my head zealously sought, I walked into a grocery store. I wanted to buy a vegetable that could be pickled into a dish of instant kimchi. Napa cabbage was commonly used for kimchi, but I wanted lettuce because its soft leaves could absorb the spices fast. With the electric rice cooker I borrowed from a Korean graduate student, I could make bowls of hot steamed rice and mix them with the spiced lettuce in a large brass bowl. When it was finished, I could take it to my bed and devour it on the comfort of the soft mattress with a pillow behind my back. As a prisoner in solitary confinement would live for the joy of greeting his friends and family who handed him packages of delicious snacks through the iron bars, I endured American junk food during the day for the anticipated pleasure of eating the semi-Korean meal I managed to improvise at night. As long as it smelled like one of the dishes on the table at home, my stomach would be moved by my effort and stop rejecting all the American food I swallowed. It would accept some of the canned beans and most of the frozen broccoli, and handle, though with reluctance, the spaghetti noodles covered with bloody red pasta sauce and greasy meatballs. The bologna and salami, which came between little sheets of cheap American cheese, would be made a bit easier to process, and the mustard and mayonnaise on the bread would look less alien, digested a little more painlessly with the chunks of spam in the over-fried eggs.

"There's nothing that's not big in America," my Korean friends marveled. "In this country, cars are huge. Grocery stores are as wide as an ocean, and shopping malls are as long as a sea. Potatoes are as large as a child's face. Parking lots have a hundred floors, and bookstores have a thousand aisles. A university campus is stretched out for miles, a building rises ten kilometers high, a river runs twice as deep as the whole length of Japan, and mountains are larger than the whole country of France."

"Even people's bellies and thighs are huge," I added. "Look how enormous their dishes are! They can eat so much – and so much grease at that!" To show off my insight, which by now I had the overt vanity to define as being first rate, I said, "Maybe, that's one of the reasons why this country lost in Vietnam. The Viet Cong could easily crawl in and out of the little caves they dug in the jungles because they were so small, but the American soldiers couldn't even tell where the caves were. They had to use specially selected soldiers who were built small enough to crawl into the shafts and shoot the enemy hiding there."

Yes, everything in America was big, and I felt I was getting bigger, living in that big country and eating all that greasy food. I was afraid I would add a couple extra inches to my waist and thighs in a short time. As one of the Korean graduate students joked, even the Moon looked bigger in America, and I felt excited to be living in a country where the mysterious planet looked not only larger but also clearer. Because there was less pollution in the air, the stars appeared more sharply and fully to the earthlings here, giving my Korean friends an opportunity to jest about how small even the planets looked in their very small country. Besides the occasional pleasure of devouring the hot steamed rice with the spiced leaf lettuce, I had the monthly privilege of watching the full moon—the same moon with a rounder shape and a bigger size—through the window in my dorm room, and I thought I was adding a list of small *happinesses* to the treasure of grand *joys*. For the *joy* of achieving, I endured not only breakneck routines of studying every minute but also the constant complaints from my digestive organs. For the *happiness* of living itself, I had those special moments of having the same stars I saw back home look bigger and the same food I had taken for granted taste better.

In an attempt to save every penny, I could, I didn't even buy a sheet. To cover the hideously ugly black stripes on the faded gray mattress, I instead spread a large picnic blanket I had picked up for a quarter at a garage sale, fixing it firmly on the mattress with a dozen clothespins. I was in the habit of recalling the promise I had made to my parents:

"All you have to give me is half of the money you'd have to spend on getting me married off to a stranger you find through a matchmaker. With three thousand dollars, I can finish my master's degree. You watch!"

I chose to come to the State University of New York at Albany because it was the only school that gave me a financial aid in the form of a tuition waiver. In 1980, I wasn't at all different from most Korean students who chose to attend a graduate school in America because it offered financial aid in one form or another. To an English major from Korea, a tuition waiver was a rare gift because American universities almost never offered any financial assistance to graduate students from non-English-speaking Asian countries. While they generously provided assistantships and fellowships for Korean students in math and sciences, those who studied the subjects which Asian students were known to be good at, they remained convinced that graduate students from a non-English-speaking Asian country didn't deserve any form of financial aid, including a teaching or research assistantship, or a fellowship of any kind. Such students had to work extremely hard before they could be considered for even the smallest paying jobs or assistantships from an English Department. Even the most outstanding Korean graduate students in English who could speak and write in perfect English had to wait for two years at least before they had a chance to earn a teaching or research assistantship on the lowest level.

Nor did the Korean government support English majors. In a desperate hurry to industrialize the country, they only promoted sciences and technology, providing financial help only for students who they believed would help bring the fastest economic progress. While supplying generous scholarships for the graduate students who went to Western countries to study subjects such as math, economics, engineering, chemistry, and computer programming, they showed zero concern for the ones in liberal arts and other fields that seemed unrelated to the country's industrial developments. Under these circumstances, imagine how glad I was to receive the tuition waiver from the State University of New York at Albany! On the day I received the offer, I was ready to leave.

I would have come to any university in America, however, regardless of whether or not I received any financial help. In 1980, I was twenty-four years old and I wanted to live out my twenties in another country. I was afraid that if I stayed in Korea, I would end up surrendering to the intense pressure to get married and miss all opportunities to pursue a life of my own. To the vast majority of Korean women of my age, marriage meant an abrupt end to their careers and a lifelong devotion to the exclusive duties of supporting their husbands and raising their children. Once married, women had no place in society, mentally confined within the four walls of the house. They were forced to stop working outside the home, forever deprived of the chances to be anything other than a domestic being. If I could leave the country before this pressure began to fall on me, I thought I could escape such a stifling existence and at least continue my studies. If I could come back to Korea with a PhD in my thirties, I would be able to get a respected job and earn a certain status with which I could beat the frustrating norm with secret, cynical laughter. I would be called by the dreadful name, an "old maid," but as an old maid with a terminal degree and economic self-sufficiency, I would be armed with an achievement that would be powerful enough to silence those who felt tempted to call me by such a name. With half of the money to be spent on having me married to a stranger, my parents could give me a chance to be such a powerful woman.

In his letter, Father made it clear to me that a check for another two thousand dollars was coming to help me out, but I knew this check was an accumulation of the coins he had gathered day by day. It was made of the change for coffee and snacks, of the loose money that should have bought Mother and Father warm winter sweaters, of the small cash that could have bought them the pleasure of a cold drink on a hot summer day. "We'll help you create an environment in which the only thing you have to do is study," he kept writing to me. "Don't feel burdened. We *want* to support you."

But I was determined to fulfill my promise to them. I knew that using a picnic blanket for a bed sheet wouldn't cut down my costs in the end, but the three quarters I had saved by doing so made me feel as if I had done something to pay my parents back. I had a chance to lessen my feelings of guilt, an opportunity to show at least part of my gratitude and duty, and a few minutes of time every night to remind myself of the efforts I owed to my family. I was by no means seeking pain, but sleeping on the picnic blanket pinned to the mattress kept me in touch with what I gladly endured to achieve what was in my destiny. I was a proud descendant of the ancient Korean warrior whose legendary life had been handed down to me by my grandmother.

"About a millennium and a half ago, there lived a general named Taebeck. He was exiled to a remote island after his king was assassinated by his treacherous vassals, but he never gave up the hope of re-crowning his lord. To keep his mind focused on what he had to do, every night for ten years, he chose to sleep on a hardwood floor without a mattress."

I was no General Taebeck, and my picnic blanket had nothing to do with his hardwood floor, but the legend served the purpose I wanted to believe in. To overcome the guilt and shame I felt about being still financially dependent on my parents, I needed to attach a special meaning to the life I was living then, and the legend of the general came as a natural substitute for an active self-disparagement. It helped me shift the shame to gratitude, to a sense that my economically incompetent present was in actuality a preparation for a brilliant future. I was an exile on her way to a victorious comeback, a brave warrior who refused to sleep on the comfort of a soft mattress. I was a woman whose awareness of where she was going was manifested even in her bed.

I kept telling myself what an opportunity I was blessed with. Because the university awarded me a full tuition waiver, I was allowed to minimize my parents' burden, and thanks to my humorous compatriots from Korea, I could revel in the miracle of witnessing the different sizes of the full moon. I was a homeless person who had the pleasure of falling asleep with the cool outdoor breeze a rich person was barred from, and I had in my spiritual possession more than any of those wealthy people who were deprived of the freedom of being on the outside. "I have more in my experience than those rich Americans who've never had to leave their country," I convinced myself. "Look at what I've got. I am bilingual, and I know more than one country. I can see America as a Korean. I can see Korea as an American. Most Americans don't see how barbarous their country can be. Most Koreans don't see how primitive their country can be. But I can see how advanced and backward both countries are. I see the many faces of each country – many more than I would if I had been only in one country." Undoubtedly, my dialogue with myself was a defense mechanism I constructed in my mind, but it served as a force of self-preservation, as powerful as a medicine curing a painful illness. It marked the first step of my long life in America, during which a succession of self-defensive monologues turned into a genuine will for survival and finally success.

Ironically, what struck me as being one of the most barbarous faces of the Americans was what they saw as being one of the most civilized faces of the nation. To this day, I remember the shock I felt when I wandered into a large grocery store in America for the first time. An entire aisle stocked with pet food seemed a criminal extravagance to a young foreign student who had grown up in a country ravaged by war, where food for people was scarce and anything other than the absolute necessity was a luxury. In Korea, dogs and cats were given leftovers from dinner tables and allowed to roam streets alone without a leash or identification, and female animals were let loose to have one litter after another. Some adults loved their pets and more children proudly paraded their little furry friends in their arms, but spaying them was the last thought to occur to these animal lovers, young and old alike. Taking animals to a vet to rid them of their procreative function seemed not only an outrageous extravagance because there were so many sick people who couldn't afford to go to doctors, but also a violation of a natural order because one shouldn't deprive an animal of its most basic right – that of multiplying its species. Animals should be treated like animals, Koreans would say. Spoiling them wasn't fair for people. Standing in the middle of the animal food aisle on a cold winter day during the first month of 1980, I couldn't help thinking about what a frivolous country America was.

With humorous anger—because I knew animals were far from human anyway—I put a criminal scene on trial in my mind. On notebook paper, I drew a rough sketch of a courtroom in which a dozen cats and dogs were seated on the witness stand while the defense lawyer for the pet owners and the impassioned prosecutor kept arguing in front of the stoic-looking judge. "The defendants spend thousands of dollars a year on their cats and dogs, but they won't invest a penny for their elderly mothers in a nursing home," the prosecutor fired up. "Taking the animals to a vet even at the slightest sign of indigestion, they won't visit their sick mothers—not even once—for ten long years until they have to attend the funeral and meet with their brothers and sisters to claim their inheritance. One wonders whether they would even have gone to the funeral had it not been for their share of the money. One asks how often they must have exclaimed, 'Oh, my pretty doggie! Oh, my lovely kitty!' and how rarely they must have picked up the phone to say hi to their elderly mothers dying alone."

As the defense lawyer rose from his seat on the other side, I fed him the following lines, "According to the prosecutor, taking care of one's pets while leaving one's parents in a nursing home is a criminal behavior, but allow me to prove the falseness of his reasoning. As you are well aware," he started in a low key loaded with smoldering intensity, making eye contact with each of the jurors. "The United States is a country of, by, and for the youth. Because the youth is given the power to set the norms against the models the old folks want to pass on to them, this country can create new rules and paradigms with much more ease than any other country in the world. We have a melting pot where everything constantly changes because young men and women are not ashamed to separate themselves from the elderly, including their own parents and grandparents. Look at the third world countries where few things can change in a century, and senile octogenarians try to control young men and women in their twenties and thirties. In these backward countries, old people are domineering beasts sitting upon young folks' backs. The last thing that should happen in our homeland is this sort of absurd situation." He was speaking on my behalf about my own grandmother, whose destructive presence in the house threw the entire family into a yoke of suffering until her long-awaited death at eighty-five. "Pets deserve to be given great care as they are the devoted companions of the youth who need the privilege of being apart from the elderly. They are the creatures inspiring young citizens of the United States to accept the curse and blessing of being solitary, the soul mates helping their human friends to engineer a new future for their peers and descendants." The trial always ended in a hung jury, my judgment always lost in a swamp of ambivalence.

I was disturbed by the sight of old people sitting alone on park benches with their dogs. They seemed to have no family or friends, always hungry for strangers willing to offer them a few minutes of their time, eager to unload their life stories upon anyone with hearing ears. They were enormously proud of their children, with whom they appeared to have very little contact, and they were tremendously fond of their grandchildren, many of whom were being raised by step mothers or fathers after their parents' bitter divorce, and didn't care about the wellbeing of their grandparents in another city. Their only companions seemed to be their dogs, their only conversation occurring with the passers-by who complimented them on their canine children. I was afraid that the two monosyllables they gave to the strangers kind enough to pet their dogs, "Thank you," were probably the only thing they ever exchanged with another human being for the whole day. "Maybe, however, it's a necessary evil," I again entered a dialogue with myself. "In America, there's at least a clear tradeoff. For a free, unhampered youth, they have a lonely old age. It might be a more reasonable set up than the one we've got in Korea, where young men and women find it difficult to make the best of their youth because of their obligation to the old. Their old age is less lonely, blessed in comparison to that of Americans, but the Korean youths don't get to taste the hot years granted to American youths." Such rationalization didn't make me feel less disturbed. It was a vain attempt to persuade myself to believe that I had moved to a better country, a philosophical justification I tried to create in order to make myself accept that I had done the right thing by jumping across the Pacific. That Americans noticed dogs before they saw their human friends struck me as a bizarre personality trait, and I figured that probably elderly people brought their dogs to the park to attract attention.

No matter how hard I tried to deny it, my new country was hardly better than my old one, and my struggle to accept it became an emotional war to be fought ever more fiercely. I found myself not only unbearably lonely but also physically stressed out. If the emotional isolation surrounding me was like solitary confinement, the work I had to crank out each day to fulfill academic requirements was like a gun pressed to my head. The new environment was a Mohamed Ali I had to fight with no training. I was a baby, bound and bare-fisted, combating a freely moving, unbeatable monster. A line of information took a non native speaker an hour to digest – a far cry from the one second it could take a native speaker. For me, writing a paper was a challenge close to a nightmare. Catching up with reading was a constant grind, and trying to understand professors' lectures was comparable to the aggravation of listening to Greek. The more I listened, the harder it became to decipher what they were saying, and the closer I got to figuring it out, the further the concepts seemed to drift away from me. Having to ask a classmate to repeat what the professor had explained in class for me was humiliating, and being forced to copy another student's notes made me wonder whether I was at all qualified for graduate work in English.

I felt torn by doubts. But giving up was the last thing I could contemplate doing. Like a member of a secret masonic order for whom failing was not an option, I was determined to succeed, to wave the flag of victory at my family and country against whom I had made the brave—and reckless—decision to leave for the United States. It wasn't self-confidence but my furious will to save face, to prove how wrong they were in not believing in me that strengthened my resolve to stay on and earn a master's degree in a field that was deemed nearly impossible for a Korean who virtually started to speak English for the first time at the age of twenty-four. It was the fear of failure and more accurately, a desire for self-display that made me endure the blood-draining routines.

I could see I tried too hard. I totally forgot about people in my pursuit of the English language and completely ignored human relationships in an attempt to master English. Even though I knew my roommate had to get up at six, I sat up until three in the morning, and it never occurred to me to apologize to her. Like a racecar driver speeding to finish the line even after killing another driver, I didn't bother to recognize how I was hurting her. I was oblivious of the basic courtesy a human being owed to another. Remarkably and very thankfully, my roommate never exercised her right to report me, either motivated by a sense of compassion—or pity—for a desperate foreign student or resigned to waiting until the semester was over. Whatever her reason, for the past thirty-eight years, I have found myself wishing for an opportunity to apologize to her.

"There's something wrong with that Korean woman," I overheard her say to another woman in the hallway. "She radiates energy one moment, but looks dead the next. I wonder if she's crazy because she turns from happy to sad in one second. She has a problem sleeping. She has to turn in her bed a thousand times before she can finally shut her eyes." After observing how I ignored everything else except studying, she went on, "That Korean woman is a slob. Her side of the room is like a giant cocoon of filthy clothes, but when she leaves the room, she manages to look fresh somehow. She seems to think she's a beautiful butterfly that can step in and out of her ugly cocoon anytime she wants."

My roommate was right. Besides my body and hair, the only clean thing about me was the typewriter I switched on every evening to save the words I gathered. I adhered to my writing—my only weapon—until every syllable jumping out of my typewriter appeared to be a perfect match for the thoughts flying out of my mind. To fulfill my destiny of tearing down the walls between individuals and nations by perfecting my English, I paid no attention to anything but the magic of language.

Only printed pages mattered in my cocoon because I knew that only on printed pages could my visions for the world exist. I wanted to create a world where there was no slavery, but I knew such a world could be found only in dreams. Knowing that the world I envisioned was only an *idea,* I still wanted to pursue it in my academics. As a way of affirming the truth, rather—that reality could not be sustained without slavery, some sort of slavery anyhow—I tried to embody in my blank pages a place that could be maintained without slavery. To be faithful to the world I constructed in my head—to the nation I named a republic without slavery—I rejected my roommate's offer to clean my side of the room. Knowing that I would never tear down the messy cocoon surrounding my desk, she wanted to do it herself. But I refused to violate the founding principle of my republic by letting anyone else do my chores. I knew I was being absurd, carrying myself to the point at which a virtue became a vice. In my mind, I even recited a famous Korean saying, "Too much good is bad. You're going too far." Watching myself going too far, I didn't stop. I couldn't stop. Because it was impossible—because I knew it was impossible to build my republic in this world—I pursued it in another world that lay in my typewriter.

I was an unsightly person in class as well. To disguise my frustration and insecurities, I talked loudly when I had nothing to say, often raising my hand compulsively just because nobody else did. The high degree of tolerance my professors and classmates displayed for me started to occur to me a few years later, when my ears stopped missing easy words. Because I could grasp only half of the content being discussed in class, I was frequently out of context. I was so irrelevant sometimes that everyone else in class, I suspect, had to fight the urge to laugh. My professors and classmates were perhaps astonished by the astute comments that popped out of my senseless mouth every now and then. It was most likely this sporadic quickness in my words that made them abstain from frowning at me, and I myself at times got a glimpse of what I might be capable of achieving through these perceptions that shone randomly through my apparently thick brain.

So, when I received an Incomplete from one of the courses I took in the first semester, I wasn't as devastated as I had thought I might be. Nobody told me, but it wasn't hard to see that my problem was too many crowded concepts in one place. I was being too ambitious for my level of vocabulary and syntax, and I could tell that I had to wait until my sentence complexity grew mature enough to embody the vortex of seemingly disconnected knowledge in a connected manner. A few days after the grief of reading the shocking grade in my transcript, I started to separate the chaotically entangled ideas from one another, making two sentences out of one. "Richard Smith was an American who thought America was too vulgar for him to live there, who questioned the virtues of the materialism and commercialism which was binding his free spirits, and who believed it was his destiny to move back to Europe from where his ancestors had come two scores and ten years before, and he was firmly resolved not to come back to America, where he was afraid he would be unfortunately polluted by the same mercenary culture that would enslave his spirit struggling to free itself from the physical environment..." became "As an American, Richard Smith was tired of the vulgar materialism and commercialism in his country, which he loathed, and decided to return to Europe, from which his ancestors had sailed for America five decades before. He was firmly resolved not to return to America, which he would probably be frustrated with again upon his return, which he would wish to leave again, and which he would certainly escape from again."

After revising the same sentence a dozen times, it still didn't sound like English, but it became easier little by little to cut away the redundant excesses and sharpen the core meanings. Grammatical problems gradually went away, while faulty sentence complexities slowly gave in to a much leaner, clearer style without the fattening modifiers that came out of anxiety. To use a cliché, I was blowing away at the dirt surrounding a diamond, trying to chisel away at the first layers, the final layers, and the ones in between. Until now I never reached the final layer, but remembering the stages my writing went through, I get a good laugh, and this laugh is sure proof that I am marching closer to the ultimate shine of the jewel. Perfectly grammatical but not making much sense, one of the sentences I wrote during these long, laborious stages would make anyone laugh. "Richard Smith undertakes a reverse pilgrimage to Europe, from which his forefathers had come in initial pilgrimage to America half a century before, hoping to see a lot of progress for humanity and spiritual prosperity. How ironical that the same hope takes him back to Europe, that the same longing for a true civilization, founded on justice and equality, makes him return to his ancestors' land with no hesitation!"

Without arrogance or condescension, I could say that I felt I had a third eye planted in my forehead, an extra vision that instantly empowered me to penetrate into the heart of the matter. A gift possessed by very few of my peers, this third eye enabled me to make connections between seemingly disconnected realities, to perceive the core of the problem lying under the surface like invisible wires running through a ballast. It wasn't just messages from individual authors that I understood. My knowledge extended to the historical contexts in which these authors' lives were shaped and their styles were created, surpassing into the inter-textual continuity, and linking the apparently very dissimilar contents and subject matters. Armed with the bare minimum necessary to learn a foreign language, which for me was a copy of the notebook-size American Heritage Dictionary, the laser-sharp concentration that made my eyes glitter with the focus of a hungry cat going after a mouse, and the pocket-sized book I carried to jot down a list of the new words to memorize, I could read between the lines in a single volume as well as the relationships among various authors in multiple volumes.

Because my dreams were made possible by my nightmares, I endured. I endured until the vain twenty-four-year-old became a modest thirty-eight-year-old English professor, until I forgot to count how often I cried in despair, "What has changed in my life in America? Every day I am working until the pain in my eyes, so familiar from the days of my childhood, is unbearable. If anything, it seems only worse. I'm not even in my own country." Too many times, I was struck by the irony that to be free from my country, I was imprisoned in another country. Proudly, I had chosen the option of leaving Korea, where I would have been faced with severe pressure to marry and have children and be nothing but an "unpaid maid" (what I called a housewife), for a country where I thought I could be a person of my own. But I seemed to be an unpaid academic slave, worse off than an unpaid domestic maid.

But I refused to let this irony stop me. Rather, I used it to reinforce my style, which was based in clashing two antithetical forces together and generating a powerful nuclear reaction. Similarly to the emotional prison of the women in my family and my country, I created my own emotional prison in America, and out of the energy sprouting from this headlong clash, I reaped the harvest of an iron will. I even felt a strange sense of gratitude. Because of my fear of these emotional prisons, I could redouble my effort to escape them, and because of my nightmares of being locked away in them, I could run so unceasingly toward my dreams of being free. By keeping myself zeroed in on this inextricable link between my nightmares and my dreams, I could create a life of my own.

I must have carried a touch of optimism in my new prison in America. How else could I have forgiven myself with a smile after I made mistakes that so thoroughly violated the standards of behavior I believed I held? I couldn't have looked into myself with such relentless honesty without a degree of faith whispering to me that I would someday be strong enough to look back and laugh at the immature newcomer in graduate school. I could in my heart apologize to myself and to my professors who were forced to tolerate my very unprofessional, rude behavior, and I could tell myself that I should be a better person. I could actually write a letter of apology to one of my professors to whom I had thrown a barrage of violent words. About a year after my first semester in graduate school, I carefully cut a piece of paper from my notebook, wrote several lines on it, and folded it into a paper boat to let it float on the Hudson River in Albany. I wrote the words six times to make sure it wasn't an act of easy self-absolution. "When I received a B instead of an A from you, I felt I was betraying my parents who had saved every penny in their possession to send me to graduate school in America. It was my first semester in graduate school, and I lost my mind over the fear of failing. I raged at you. I yelled and screamed at your fair evaluation of my performance. I overreacted. I would be grateful if you accept my apology a year too late." What really mattered was how sincerely sorry I felt and how diligently I put this feeling into practice. I didn't have to let my professor know how determined I was to make it up to him – and to myself. I just had to *do* it.

Perhaps, I also knew I would make the same mistake in the coming years before I would be able to put an end to it. I had many more years to go to finish my PhD, and I was going to suffer the same intense agony over my grades and rage at my professors over the less than perfect grades in the same belligerent manner. Perhaps, I knew I would repeat the same ritual of apology, of writing letters and making them into paper boats to float on the river. Perhaps, I knew I would laugh again at this letter, too, and at the paper boat disappearing down the river.

Laughing was good for *knowing,* too. Each time I laughed over the tumbling paper boat, I rehearsed new English phrases I had picked up from a native speaker. To add new color to the old laughter, I chanted, "What's up?

What's up? What's new? What's new? How weird! How weird! That's lousy. That's lousy." Zealously, I sang over and over again the words I couldn't have learned how to use in Korea, "He's an asshole. She's a bitch. Any asshole can do it. That's a dumb bitch. Like a dumbass, he put all the eggs in one basket. Being a stupid bitch, she drank and drove." Learning by repetition, I made myself into a broken record, "Oh my, oh boy, oh my goodness, oh dear, oh my, oh boy, oh my goodness, oh my God, oh well, oh no, oh boy, oh yes, oh dear." Not yet knowing where to place these interjections, I combined them with the four-letter words some fun-loving native speakers enjoyed teaching me, "Oh my, all the shit is coming. Oh my goodness, the crap is working. Oh dear, bullshit has legs. Money talks, bullshit walks. Oh yes, he's full of shit. Oh no, she's shitting me."

There was nothing I wanted more than a perfect command of English, and there was nothing I desired more than a complete mastery of the colloquial English or the vulgar slang rarely found in books. I knew this sort of language had nothing to do with the educated language I longed to learn, but it thrilled me to feel it dancing on the tip of my tongue. It made me feel as if I were indeed becoming an American, an insider speaking English with a linguistic instinct forever elusive to me. While speaking these words, I had a chance to delight in the *sense* that I was *in* America, not merely observing the country from the outside. I was blessed with the opportunity to forget what I wished to forget more than anything else, that I was a foreigner who had to think before I spoke, a sure sign that I was an alien speaking in my second language. It was a time during which I could stop the process of having to filter what was in my head into what finally came out of my mouth. It was a moment of relief during which I could forget the curse of having to work so hard to become an American. I *was* an American. I didn't have to *become* an American. I had the leisure of having my tongue do the work of expressing myself. My tongue could deny the difficulty in my head.

As laughter, however, is the other face of sorrow, my insatiable urge to laugh rose out of my sorrow. I laughed because I was lonely. I laughed because I was sad. I laughed because I was frustrated. I laughed because I was at once so bright and so dumb. With a third eye on my forehead, I was so perceptive about all the complex problems regarding humanity, and yet I was so blind about simple matters concerning human beings. I was a walking contradiction whose brilliance concealed her stupidity, a studying machine whose cheerful mask belied her true face laden with pain. I often flattered myself, thinking my mask was so good that no perceptive eye could have seen the face lurking beneath the veneer of manufactured jolliness. But people weren't as easily deceived as I hoped they would be, and I could tell some people could see what lay inside. My roommate, who saw me living in a cocoon of filthy clothes, was one of these people.

Chapter 3
Intruder in the Garden of Eden

Despite being on a tight budget as well, Big Brother and his wife graciously invited me to live with them over the summer. I accepted their invitation without a shred of hesitation, determined to finish my master's degree with the one check I had brought from Korea, to minimize my parents' financial burden. As selfish as my decision to live off Big Brother and his wife seemed, I reasoned that I was helping my parents and would eventually help Big Brother and his wife. As the oldest son and the oldest son's wife, they were the ones ultimately responsible for my parents' economic sufficiency – and the ones responsible for supporting them until the end, if necessary. There was virtually no difference between my parents' money and theirs. If I could restrict my expenses for a master's degree to the one check my parents had been able to give me, I could contribute to not only my parents' monetary ease but also their oldest son's future financial comfort.

Because Father was headed toward a decent retirement, there was little possibility that my parents would be economically dependent on any of their children, but Big Brother was always mindful of his duty. If anything unexpected happened, he was the one the mission of rescuing the family would fall on. He was the one who would be assigned to take care of the aged parents and younger siblings. Very dutifully, he believed his money was his family's money. Very judiciously, he believed his money had to be spent carefully. Even when he was the one who earned it all, he refused to spend it on anything that wasn't for the good of the family. With a full fellowship at Harvard and a couple thousand dollars a year from my parents and his wife's parents, he could afford some of the small luxuries that graduate students of modest means could buy. But he rigorously restricted his indulgence to one six-pack a week he would enjoy with his wife every Saturday night, the sneakers he needed to play tennis with his friends, and the cotton shirts and shorts he wore to the gym, where he exercised vigorously every other day to keep his energy up. As much as he loved classical music, he said he could wait until his graduate student days were over to buy a decent stereo, and as much as he would like a brand-new car, he said he could drive the ragged-looking secondhand Buick until his graduate school years were over.

Agreeing with him entirely, his wife also economized wisely, gathering coupons for groceries and finding sales on clothing. Being from a solid middle-class family, she was used to a level of comfort and affluence that made it less than easy for her to live on a stringent graduate student's budget, but with an instantly acquired expertise, she managed to give their old one-bedroom apartment a facelift at little cost. A large handmade white coverlet draped over the gray secondhand couch gave the furniture a fresh look, while the glass top of the worn coffee table lent a bright, cheerful look. A simple rack held the flowers that she watered regularly with the right amount of Miracle-Gro. Their long, broad leaves were pruned with the precise movements of nurturing hands, and their stems shot out of the rich, dark soil that had been jammed in the variously shaped pots. She had also woven wicker baskets of several different sizes that she filled with wildflowers picked from the parks in Boston and hung on a wall, perfectly contrasting the Picasso and Matisse art on the other side. Big Brother's wife had pasted the prints on canvasses, pressed the surfaces until they were immaculately smooth, and hung them by wires deftly placed on the back edges. His desk was made of a door, but she had very carefully selected beige filing cabinets as legs and used a fine brush to draw a pattern of thin light-brown branches to match the dark brown streaks on the window curtains she had made.

Everything in the apartment was made of cheap materials, but everything looked tasteful. It shone with the painstaking richness of a homemaker's attention to detail, with the elaborate wealth of a wife's devotion to the family's habitat. Big Brother's wife had built a haven for herself, a warm refuge for her husband, and a welcoming cradle for their baby. She had created a home in their new country. She was happy. She never complained about their lack of means. If there was one thing she wanted, it was for her and her husband to go more than once a year to watch the Boston Symphony play Beethoven. She said that once he received his PhD, they would be able to fly to San Francisco and stay in the city for a week to watch the San Francisco Symphony perform

Rachmaninoff and Tchaikovsky. Until then, she was satisfied with the whiny little sounds from the boom box.

It didn't take me long to realize that I was an invader in their home. To this day, I have no way of describing how I felt except by resorting to words from the Bible. I was Satan furtively watching the happy couple in the Garden of Eden, an outsider coveting and yet unable to achieve the condition that blessed the insiders. I was an old, wicked adult, jealous of the simple lives of children, only I wasn't going to try to seduce the wife to taste the apple of knowledge because I had none of Satan's malice. If anything, I wanted to banish myself from the garden to make it up to the inhabitants whose peace I was disrupting. I wanted to punish myself for looking *in* from the outside.

Surrounded by Korean graduate students and their wives, whose lifestyle was a precise reproduction of what I had fought so hard to leave behind in Korea, I tried to define myself by separating the two adjectives that best described my life. I was *alone*, not *lonely*, and I was going to create a life in which being alone was a powerful existence. I reminded myself of what separated me from the Korean graduate students and their wives, and I remembered what would have happened to me if I had followed the path my family and my country had laid for me.

I went back to where the Garden of Eden was conceived for Big Brother and his wife for the very first time, my family's house in 1978, the year before the couple married and left for Boston.

Father was glowering at me, the muscles beneath his eyes twitching mildly from suppressed ire.

"There goes the famous scowl of yours," he said. "After meeting with half a hundred women for over a year, your big brother is finally getting married—to a very good woman at that—and you show nothing but a long face. Why are you so unhappy when everyone else is so happy?"

I was far from being unhappy. I was at a loss. I wished I could neatly separate the conflicting feelings that swung like a pendulum in my mind. On the one hand, I was overjoyed for Big Brother, the beloved leader of my brother and sisters, the man who was entitled to a life of abundant professional success and personal satisfaction. But I was angry at the system that automatically endowed him with plenitude and robbed me of such riches. I was wrathful at a culture in which men were given easy opportunities for a career and a family, while women were forced to choose one or the other. Although I wasn't nearly as brilliant as Big Brother, who was "one of the three geniuses from K high school," I thought I had a good reason to be angry. The inequity was too great. Without a shred of question, my country preferred men with mediocre abilities over women with extraordinary gifts. My country unanimously granted the privilege of family and career to men while summarily denying it to women. I wished I could erase the loud dissonance in my head as neatly as one could wipe out lines on a blackboard.

"You're not jealous of him, are you?" Mother intervened. She added, as if to cancel the absurd question she had blurted out, "Who would feel bad about her brother getting everything he wants unless she's a truly malicious person? You're just anxious over your new sister-in-law coming to join us. You want to make a good impression on her and you don't know how to."

Mother was right. The gods knew I not only welcomed Big Brother's wife but also thanked her for being so ready to dedicate herself to him. Immediately after the wedding, she was to fly to Boston with him, where he would be working on his PhD in economics with a full fellowship from Harvard, and then return to Korea with the proud—and expected—proof of her wifely achievements. If everything went as smoothly as the couple—and everyone in my family and hers—hoped, she would be returning with a child, preferably a boy of about four years old, and her husband, exuding satisfaction and confidence, would be holding a portfolio full of astonishing transcripts and glowing letters of recommendation from his Harvard professors. Much like most Korean women of her generation, including the ones with plenty of talents but no ambition of their own, content to be adjuncts in their men's lives, she was going to be an ideal wife for Big Brother.

Because she was marrying an oldest son, it was all the more fortunate that she fell nicely into the Korean-wife type and automatically relegated to the role of a primary caretaker. She was expected to look after her husband's parents and his younger siblings, to sacrifice her and her husband's personal wishes to serve the common good of the family, and if necessary, to share her husband's earnings, however large or small, with the rest of the family. As an individual, she would be the last person to count, but as a daughter-in-law, she would be the first person to matter. For the wife of the oldest son, a career outside the home was bound to be a serious detraction, a barrier to the time-honored system that had to be perpetuated with no interruption. While none of my family members, not even Grandmother, believed she should be a traditionally subservient housewife, in an apron smeared with the grime of a kitchen stove, we all assumed that she would stay within the boundaries of a filial daughter-in-law and a loyal, self-sacrificial wife whose top priority was providing what her husband needed.

By the time Big Brother was about to be married, enough social changes had taken place to abolish the virtual domestic slavery that had been required of women in the past, and few people, except some old country folks still practicing a medieval lifestyle, demanded that their daughters-in-law, including the one married to the oldest son, do much more than taking care of their own immediate nuclear families. Doing a good job for her husband and children was thought to be enough to draw praises. Although an oldest daughter-in-law was entrusted with the primary duties of ensuring her in laws' general welfare, she was no longer responsible to serve her in-laws on a routine basis.

Marrying at such a transitional time, Big Brother's wife was facing the prospect of a relatively painless marriage. She could, with reasonable certainty, expect fewer family obligations and a lesser degree of servitude than her peers who married into families under needier circumstances. Father's steady job had him well on his way to a comfortable old age with a modest retirement. Mother was covered as well, being named as the sole recipient of his pension after his death. The children, too, were thriving, headed in the right direction. With an older sister married to an economically stable banker and three younger siblings safely marching toward a life with not only financial security but also prestige, Big Brother had none of the extra burdens assigned to an oldest son. The job waiting for his bride was that of a supportive wife and a nurturing mother, no more and no less. If one thing should have concerned her at all, it was the usual, sometimes pressing *sense* of responsibility that lay upon an oldest son that made him occasionally neurotic. But for a woman with a cheerful disposition, it was a flaw that could be ignored without much difficulty. Nothing was perfect, she probably said to herself, looking forward to a happy marriage with few responsibilities to her in-laws.

I never harbored one iota of negative feelings toward Big Brother's wife. Clearly, she was wise in choosing to follow the conventional path for a woman and smart in selecting such a promising young man with few family obligations. As an honors graduate of K girls' high school and a *cum laude* from Seoul National University, both of which were the very best institutions in the nation, she—as well as everyone else who knew her—was acutely conscious of her worth as a spousal candidate. A man without a demonstrated potential for a highly successful future didn't dare approach her, and she herself never allowed such men to enter her mind as anything other than a casual friend or a chance acquaintance.

"What a clever businesswoman she is!" I exclaimed as the weeks went by and the wedding day drew nearer. "She is so good at figuring out what she wants and so fast in grabbing it." But she wasn't different from most women in my country, whose ultimate goal was to marry men with a proven ability to provide for their women. Very few women, even the most talented and independent ones, sought to achieve what they wanted on their own, unable or refusing to bring themselves to believe that they could be defined by themselves, not by their men. Only the ones with her exceptional qualifications were entitled to look for more – for superior men who were equipped to bring them not only economic security but also considerable social status and prestige.

For Big Brother's wife, I should have felt the same contempt I felt for women whose chosen lifelong vocation was unpaid servitude. But ironically—very ironically, indeed—I found myself letting out a sigh of relief, exclaiming silently, *How lucky we are! Big Brother has a jewel. She is bright and capable, but she's going to be satisfied with her husband's success alone.* I thought happily, *If she had ambitions of her own, it might be bad for him and the family as well. He'd have to take a chunk out of his studying time to help her with the chores, the children, and whatever else she wants to do. If that happens, the whole family will be disappointed because it'll slow him down and most likely take him longer than five years to get his PhD. We don't want him to be delayed.* Korea endows glorious titles upon the faithful wives of diligent graduate students who are to be professors someday: "PhP for Pushing Husband to Pass," "PhP for Pushing Husband to Publish," "PhT for Pushing Husband for Tenure," and "PhP for Pushing Husband for Promotion." Luckily, Big Brother's wife was prepared to receive all those honorary degrees.

When I wore the scowl Father hated so, it was directed at the hypocrisy I saw in my own mind. I was, after all, no more than a conventional Korean woman whose only concern was her family's safety, and I was disappointed in myself. I was eagerly approving a choice I despised, and violating the very principle I believed I was ready to defend with my life. Because she would be my brother's wife—a pillar of our home—I gladly made an exception for her, relieved that she was content to be what I called an unpaid maid for the rest of her life. By putting my family's comfort—and our social status, since Big Brother's success would determine our social status—above the much-needed progress for humanity, I was being a hypocrite. It troubled me to think how unwelcoming I would be toward my soon-to-be sister-in-law if she had been one of those women with my style of an unyielding dream for self-realization. For my own convenience—and for my family's—I would have rejected a career woman who would work hard to help our country to move forward. I wasn't different from anyone I held in contempt. In a country where a woman's individuality was incompatible with the family's wellbeing, the discord in me was only natural, but it was hard for me to handle it at the very idealistic age of twenty-three. It wouldn't be until a decade later that I would treat this discord with laughter.

I was happy for Big Brother. The sense of security his wife's unceasing devotion would provide and the delicious warm dinners her nurturing hands would cook were certain to keep him in a balanced state of mind. He wouldn't develop the kind of egocentric attitude that I had been forced to cultivate to hold on to my dreams of self-realization, and he would have no need to throw himself into a fit of rage because there would be fewer issues in his country's system to anger him. As a man whose privileges came naturally, he was destined to be one of those few men who would experience generous givings as a routine practice. He was bound to be a man of renown. He worked hard—very hard—and he paid prices as the oldest son of the family. But in terms of having what his country could give a man, he was blessed. He wasn't a woman. Because he received more, he could give more.

I could easily envision Big Brother with a winner's enveloping aura, with the ends of his long, thin eyes slanting into a relaxing, yet inspiring smile and his broad upturned lips opening to speak welcoming, yet slightly distancing remarks that put his listeners at respectful ease. His audiences, whether close friends, acquaintances, or total strangers, would be at the mercy of this magical combination of awe and love, in the presence of that magnificent leadership evoking fear and liking at once. In contrast to me, his little sister whose life held daily fights for equality and chronic depression, how magnanimous and noble he would look! Compared to his face, reminiscent of the morning sun, mine was a dark room with dim fluorescent lights. Mine would be a face marked by battle fatigue, with eyes reeking of vengeance and teeth clenched with an unresolved wrath.

Bitterly and yet wholeheartedly, I congratulated him, picturing him and his wife landing at Seoul International Airport in a few years' time with a four-year-old son and a PhD from Harvard. All in all, he was my beloved, honorable Big Brother, whose many generous acts of giving and caring proved his love for me. Unable to deal with my loneliness, I once again found myself falling back on my usual coping mechanism, alternating between a loud, high-pitched laugh and a deep, long furrow between my brows. Those in my company didn't know whether to laugh or frown, anxious in an effort to decipher my true intentions.

On Big Brother's wedding day, Mother pleaded with me, "Just for today, try to look cheerful. Looking at your sister-in-law alone would make you feel better. There is no woman in this world who doesn't look pretty on her wedding day, but she looks prettier than any of the brides I've ever seen."

Mother wasn't exaggerating. Big Brother's wife, whom I now called Big Sister-in-law (because in Korea, one doesn't call one's older siblings' spouses by their names, just as one doesn't call one's older siblings by their names), was beautiful in a special sense. Having seen her before without makeup, I could tell that it wasn't the bridal makeover or the snow-white dress that created her perfectly symmetrical features and virginal aura. It was what was inside, the wit and intelligence that had been molded by a lifetime of a good upbringing and a prestigious education. In her, one could see the presence of her father, a university professor well known not only for his outstanding scholarly achievements but also for a gentle, embracing personality, and the influence of her mother, a wise, gracious woman whose unconditional love came with just the right amount of rigor.

But of all the things in her face, I especially liked her nose. Unlike mine, which was flat and wide with a soft tip, hers was small but cubic, with a distinct narrow shape, and I thought it brought her the look of a sharp mind with a highly refined air. For some reason, I had the idea that a prominent nose denoted a high level of intelligence, while a flat one revealed a substandard brain. Big Brother, too, was a victim of this same superstition, and every now and then he would make fun of his own typical Mongolian nose.

"My face is fine, except for the nose," he would say, and I would return half-jokingly, "Yours is better than mine. Its tip is narrower and harder, and it doesn't go all the way down when you push it."

Big Sister-in-law would have had a perfectly oval contour had it not been for the almost imperceptible pair of dents on the sides of her forehead and the slightly protruding jaw that created semi-square edges toward the bottom of the cheek lines. These features brought a tinge of masculinity to a face that would have been the ultimate incarnation of femininity, adding a peculiar charm. They awarded her an air of a decisive, quick-moving mind, a quality that was normally characterized as male. Once exposed to the pleasure of her companionship, one could see that such a contour might indeed be a sign of a soft-spoken, yet resilient personality. Anyone could tell that her eyes were unusual as well, shimmering with a pleasant mischief and always ready to declare keen insights with a delightful sense of humor.

At times, they disappointed me because I was afraid they showed her feelings too easily and too quickly. They didn't seem to be windows shading a deeply concealed heart reluctant to rise to the surface. But this rather transparent disposition I saw was good for both of them. It occurred to me that if her disposition matched Big Brother's seriousness, he may go insane in less than a few months with her. With her sunny outlook, she would put a brake on his somberness at the right point and stop him before he took himself too seriously. With a voice that reminded me of a breeze that makes a crisp swish over tall trees in a forest and cools the sweat on a farmer's torso, she would calm him down, and before long, the couple would discover that they fit each other as perfectly as a pair of hands and custom-made gloves.

Watching Big Brother and his wife truly happy with each other, I realized that most people, however brilliant, were content to travel on the road their culture had marked for them. It occurred to me that women with my will to differ might be an arrogant lot who refused in vain to settle in their place. Even women who graduated from Seoul National University with honors were modest enough to sacrifice their achievements to follow their husbands, so what was my ground? With nothing but discipline and determination, and sometimes words that brought my family to the brink of madness, I seemed hardly adequate to achieve my dreams. How could I dare to hope to have a career full of remarkable achievements and a family that was equally noteworthy for its smart, loving children? I found myself in despair, resentful of my own shortcomings and high expectations.

Big Brother and his wife weren't just set for an ideal marriage, they were set for an *ideal arranged marriage*. They would be a couple to prove the everlasting effectiveness of the custom founded on the belief that once a man and a woman were brought together by their social circumstances, love between them would naturally grow over time. Love, according to most Koreans who firmly believed in arranged marriages, was the slow and steady intimacy that developed like a viscous chemical amalgamating the individuals together. It wasn't passion. It wasn't romance or fire or even friendship. It was the undefinable, invisible, and yet fierce substance forming in the space between the spouses, the intangible morass blooming in the zone welding the two separate beings into each other. Love was the magic of time accumulated, these believers declared, and arranged marriages were certain to maximize this almighty power of time by carefully measuring the couple's compatibility before vows were exchanged. They acknowledged that to those who didn't believe in arranged marriages, such measurements might seem absurd or even vulgar because they were calculations based on external conditions. They didn't take into account the couple's internal needs and demands, and they didn't seriously consider their emotional and physical compatibilities. But what could forecast a solid marriage more effectively than a combination of factors deeply grounded in reality? In arranged marriages, one's social qualifications—such as the level of education, income and wealth, family background and heritage, occupation and major, and one's track record in academic excellence—were carefully matched and used to forecast the chances for a marital success. The probability of errors in such a careful deliberation was much slimmer than in a marriage born of passion and romance. In all probability, Big Brother's marriage was bound to be a success.

Essentially, Big Sister's marriage was of the same kind as Big Brother's. As Big Brother and his wife were brought together by a friend of Father's who was well-acquainted with the groom's parents and the bride's, Big Sister and her husband were introduced to each other by a relative of my family who was also the young man's work colleague. Both Big Brother and Big Sister finalized their decision to marry after Father, having run a primary investigation upon his future children-in-law, issued his final approval. But I was disturbed by what seemed to me a striking difference in his attitudes toward his son and his daughter, which revealed an overt sign of preferential treatment and discrimination, a mark of obsessive zeal for one child and a nearly callous disregard for another. For Big Brother, Father was painstakingly meticulous in evaluating his future daughter-in-law. But because Big Sister was a two year-college graduate, he was much more lenient and, in my mind, almost too generous—and certainly loose—in assessing her prospective husband.

There were procedural differences in the ways the matches were conducted. In Big Brother's case, the prospective groom and his wife had to be outstanding not only in their academic credentials but also in their social class and family backgrounds. Expectations on both sides ran higher and the search took longer. Because it also involved dealing with some very influential people in the inner circles of Korean academia, it had to be carried on with more caution and courtesy—and more secrecy, if necessary. Big Brother's pairing couldn't be accomplished in the short time Father had invested on locating Big Sister's husband. With his daughter, he had felt he had little time to wait. For her to miss the youngest possible marriageable age seemed tantamount to losing the best chances to meet a man worthy of his admiration. For a woman with only a two-year-college degree and without much claim for anything exceptional, youth was her only asset. Father was in a hurry to grab the first man he thought was right for his daughter, and when he believed he met such a man, he made a snap decision for fear of losing him.

With his son whose price in the marriage market was much higher, he was much more at ease. Confident that he would find a woman he could eagerly endorse, Father took his time. Overjoyed by the reports from his matchmakers, who called to tell him about all the women looking forward to meeting his son, he could well afford to turn down anyone who didn't deserve serious consideration. When Big Brother eventually settled his eyes on one woman, about whom neither father nor son had any doubts, he was relieved because the year-long search was finally coming to an end, but not because he had been worried about the possibility to have to grab the second best.

Although Father was the one who made calls to the matchmakers to gather details about the women and arranged their first meetings with his son, he had enough leisure to abstain from presenting anyone with overt favoritism. He didn't feel inclined to handpick anyone, although he evaluated certain candidates more highly than others. Nor did he wish to meet any one of the women in person until his son was ready to make the initial decision on whether or not to meet them. Concerning the ones Big Brother wanted to see, Father suggested, without the bombastic tone I had heard him wield upon Big Sister, that Big Brother try to go out with them more than once so that he could have a second impression. The day his son came home from the first date with the woman he felt was meant to be his wife—the one who indeed became my sister-in-law three months later—Father didn't forget to advise him gently to take it slowly.

"After several more dates, you'll see how you'd get along as friends. You'd better be sure you can be good friends before anything else." In fact, it wasn't until the hopeful couple felt fairly certain about their potential to be lifelong mates that Father expressed his interest in joining them for a cup of coffee.

In the investigation process, too, Father was much more meticulous and serious than he had been with Big Sister. All he had bothered to look into regarding his prospective son-in-law was his college transcripts, his reputation at work, and his annual income. Regarding the young man's family, Father didn't care to go further than being informed about the most bare facts, like the ones people exchange during their first casual meeting – that the young man's father had passed away in his thirties, that he was the youngest in his family, that his mother had raised five children alone, and that he had been groomed to be a banker since he was a freshman in college with a full scholarship. In selecting his son-in-law, Father never conducted a secret investigation, not in the least the kind of thorough, far-reaching detective work he chose to undertake for Big Brother's future wife.

For Big Brother, there was a KGB-style investigation on the prospective bride, the "backdoor inquiries," as Koreans with marriageable children called it. Because a bad marriage for Big Brother would mean trouble for our family, Father couldn't be too careful. The day after Big Brother came home from his second outing with future Big Sister-in-law, Father began to make his moves. First, he made a phone call to a former college classmate of his, who had been teaching at K girls' high school for nearly fifteen years, to ask him if he could dig up the young woman's attendance records. Second, he called a longtime friend, a professor at Seoul National University, and persuaded him to check out her college transcripts. Finally, he got hold of the personnel directory of the company where she worked, located a name that sounded vaguely familiar, and upon learning that it was one of his former students, he contacted him to learn about her work performance. To his satisfaction, Father heard adjectives such as "punctual," "diligent," "sociable," and "competent," but he was absolutely delighted by the last two sentences that concluded the half-hour long description. He quoted the man, dropping the phone, "'She's got a bit of an arrogant air about her, but it's a turn-on in her case. It's a nice way of letting people know that she's not fit for an average man.'" Father exclaimed, his voice quivering with excitement, "What a lucky boy our son is! He's going to get such a highly priced bride!"

One thing he couldn't be entirely certain about was the intimate details of her private life – her sexual past, to put it bluntly. He knew everything about her, including her excellent grades from high school through college, her good reputation at work, her very well-educated and refined family, her fine etiquette and ebullient optimism, and her strong constitution. She had had only three absences in high school—one each year—a sure sign that she was not only hardworking but also healthy. Her siblings were also smart and in good health, currently attending or having graduated from prestigious colleges with outstanding grades, boasting of perfect attendance wherever they went. Discipline and a brilliant brain were in her genes, and Father had no doubt that if she became his daughter-in-law, his grandchildren would be born with the same endowments and be raised with just as much drive.

"If she has a boy," Father mused, "and if this boy has his father's talents and his mother's gifts, he'll have two different brains in one. It'll be something – something indeed!"

Surprisingly, Mother snapped, in one of those rare moments she obeyed her impulse to disagree with him, "You're pushing your luck! Greed makes the gods angry. If he has two brains in one, something terrible will happen. Don't wish for a tragedy!" Clacking her tongue, she glared at him, but as he broke into a sheepish laugh, she concluded, "There's no way we can find out how virtuous—or fallen—she is morally, but we can pretty much tell. If she's a professional playgirl, she'd be notorious in Seoul, and we would've heard of it by now."

Father agreed, "Judging from her family, she's most likely a decent woman. I just wanted to be sure that she's not a habitual heartbreaker, and I feel pretty sure she's not. Even if she'd dated a man, she's not the type who'd be loose enough to have sex with him before getting married."

It didn't occur to Father or any of us that the young woman's father was making the same backdoor inquiries about Big Brother. Not long after the wedding, upon learning how thoroughly the renowned professor had conducted his secret police work on his future son-in-law, Father burst out laughing and exclaimed loudly, "That proves how good my methods were! He copied mine, verbatim!" Indeed, the professor had followed the same steps, starting with Big Brother's high school attendance and then following up with phone calls to the bank where he was working full time while studying to finish his master's degree. He also got hold of an old friend at Seoul National University to find out how well he was doing with his graduate work, and as the answer was quite satisfactory, he moved on to the most natural question for the bride's father to ask: What was the young man's moral reputation?

"For a father with a married daughter, you know what the most frightening thing is?" Father asked. "It's the possibility of her running back to him with tears in her eyes because of the other woman in her husband's life. He had to be sure she wasn't marrying a womanizer." He paused, his lips curving up from joy and his eyes full of proud twinkles. "There's no way you can tell how a man will change in the future, but you can guess it from his behavior in the past. You can almost trust the cliché, 'Once a womanizer, forever a womanizer.' Likewise, you can almost trust the reverse, 'Once a faithful fellow, forever a faithful fellow.'" When he secretly interviewed people who were familiar with the details of Big Brother's daily routines, he felt reasonably certain that his daughter was going to be in safe hands. Since some of these people were cooks and cleaners at the boarding house where Big Brother had lived alone for about a year while teaching at a local university with a master's degree, he knew he had credible sources. He had no doubt his sources were telling him the truth when they said they had never seen him bring a woman to his room or sleep out of the dorm even for one night.

As much as I detested it, this KGB-style investigation was enormously effective in increasing the probability of a successful marriage. It left nothing to chance, except for perhaps the most unforeseeable factors such as sudden, irreparable changes in the couple's feelings for each other or unexpected disasters, including a spouse's premature death or fatal illness. While an arranged match was a business transaction, the backdoor inquiries were the procedural steps. Because everything, even the intimate details of one's private life, was scrutinized, these inquiries had little room to yield inaccurate data, and hence, few erroneous forecasts about the compatibility of the man and the woman being paired. As long as the couple liked each other and mutually felt some sort of physical chemistry, it was predicted that their marriage would be on solid ground and that its longevity could be safely envisioned, if not guaranteed. Since uncertainties coming from a class gap or unstable socioeconomic circumstances were eliminated from the beginning, divorces were rare and death or unforeseen calamities remained to be the only forces that would separate the couples.

But to an idealistic college girl, the secret investigation seemed nothing but a series of vulgar calculations and deliberate deals. "How could anyone be married like that?" I wondered. "Two people have to fall in love before they talk business. In an arranged marriage, they talk business before they fall in love. How can they do that?"

But these questions didn't trouble me nearly as much as the ones that followed. Individuals with a "record" wouldn't have much of a chance to pass the scrutiny, and those who had had a premarital affair would have a problem finding a spouse through a matchmaker. If they were found out, they would be instantly rejected, and in some unfortunate cases, bring dishonor to their families. If they could hide it, it would be OK, but could they? And even if they could, should they?

To me, an arranged marriage was intolerable because it didn't allow room for mistakes. One publicized blemish was enough to ostracize a candidate from the marriage market, while one outstanding merit was far from satisfactory to those seeking a whole package. The secret police work granted probabilities only to the formula, to relationships fitting the paradigm set up by cultural norms. To be welcomed by a matchmaker, a man had to be a provider and a woman the keeper of his provisions. Anyone interested in creating a different pattern was advised to seek a love marriage. For women with my career goals and personal aspirations, even love marriages offered little hope because once married, they found themselves falling into the grip of the culture and sooner or later leaving work for their family.

For those who fell nicely into the formula endorsed by matchmakers, arranged marriages worked very well. Big Sister's marriage has lasted nearly five decades, and Big Brother's has stood the test of more than forty years without a single rupture to raise serious doubts about the blessedness of their matrimony. Compared to Big Sister's marriage, which faced several crises because of her husband's reckless spending habits and his siblings' vulgar behaviors, Big Brother's has been a jolly ride jammed with fulfilled hopes and jubilant spirits. But in the end, the outcome of both marriages has turned out to be no different. After all, Big Sister and her husband have been getting old in the same house, having lived more years together than alone, and Big Brother and his wife have been well on their way to an old age united in pleasant memories. Both of these couples will stay married until "their hair turns as gray as the roots of green onions," to prove the magical longevity of the custom my country has practiced with such ruthless, unforgiving uniformity.

Imagine how alone I felt in the home of the couple whose marriage was a prime example for this fully blessed journey. I felt I was a Satan disrupting their sacred, happy routines.

Chapter 4
Einstein's Wives

With little variation, the dozen or so couples in Big Brother's inner circle at Harvard had been married through the same route and stayed married in the same monotonous pattern (except for one couple in a love marriage, whose match would have been unlikely in an arranged marriage because she was from one of the lowest departments in a third-rate university and he was from one of the best at Seoul National University). In each couple, husband and wife were deeply committed to each other. Most of them had small children, one or two born within the first two years after their move to America, and having been educated at elite schools and with prestigious upper-middle-class backgrounds, their successful and privileged future (and that of their children) was practically guaranteed. Anxiously awaiting the days that would bring them the shining proof of their wifely duties and achievements—the days they could finally see their husbands' diplomas—the spouses of these graduate students gladly sacrificed their wants and needs for those of their husbands.

The women created an environment in which the only thing their husbands had to do was study, eat three warm meals a day, and sleep comfortably. The women shopped, cleaned, and washed. They drove their children to doctor appointments, put them to bed at night, and woke them up and washed them in the morning. They even took them out for a walk or to play at the park to give their husbands some quiet time in the evening when term papers were due. At hectic times, such as the end of a semester, they even typed their husbands' handwritten papers, cranking out one error-proof page after another. Having learned typing in college in preparation for their role as a competent wife, most of them knew a lot more about how to put together an attractive-looking paper than did their brilliant husbands, who had little knowledge for anything except their narrow academic fields. Without their wives' slave labor, they couldn't have done what they were doing.

While a peddler's wife toiling beside her husband to make a living had my compassion and respect, these women who solely thrived on their husbands' social status earned nothing but my condescension. Poor and uneducated women had no choice but to marry men who would provide for them, but I could harbor very little understanding for well-educated women from privileged backgrounds who volunteered to be nothing but adjuncts in their men's lives. Further, they felt free to grant themselves a false sense of superiority. They would proudly boast: "My husband is a PhD," "My husband is an MD," "My husband is a CEO," and "My husband is a JD."

I didn't *want* to blame them for assuming their roles without question, and I found myself spinning in a never-ending vortex of the contrary feelings toward them. Although it was difficult for me to respect those who held a sense of superiority because of their husbands' achievements, I acknowledged the enormous contributions they made to the wellbeing of the family system. After all, living in Big Brother's apartment for a whole summer meant that I was benefiting from one of these women's unpaid labor. I thought with a touch of laughter, *If the world only had women like me, who think that a woman ought to preserve* ***a sense of her own self****, whether she is a full-time homemaker or an all-time careerist, it would fall apart in one day.*

I reminded myself over and over again, "If I'm condescending toward these women, I'd be condescending toward my friends, mothers, sisters, and my aunts and great-aunts. I'm being judgmental against the system that makes them so obedient. We're sisters—all of us—and we must preserve and nurture sisterhood. I can love my sisters even if I don't respect them."

Still, I found myself secretly passing judgment on them. These men and women not only carried the traditional system over from Korea but also proudly practiced it in here in another country as if it were a universally superior system. While the men continued to live for both love and work, the women continued to live for love only. While the men continued to construct and strengthen themselves, the women continued to dismantle and weaken themselves. To use a Korean metaphor, while the men very proudly remained the head of the family, the women very modestly remained the tail.

Nevertheless, the Korean men at Harvard seemed to be more refined than the male Korean graduate students I had met at SUNY in Albany. Even if not entirely open minded, the former at least appeared to abstain from the atrociously vulgar racism and sexism the latter displayed. More than once, I heard the Korean SUNY men casually dropping comments such as: "So-and-so is riding a white horse," "So-and-so is riding a black horse," and "So and so is riding a yellow horse" – when talking about a Korean man having a sexual relationship with a non-Korean woman. (A yellow horse referred to a non-Korean Asian woman.) But when a Korean woman was having a sexual relationship with a non-Korean man, whether black, white, or Asian, they condemned her behind her back. Their double standard reflected the belief that Korean women were the property of Korean men and therefore were to be zealously guarded, but non-Korean women, the property of non-Korean men, were treated as sexual objects that were not granted the dignity Korean men awarded to their own property. To them, conquering non-Korean women was something to be proud of, a sign of their nation's right to extend its turf, but having Korean women conquered by foreign men meant having their national property stolen by outsiders, proof that the men who led the Korean nation were weak.

This double standard brought to mind the nauseating hypocrisy once practiced by the traditional white male in the American South. Believing white women to be their sacred property, white men brutally lynched and killed black men accused of having raped white women. They ruthlessly ostracized white women who consorted with black men, trashing them as whores to be buried socially. It is no wonder that white and black women both called slavery a patriarchal institution. While white male plantation owners were free to rape black female slaves or engage in a string of irresponsible sexual liaisons with them, their white wives had no power to stop their men from degrading the female gender – either black or white. I wondered if this was why there still was a double standard in America, in the North as well as in the South. I asked, "Is this why white Americans are more upset to see white women being raped by black men than they are to see black women raped by white men?" It was men's ownership-driven mentality that lay at the bottom of what the world so unanimously deplored, the inequality coming from a lethal combination of racism and sexism that demoralized women of all races.

Because the Korean men at Harvard didn't seem to have this ownership mentality toward women, I had a reason to think better of them. In the most fundamental way, they were sexist because they played a role in perpetuating the sexist model, in reinforcing the very conventional lifestyle of benefiting from their wives' unpaid labor. But none of them made any of the vulgar comments the men in Albany made about white, black, and non-Korean women. Their wives were also more learned and refined than those in Albany. They were my brother's wife and his friends' wives, and I reminded myself that I shouldn't—and wouldn't—disparage them.

Perhaps, my contempt for these women who lived without a sense of self was inseparable from my fear and potential of being like them. Maybe, my will to create my own social status was a reflection of how subconsciously I coveted what they achieved through their men. I realized that, in spite of myself, I was still bound to the patriarchal norms I was trying so hard to escape. I felt that if we were living in a more just society, it would be unnecessary for me to see my life as an antithesis to the lives of the women whom I thought so little of. *Patriarchy is a woman's collective subconscious*, I secretly acknowledged. *It is like water for fish, and women of the world, myself included, can't seem to live without it. As a product of patriarchy myself, I want to be kind to women as I hope they are kind to me.*

But I was unable to bridge the gap between my intellectual realization and my emotional impulse. The more I tried to respect the "selfless" Korean wives, the more I found myself straying into contempt. At least twenty years were to pass before I could bring myself into the state of a convenient, proud indifference, an emotional condition where I could let go of the contempt. Approaching my fifties and writing my memoir, I finally threw out my aversion to them like an old shoe, glad to live with the inspiring company of a small number of friends whose capacity to preserve a sense of self impressed me. They were husbands and wives, fathers and mothers, but with both love and work in their lives, they held a balance worth admiring and envying.

At twenty-four, I couldn't hide or control my true feelings, and I ended up behaving in a manner often puzzling to people. I wasn't overtly condescending or critical since I held a minimal degree of social skills necessary to put on a respectful face. Nor was I overly modest or excessively polite in a gesture to conceal my scorn. Rather, I was deviant in my emotional manifestations and vented on random subjects that had nothing to do with what really bothered me. As a rapid, strong current of water flowing in one direction would break into a violent stream, I would lose my fight against the ambivalence, and my raw feelings would rush out in a short, but noisy fashion at something entirely irrelevant. I would occasionally become a source of displeasure for my company, overstepping boundaries to butt into a topic far removed from my knowledge.

Of all the incidents my erratic behavior created, I remember one vividly. At a party for the Korean graduate students and their families at Harvard, which I was invited to, along with Big Brother and his wife and their one-year-old son, I lunged out at one of the men. This man was discussing with the other men the relationship between economic growth and distribution. "There are conservatives in America who will not allow the system to reduce the gap between the owners and the owned," he said. "They believe in trickle-down theory and stand on the side of capital. They're not interested in equal distribution." I barged into the conversation in an aggressive, condescending voice. "Distribution is just as important as growth!"

Everyone was dumbfounded. In front of everyone, Big Brother ordered me to stay out of the men's talk, and as I moved to the kitchen, where the women were eating, it dawned on me that I had been not only rude but also stupid. My belligerent remark was meant to be a cry of protest against the strict gender segregation, but not knowing how else to protest, I blurted out whatever words that came to my mouth. I had little problem pretending to accept the status quo, but when the gap was manifested even at something as routine as the dinner table, it became too much for me.

The men sat at one table to talk about history, politics, economics, philosophy, and world affairs, while the women sat at another to gossip and brag about their fancy curtains and their children's grades in kindergarten and grade school. I had joined the men's side and let out a cry against the setup that I had perceived as demeaning not only to women but also to men. And since this cry was taboo, it became a rude, irrelevant interference. I felt wretchedly lonely. I had made myself into a mere idiot, full of rage that I couldn't articulate.

What was even harder to tolerate was their overtly expressed pity—or, in their words, "concern"—for me. Because I was unmarried at a highly marriageable age, they never missed an opportunity to throw their advice at me, "You'd better get married before you get too old. I'd love to introduce you to a man, but I don't know any. I'll keep my ears open." Refusing to recognize that I had never asked them for any help, they insisted upon exercising their good will toward a woman they saw as a misfit because she was without a man.

So convinced that they were motivated by compassion and respect, they kept singing the cultural cliché upon me until it became a routine act of verbal violence. They defined me as an emotional outcast, constantly labeling me as "wrong." They didn't realize they were doing this because they were blindly obeying the norms. These do-gooders couldn't have done a better job in proving the truth in the proverb, "The road to hell is paved with good intentions."

I was in an emotional prison. When Big Sister-in-law told me, laughing but serious, "Your brother wouldn't mind running stark naked for half an hour along the Boston River if that would bring you a future husband," I decided I had to break out of that prison or choke from all their pity. Big Brother had come up with that hilarious idea out of love for me, and his wife shared it with me as a joke, but I felt pushed beyond the limit. As much as I understood and appreciated their good intentions, I was overwhelmed with frustration. I had to free myself from the cultural forces that drove them to such an extent of concern about something so absurd.

Unfortunately, my way of freeing myself wasn't ignoring them. It was falling into a trap set by my culture, and it was choosing a man who turned out to be the worst disaster in my life. Everyone I knew was married and everyone said that I, too, ought to be married because they believed that being alone was a violation of the destiny a human being—particularly a woman—was born to fulfill. They were advocating *marriage*, not *love*, and in listening to them, I forgot the difference between the two. I willingly fell into the hands of a man who I knew even then was worthless. I was desperate enough to take any man I thought would be open to being with a woman who sought happiness in both love and work. I concluded that he could be a bum or even a bully, but as long as he understood this desire of mine, he would be fine with me. A man who didn't rule out work from his wife's life seemed as rare as water in a desert, and when I thought I had finally met such a man, I felt I had no time to wait.

Chapter 5
The Low-Maintenance Women

Jonathan seemed to be a perfect candidate, someone I could establish an honest relationship with. Deceived into believing his words over his actions, I convinced myself that he was the right man for me, and he eagerly agreed because, as I was to find out later, he was desperate for a woman. He had found it impossible to engage the interest of a woman he could respect but refused to lower his standards. He waited for the miracle of meeting the one who would recognize the greatness he believed he possessed. Although he wasn't an achiever, he believed that he was good at enabling those around him to be achievers. Because he had excellent skills in recognizing talents and encouraging them to succeed, he saw himself as a wise, nurturing mentor with hidden leadership skills. He would proudly declare, "I am a man of a socially inferior but a personally superior class." To him, I was the one who could benefit from this personally superior quality of his.

Noticing that his ability to recognize others' talents came from the vacuum of self in his life, I allowed myself to be flattered by him when he said I was smart and independent. I wanted to believe that he was kind and accommodating, giving freely of what little he owned as well as socially well-mingling. Because he was skilled in flattery, he always had a flock of people gravitating toward him, and I opted to see this as a sign of exceptional social ability. Because he was excellent at fostering others' dreams, he constantly enjoyed receiving their hungry attention, and I elected to see this as proof of his effective mentorship. He had nothing to lose because he had nothing. He encouraged others to achieve because he achieved nothing. He inspired others to realize their dreams because he had no dreams of his own. And he was always sociable because he was afraid to be alone. In love with his flattery, which I so very much needed, and aware that I was in love with his flattery, I decided to lose sight of his fatal deficiency: his total lack of self.

At thirty-three, he was barely making minimum wage, delivering *The New York Times* at four o'clock in the morning, overjoyed during the holidays by the few dollars he received as tips in the envelopes he had left in subscribers' mailboxes. Occasionally, he did odd jobs, such as moving heavy furniture for ladies, mowing the lawn and trimming trees for busy homeowners, and driving long distances for disabled people and old folks. He had a license as a real estate broker, but because he wasn't competent enough to sell an adequate number of houses to fulfill minimum requirements, his boss often bypassed him for a younger, newer broker. He barely allowed him to retain his desk in the office, which he kept merely to be able to carry a real estate broker card. It made him appear to be a professional and gave him a chance to impress people. To him, his card showed his real identity and he used it to the fullest advantage. In his mind, he was a man much larger than a newspaper delivery man, a man with a buried subtle greatness that belied his outward appearance as an underachiever. Because he was a free spirit unhampered by the pressure to achieve upward mobility, he believed he was content to accept whatever came to him and to work whenever he wanted to work to avoid the unpleasant process of climbing up. In his eyes, he was one of those truly liberated spirits who enjoyed life, not a member of the mindless masses driven to sacrifice the present for the future. He believed he was one of the exceptional few who could truly transcend social norms and conventions, one who could live with the internal dignity detached from the artificial need to attain high social status.

I noted that if he were a truly free spirit who paid no mind to social standard, he wouldn't hand out his card as a token of his professional status. I buried this observation because I knew it would lower his credibility in my mind. I also ignored his overt and almost obsessive longing to be with a well-educated woman from a prestigious background. Quite contrary to what he declared he wanted, he was bent on finding a woman who could prove the status he believed he possessed and the respect he believed he deserved. That I was a graduate student with a brother at Harvard was my single most attractive asset to him.

As I complained to him about the conventional norms that made me an outcast among the Koreans at Harvard, he was quick to praise my courage to be different. He saw that I was starved for emotional support and fed me sweet words, just as a psychiatrist would pour words of comfort to a patient dealing with a trauma.

"We're in America," he said. "I'll do everything to help you to achieve your academic goals. I admire career women, and I want you to be the best you can be. In this country, we appreciate women like you."

Jonathan presented the difference between Americans and Koreans in a sweepingly cultural nature rather than as an individual one. He exploited his national identity as a selling point and I bought it out of desperation. Willingly, I ignored the fact that he thrived on what he *represented*, not on what he *was*.

Jonathan, however, was clever enough to understand that I had enough intelligence to see the flaws of the country he praised. Although he made a sweeping generalization about America in terms of its ability to accommodate women like me, he didn't forget to point at its many problems. He made it clear to me that he was by no means a poor, ignorant American whose self-representation relied solely on his national pride. With little patriotic chauvinism, he agreed with me. Like me, he also deplored the sight of old men and women with their dogs alone in the park. He denounced the United States for its backward foreign policies. He lamented the severe gap between the rich and the poor. He condemned its crass materialism and overt racism. He was sincerely enthusiastic about making his country a true melting pot. Especially fond of Asian immigrants and their children, he praised them as a group of emerging newcomers who actively contributed to making the United States more economically and culturally affluent. He found Asians more diligent and hardworking than Americans of all other backgrounds, including WASP, sweeter in temperament and kinder in manners, and he loved them for being loyal and faithful, for being so well adjusted to American life.

"Asians have never been a problem in this country," he said. "They follow mainstream American rules so well that soon, they'll beat most whites at their own game. It's because they're docile and obedient. Compliance is their biggest asset." He was proud of his overtly preferential treatment of Asians in the business of choosing personal friends and acquaintances. Having lived in Thailand for seven years as a peace corps member, he was more globally aware than most Americans who never had the experience of living overseas. He had learned emotionally as well as intellectually that America, with its merits and flaws, was merely one of the many countries on earth, an equal to the rest of the nations. He seemed more able to practice what most Americans could only preach.

But honestly, I couldn't see his true motive for agreeing with me. I knew that he meant what he said to me, but I could sense that he would give an entirely different opinion to another individual whose impression of America didn't reflect my observations. He would instantly erase his own thoughts to please another or would hide them with enough skill to bolster another's. He would even come across as admiring an individual whose values were antithetical to his. In my presence, he was sincere with his belief in a melting pot, but I had no doubt that he would instantly change his belief in someone else's presence. I couldn't trust him. Flattered nevertheless by his compliments for Asians, I listened on to him. "If he thinks so highly of Asians," I reckoned, "it would work for my advantage. With his insights, he can help me establish a balanced perspective about my new country, to understand and represent those American authors who praise and criticize their country. He can help me to become a balanced critic of American literature."

I calculated what he could bring me as he calculated what I could bring him. Usually, it is through hindsight that one realizes one's true reason for getting involved in a relationship, but with Jonathan, I knew, even at the very beginning, that there was nothing but a businesslike deal between us. Like most relationships of convenience, it was disguised as love and romance, expressed in the form of exchanging sweet words and charming gifts. He would bring me a bowl of blueberries he had picked at a friend's garden, and I would eat them, pretending they were delicious. I would buy him a small package of pickled herring, his favorite snack, and he would devour it in no time, smacking his lips loudly to show an exaggerated appreciation. He was in love with a young, well-educated Asian woman from a prestigious background, not with me. I was in love with an Asia-loving, seemingly open-minded American man who I thought would be able to help me rise in America, not with him.

His problem, which turned out to be a fatal flaw that cracked the values he so loudly upheld, was his inability to actually be who he believed he was. Instead of realizing his dreams, he just kept flirting with the possibility of achieving them. He lived in a fantasy world where he could thrive on good intentions alone. Having squandered every penny he had earned from teaching English in Thailand, he was living from one meager paycheck to another in a rundown apartment with poor plumbing, waiting for a prestigious job to come his way.

It was primarily his vanity that made him so unrealistic, but his lifestyle in Thailand also boosted his sense of superiority. During his seven years in what he called that "great" Asian country, he had learned how to exploit the privileges of being an English-speaking white male and mastered the art of being a highly spoiled and falsely respected bum. He would reminisce, "Every day, my live-in maid would go to the market and buy fresh fish and vegetables. I didn't have to lift a finger to enjoy such great dinners."

Every day, he was bowed to because he was a white male in a third world country, and every day, he had plenty of money in his pocket just because he could teach the language he was born and raised to speak. But back in America, he was nobody, and he couldn't accept the change. As a way of reclaiming the superior status he had enjoyed in Thailand, he considered nothing but a white-collar career for himself, believing that he was above the menial labor he was perfectly fit to do. The occasional part-time work he chose to do to support himself, such as delivering the paper and finishing floors for a remodeling company, was only temporary as far as he was concerned. He was precisely what people call an Asia bum, an American who was spoiled to live beyond his means because of the way he had lived in an Asian country.

I was also to be blamed for his delusions. I had allowed myself to be swayed by the Korean graduate students and their wives and grabbed the first man who came along, disregarding the discriminatory instincts I should have been able to exercise as a young woman with such a strong, rebellious mind. It should have been clear to me that he was a racist-sexist. As he constantly tried to impress me by saying that Asia was a better place than America because it was wiser and more spiritual, he incessantly tried to please me by saying that Asian women were better than American women because they were more respectful and caring for their men. As he projected into Asia what he thought America could not be, he assumed that Asian women were what American women could not be. He was a thoroughbred racist and sexist man whose narcissism as a white male was cunningly concealed by his rhetoric of praise and glorification.

While I was with him, I remained totally oblivious of what was to become so obvious to me a few years later. He turned out to be a perfect specimen of the men I learned to avoid. His was the typical male mind I was to devote my entire life escaping. In his attitude toward women, he was the epitome of the traditional mind-set of so many American men. In their behaviors as well as in their words, they would take me back to second-class citizenship, back to a place with the same old prejudices. Jonathan proved to be one of these men—the worst of them all—who delighted to show me the ugliest face of America.

"Asian women are feminine, but American women imitate men too much," he would lecture. "They are too carefree with their bodies, ready to sleep with anyone they want. But Asian women are more careful, more reserved and discriminating. You don't go to bed with someone unless there's a promise of a long-lasting relationship, and once attached, you don't mess around on your men as American women do. You believe in commitment. Whatever happens, Asian women stand by their men and abstain from indecent conduct. But American women don't. So fickle and demanding, they run around with other men the moment they spot a problem with their current men, no matter how small. Something as trivial as not being able to reach an orgasm in bed would make them compelled to find another man."

Asian women, according to these men who so preferred them over the "loose" American women, were more traditional and hence more tolerant of their men's flaws. They were gifted in bearing with the unilateral burdens of a relationship in ways that were nearly impossible for their spoiled American sisters. They were the faithful, demure lot that rarely complained about being robbed of their pleasures as they selflessly assumed the duties of taking care of their men's needs and desires. Being less demanding in bed, they were expected to accommodate their men more, to endure longer and to stand sexual negligence with a finer grace and a kinder acceptance. For them, carnal frustration was more foreign and men's selfish attitudes more familiar. Because their sexuality didn't require the same amount of feeding as American women's, their men could obtain an instant release in bed with less work and more ease and therefore could save their energy for more important tasks that really mattered to them. Asian women made it possible for their men to get what they wanted without having to give as much in return. Being used to tyranny and oppression, these women were simply grateful – and were expected to be.

The point in such false compliments is that Asian women deserved less than their American sisters. Dividing women in two categories—selfish and selfless—they ranked one higher than the other. But in truth, the lower-ranked ones were far higher because American women possessed the privilege to be freer, to be more spoiled and demanding. Harder to satisfy, they wielded higher standards for their men to fulfill and were armed with more self-confidence and circumstantial leverages to say no to a man's inadequacies. Men who were not qualified for a partnership with a more competent American woman often sought the companionship of an Asian woman, hoping to enter a relationship in which their performance—in bed as well as in other places—could be accepted with less rigorous and scrutinizing assessments. Unlike American women, Asian women were more lenient with their claims and requirements, which meant that their men didn't have to be on their toes nearly as constantly. With Asian women, men could get by with lower standards and still be safe.

"So-and-so wouldn't be able to stay married if his wife were an American, but fortunately for him, she's Japanese. What he does would be grounds for a divorce for an American woman, but his Japanese wife puts up with it," a friend of mine said about a male colleague who was notorious for his self-absorbed behavior. He was not only a selfish careerist consumed by his ambition to reach the top in his field but also an active chaser of his graduate students, an habitual womanizer whose longing for the companionship of intellectually stimulating, attractive women clashed with his need for a stable, silent wife exclusively dedicated to his success. A Japanese wife—who seldom raised her brows at him for spending more time at his office than at home and didn't bother to interrogate him about the daily phone calls from his female professional associates—was perfect for him, and he absolutely adored her, to no one's surprise. As a master esteems his obedient slaves, he esteemed her. She was "low maintenance," easy to bend, and more sensitive to his priorities than to hers. She didn't mind being left alone most of the time because, not knowing how to be dissatisfied, she didn't—and couldn't—ask for more attention from her husband as did assertive American women. Needing less, the professor's wife could be treated as less.

With one standard for American women and another for Asian women, these American men perpetuated their own double standards, which were more degrading than those practiced by Korean men. Korean men treated men and women unequally, but American men added another layer of sexism by placing one race of women beneath another and judging them with two separate sets of criteria. I found myself fighting two different double standards instead of one.

"Is this what I came to this country for?" I raged whenever I had to hear tired cultural clichés such as, "American women are too career-driven, but Asian women pay more attention to relationships. They're less self-absorbed." A sardonic snicker would escape from my mouth at hackneyed confessions like, "I'm partial for Asian women because they're more submissive than American women," and "I thought Asian women are traditional. How come you're not?" A falsetto laugh would reverberate from my throat at remarks like, "You're so vocal and assertive, so different from any Asian woman I've ever met. On the phone, you would pass for an aggressive American woman."

Jonathan had a reason to believe he was a victim. Because I had led him to believe that I could use his support to achieve my academic goals, he followed me to Lawrence, Kansas, where I planned to pursue a PhD in English for the next several years. Because SUNY at Albany only offered an MA degree, I had to go to a university with a PhD program and I chose the University of Kansas from the recommendation of one of the professors at Albany. I knew that he decided to move with me because he had virtually zero chance to meet an Asian woman with my education and background. He knew this, but all things considered, it seemed to him that he was making all the sacrifices. He was the one losing the benefit of the connections he had established in Boston, the one leaving his home base for an unknown place, and the one accommodating my wishes because I didn't express an objection. I told him that I could use his help as a native speaker of the English language with critical insights about America. I confessed to him that he could help me achieve my academic goals. Never trying to dissuade him, I was partly responsible for the wrong moves he made. He was set on having a life with the Asian woman who would bring him a status while I was intent on spending my years in Kansas with an American man who would intellectually support my success in America. Together, he and I chose to be entangled in a mutually convenient relationship. In a strict sense, it was mutual exploitation, and knowing this, we pretended we were in love.

A foreign student who, with only a year and a half in America, knew little of the ways of her new country, I convinced myself that I couldn't do without him. He was an ugly, unattractive, and penniless man, and I was aware that I was deceiving myself. It was piercingly clear to me that under better circumstances, he would be an embarrassment and a shame to me. Why else would I have been so hesitant to introduce him to any of my friends?

It was a year later that I could admit how right Big Brother was when he called Jonathan a bum. "He'd be a perfect Moonie selling chewing gum on the street," Big Brother had warned. "He's thirty-three years old, but he thinks he's a three-year-old boy. He's a dreamer with nothing but a talent in drawing sand castles. He's a hopeless case. Moving with him to Kansas would be the biggest mistake of your life."

As I kept my peevish silence, he went on, frustrated enough to use a string of extreme vocabulary, "Do you want to be a meal ticket for a worthless parasite? You're blinded by your loneliness right now, but if you look at him half a yard away, you'll see what he is. Don't you see the sickness in his eyes? I don't know what he did in Thailand for seven years, but I am sure he got involved in all sorts of shady things. Smoking pot habitually was probably one of the smallest things he did. I wouldn't be surprised if he had done hard drugs like heroin and cocaine – a lot of them, at that. I wouldn't be shocked if he had been a frequent customer at brothels."

Even back then, I knew that Big Brother was turning to the last resort, using savage words to instill some sense into my bullish head. I knew he was deliberately insulting Jonathan because he loved me and wanted to protect me. But the more I agreed with Big Brother inside, the more recalcitrant I became outside, determined to set myself against him at every possible angle. I wished to challenge the oldest son of my family, to demolish what seemed to me an older brother's ungrounded authority over his little sister, and to show that I was brave enough to go against a big man blessed with all that unquestioned credibility. I wanted to prove him wrong and me right.

Secretly, I agreed with Big Brother. As he compared Jonathan's eyes to mushy egg whites, I silently compared his face to an ugly dodo with a huge, protruding beak. Almost entirely bald, Jonathan had a short stump of hair where his head met his neck, which gave his large, broad forehead the aura of a generous fool. Being on the round side, his wrinkled cheeks softened the stinging impression created by his extremely thin, aquiline nose that accentuated the sudden sharpness of his jaw. Caved in at the bottom, his chin made an almost perfect symmetry with the narrow top of his head, awarding his face the contour of a football standing up. Even more hideous was his profile, which reminded one of a hawk with large bulging eyes. They were predatory, but pale and quiet, diffused by an unfocused gaze with a history of drugs.

Anyone who made eye contact with him could spot the long-lasting shadows of the drugs he had taken in Thailand, which conjured all the other pleasures that must have been part of the package. He admitted that for seven years in Thailand, he had smoked marijuana twice a day with the regularities of sacred religious rituals. Because I never asked him, fearful of the truth, about the more dangerous drugs he had taken, I didn't know with certainty that he had consumed cocaine and heroin. But people could see the lingering destruction of the mind-corrupting substances.

Several friends would observe, "I can smell it in him. He still looks like a junkie." I would reply, "That doesn't surprise me. Last winter, he and I went to New Orleans for a vacation. When we were walking around the French Quarter, some guy asked him if he wanted to buy some heroin and he almost said yes."

Out of shame, I didn't tell my friends that he had confided to me that during his seven years in Thailand, he had had sex with more than 220 women, most of whom were common prostitutes and high-class call girls. It was a couple years later, with an ache in my heart, that I realized how I had known all this and yet denied it.

During the two successive years I was with him, I saw plenty of selfish behaviors that I deliberately ignored. Having been a regular at Bangkok brothels for seven years, he only knew how to have sex and therefore had never learned how to make love. As our intimate moments ended in less than a few seconds, I would protest, but he would accuse me of being insatiable. He would accuse me of picking up the demanding attitude of American women who drove their men to develop performance anxieties by being so sexually demanding. Although I was very limited in sexual practices, I had somehow picked up enough information to understand that a man's inadequate performance in bed was more likely a product of poor sexual education. It wasn't because he was callous or cruel, it was because he had never been taught how to engage a woman.

I was irate only because he refused to listen when I told him I was happy to instruct him. So overcome by the fear of being with a woman whom he defined as American, he turned deaf and blind to a woman's most fundamental rights. Claiming that he was totally satisfied with me in any way that a man could be with a woman, that he admired me more wholeheartedly than any man could a woman, he absolutely disregarded the rules that a man is responsible to keep when he regards a woman as his equal.

I could tell he treated me as an object to show off. He felt compelled to present me, an Asian woman, to American women as a sign of victory. I could hear him declare in a loud silence, "Look at me, you American women! Instead of one of you, I have an Asian woman who respects men the way they ought to be respected." By being with me, he meant to take revenge against American women whom he hated so, and bolster the behavior he believed a man had the right to adopt. He believed he had the privilege to brush off a shrew who demanded sexual satisfaction against her man's will. He believed he was entitled to denounce an overweening broad who ruthlessly attempted to destroy the proud masculinity of the superior sex. So overwhelmed by the need to make a trophy wife out of me, he didn't even care about the reason why I chose him. He was the one in fact who suggested that we get a marriage license. Because I had come to America with the F-1 visa granted to foreign students and because I didn't have a job to support the credit hours required for my degree, I was faced with deportation. I was left with only one option: to get a green card by marrying an American citizen. Once I was legally married to him, I was bound to him, and he used my bondage to his fullest advantage. He believed he owned me.

Still, I didn't refuse his invitation to seek a counselor. Still, I deceived myself and agreed with him that once married, we were married forever. Still, I bought the notion he held so dearly, that I, being an Asian woman, would continue to remain committed to him, no matter what. Still, I told myself that he could learn to see me as a woman, not as an Asian woman, as an individual who was entitled to the rights of all women. I kept hoping against hope and went to a counselor with him.

"You feel you owe him because of the green card?" the counselor whispered in a decisive tone when he was alone with me after a joint counseling session. After hearing my story about his manners in bed, he suggested that I consider all of my relationship options. So transparent was Jonathan's male conceit that even the counselor couldn't bring himself to do the job that he was supposed to do and advise me to work out our conflict. He asked me very bluntly if I wanted to date other men, and I replied with a long silence, stunned by what seemed an outlandish question to a woman who had been married only for a few months. "If you stick with him, you're going to sabotage your own future. Do you want to throw your future away?"

Even then, I could tell that the counselor was acting on a sudden impulse to protect me. He saw that Jonathan used his American citizenship to obtain a woman—a kind of woman—whom he otherwise could not have had a chance with. He saw that Jonathan had initiated the marriage plan, knowing that I had no choice but to go along with it. He must have also recognized that I was using Jonathan just as he was using me, coming to the conclusion that this relationship was emotionally bankrupt. The counselor knew that between the two of us, the woman had more to lose than the man. I was sacrificing all the abundant opportunities in store for me while he wasn't sacrificing any, having virtually none to begin with. He could see that I was caught in a trap.

In our counseling sessions, Jonathan continued to attribute our marital problems to cultural differences, while the counselor continued to see through the self-justification Jonathan used to avoid looking into himself as an individual. Jonathan claimed it was because he was an American that my brother and my family didn't welcome him as my husband. He maintained it was because the two countries had developed conflicting definitions of gender roles that it was difficult for me to accept him as he was.

"Koreans draw a rigid line between men's and women's jobs. They believe men should be the providers and women the provided for. They don't appreciate the mixing of these two roles. When a man and a woman try to share the same roles, as we do in this country, Koreans laugh at them. That's why her family doesn't think I am a suitable man for her."

The counselor could easily see what was happening—that both my family and I, in my subconscious wisdom—regarded Jonathan as being disqualified because he was a hopeless bum, not because he was an American. I knew he saw who Jonathan was. I knew he recognized my internal confusion. Accepting him on a conscious level, but rejecting him on a subconscious level, I was torn by an impulse to agree with him and an urge to vehemently disagree. Turning to me to correct what Jonathan—and I, against my true feelings—observed, the counselor said, "It is a huge problem in America, too. Men are required to be breadwinners and women are expected to be homemakers. When they blur the line, they come under fire. It's not a cultural problem. It's a universal one."

It wasn't until I was caught shoplifting that I started to act upon the realizations the counselor had brought forward in me. So disturbed by the impostor that was my so-called husband, I searched for ways to assuage my anguish. I found myself cultivating a pattern of behavior that manifested who I thought I had become, a vulgar, reckless woman who had betrayed her moral standards. If I made myself into such a person, I would be justified in choosing Jonathan. I wouldn't be ashamed of being with him because I would be on his level. Driven by a subconscious will to be who I thought I had to be, I transformed myself into the stranger my environment made me. I resorted to any means to demean myself. I habitually got drunk on the cheapest beer, invited danger by walking alone at night, and frequently roamed around with a wine bottle in broad daylight. I even pretended to be crazy, talking to myself and running on the streets on hot summer days.

One night in July, during one of those notoriously blazing Kansas summers, I decided to steal a can of beer at a convenience store after convincing myself that I was unbearably thirsty. I was eager to test how far I could fall. I easily persuaded Jonathan to go along with my plan to steal. It was his style to lose his moral sense whenever his company demanded it of him. With Jonathan shielding me from the cashier's sight, I opened the refrigerator door, took a can, and hid it under my loose top. I had secretly planned to be caught by the surveillance camera and one of the men at the cashier's desk. Luckily, the man was patient enough to hear out the story I had rehearsed to make him feel sorry for me. I told him that I was an alcoholic, that I had been overwhelmed by the desire for a beer that I couldn't buy since it was Sunday (alcohol wasn't sold in Kansas on Sundays), and that I would join Alcoholics Anonymous the following morning if he was kind enough to let me go. As he allowed us to leave, I was relieved that my self-styled misdemeanor had come to an end without a police officer's report. But as I went back to the reality of my choice in a man, I was sad again. I had a chance to realize that Jonathan didn't even have enough sense to figure out that I had intended to be caught, nor did he have the strength to chide me for wanting to be caught.

I was at once a victim and a victimizer, as abusive to him as he was to me. I often yelled and screamed at him out of my own guilt and pain, but then I turned kind in a wink as if he were the love of my life. Still bound by the notion that a woman was to stay married to one man, I probably reinforced his delusions by acquiescing to his remark that Asian women believed in commitments. He automatically assumed that I, being an Asian woman, would remain faithful to a man, however unfit he might be. I didn't possess the wisdom to correct him by rebutting, "Women—yellow or white or black or purple or anything—are *trained* to be loyal to their men, however abusive they may be." Nor did I have the sense to put him in his place by asking, "Do you think I will stand by a worthless bum like you just because I am an Asian woman?" So afraid that I would be accused of mimicking the American women he hated, I kept my begrudging silence.

"I want you to be a great achiever," he would sing. "I want you to realize every dream you brought to this country. America is your home now." I wished I could be half as enthusiastic about my new home as he was. Coming from a man who, at the age of thirty four, was substandard enough to live off the minimum wage I made as a part-time student worker on campus, such encouragement was nothing but a lie. He selfishly went back to school, breaking his promise to be the breadwinner and support me through graduate school. I was to be three different beings all at once—a highly achieving superwoman, a provider, and a maid. Even his sister called to chide him.

"I wouldn't go back to school at your age," she said. "You have no time to waste now. Go back to being a real estate agent. Didn't you pass the Kansas test for real estate?" But he insisted on getting a second undergraduate degree in architecture, on competing with men and women half his age and twice as bright. I had every reason to doubt that he would ever finish.

In retrospect, I can hear clearly what my friends were telling me in chorus when they were advising me to leave him. Hardly aware of the details of his behavior—and my own behavior—they tried to help me see him for who he really was, to see the sham in his rhetoric. He made them queasy, and they instinctively shunned him but could not explain why. Some of them even took the risk of hurting my feelings by saying, "He's a creep."

But guilt made me overlook what they saw. I had allowed him to move to Kansas with me, accepted his marriage proposal, and aided in perpetuating his delusion that there was a firm commitment between the two of us. I was unable to bring myself to "get rid of him," to act upon the instinct that my friends articulated in such a strong consensus. Nor was I capable of considering another side of the matter. So absolutely certain that I—an Asian woman who believed in commitments, after all—would remain by his side, he had volunteered to marry me and get me a green card without an ounce of hesitation. I couldn't help but feel responsible for what he did. As much as he "pushed" me into marrying him, waving his American citizenship over an inexperienced foreign woman, I ended up taking advantage of the offer. I was not a victim. I had let him come along and encouraged him with my acquiescence.

I remained trapped in a relationship with him for only one reason—anger at my family and my country for punishing independent women—and I had agreed to marry him for no other reason than my own self-preservation. But as the years went by, one thing became absolutely true to me. I wouldn't have condemned him nearly as harshly as I did if I had been given one reason—just one—to believe that he was not a practicing racist-sexist. "What a nice guy!" I exclaimed, remembering all his sacrifices for me. But recalling all his racist-sexist comments and actions, I moaned, "What a creep!"

I turned creepy to get rid of the creep. Although it took me years to face why I did what I did, I must be honest enough to admit that I was perhaps aware of what I was doing. I would like to think that I was merely possessed by an impulse to survive, to escape the emotional jail. As time passed, I learned to confront how willfully deceitful my actions had been. Just three months after our five-minute wedding at a Kansas courthouse, I told him that I had decided to live by myself, to move out of the shabby one-bedroom apartment where we were cohabiting. I knew that we would be accused of lying to Immigration if he annulled the marriage, but I knew that he wouldn't dare because he couldn't bear to lose me. I relocated to a tiny one-room apartment with a kitchenette and a shared bath. I then actively sought the companionship of a man I had known for half a year or so, plunging into an extramarital affair. Until Jonathan caught me, I invited this man to stay almost every night for nearly a month. I thought that if I invited another man over for the night, Jonathan would leave me alone out of disgust or anger. Although he wouldn't dare to leave me for good, he would at least stay away from me sexually as long as I was with the new man. I was determined to continue my extramarital escapade until I received the green card in my hand, until Jonathan could no longer feel he owned me. Then, I would dump him once and for all and call the police if he tried to come back to me.

But he didn't leave me alone. He would soon beat me at my own game. He continued to push himself on me sexually, with increased force and more cruel indifference than before. He made it clear to me that he meant to use the green card to blackmail me and could get away with sexual assaults of any kind. Perhaps he was trying to humiliate me by reducing the short process even further, making it no more than half-a-minute-long coitus. He was trying to denigrate me by behaving as though what he was doing was perfectly normal. After the one-sided copulation was over, he would nonchalantly pull his pants up and say in a singsong voice, "Some friends and I are having a picnic at Perry Lake this afternoon. You want to come?" It seemed that he had made a deliberate decision to enjoy violating me, to delight in the power that brought the most instinctive fear in a woman. His revenge was to maximize, with a piquant glee, the pattern of his sexual behavior that he knew had hurt me in the past. Although he never even tried to learn why and how his way of "making love" was so demoralizing, he knew how to use it against me.

Despite all this, I must admit that he wasn't deliberately evil. Being a devoted practitioner of his religion of racism and sexism, he was a morally sick man, but he didn't have the courage—or the character, to be precise—to confront his sickness. He wasn't even aware that he was a sick man. The thirty-six years that have passed since then have given me a sense of pity for a weak man who had nothing but brute force to resort to as a weapon over an equally powerless woman. With no credit card, no bank account, no property, and no intelligence or wisdom to offer a woman, Jonathan found himself in possession of one thing—the physical power to beat a woman into submission—and he wielded it accordingly. He knew that as long as he held that one power card over me—the green card—he would be able to keep me pinned down. And he knew that the day I received an envelope from Immigration, after a few more months, he would no longer hold that power to obtain that highly convenient, cost-free sexual pleasure from me.

Chapter 6
The Magical Gift of Being Alone

It took me almost two decades to be able to talk about my destructive and traumatic married year with Jonathan. Shame, guilt, and pain haunted me and the fear of stigma followed me until I finally reached a state of mind where he became—almost—a person of the past, a specter without the power to be real. Twenty years after it all, I found myself in an emotional condition where the memory of my experience dissipated effortlessly in the little time it takes water to evaporate from a duck's tail. If pity is a sign of forgiveness, feeling pity toward him probably meant that I forgave him – and myself as well. Jonathan eventually became little more than a skeleton in my closet. As much as he would snake his way back into my memory at times, he lingered there only as long as he could arouse a feeling of contempt that could barely hold my interest at all.

Somehow, the man I thought so little of contributed the most to my growth in America. With his vices, he abetted me to plummet into the deepest nadir, yet with those same vices he helped me rebound to the highest point within my reach. It was in part because of him that I became a tumbler that was pushed as far down as possible and sprang back as far up as I could imagine.

To redeem myself from the mistake of having been with him, I redoubled my already zealous drive for intellectual achievements. It was largely my own determination and effort that made it possible for me to be who I eventually came to be. But I was undoubtedly driven by another will, another very powerfully motivating factor: I had to succeed to show myself and my loved ones that I was much more than the person I became when I was with Jonathan.

In time, I was able to see the one area in my life where he had made his contributions. As the first person to introduce me to the dark side of America, he indulged my curiosity about the big bad country, happy to feed my appetite for knowledge that would have been tiring—and repulsive—for anyone else. Without the seven-year-long experience in Thailand filled with prostitutes and call girls, exposing him to the thrills of enjoying the most corrupt elements of a nation's sex industry, he wouldn't have known how to introduce me to the other side of the new country. America was a huge sphinx to me, and my desire to witness its good and bad was as strong as my drive to succeed in its academia. I don't know how I could have discovered the seedy underbelly of Boston without him. I don't see how I could have appreciated the sunniest side of the country without the shadows he guided me into. While attending graduate school and learning about the highest ideals that one should aspire to practice, he exposed me to the lowest reality to which one could fall. With Jonathan, I visited immoral dungeons that reeked of decadent debauchery as often as possible. At strip joints, I beheld, for the first time in my life, stark-naked women dancing on stage one by one. In theaters on the same street, I watched pornography with unspeakably raw scenes of human copulations. For the simple reason that they were forbidden by law in Korea, these "genres" of nightlife fascinated me and made them sufficiently worthy to be included on my list of things to know and understand.

Although none of the actions I saw in these dimly lit places whetted my sexual appetite, they certainly awakened me to accept the undeniable reality that our hunger for sex is overwhelming enough to perpetuate a multimillion-dollar industry. I wasn't tempted to practice anything I saw in pornography, most of which was created by men's sexual fantasy alone and failed to stimulate a woman's imagination. But the mere knowledge that there was so much made in an attempt to respond to sexual needs made me realize that I had no reason to be ashamed of my sexual drive. Yes, I had heard about the problems of pornography such as violence against women and the objectification of female sexuality, and I saw it plainly in those poorly ventilated, stench-filled theaters. But what I gained in the theaters was the realization that the sexual need of human beings was so overwhelming that it created a huge industry that thrived on reproducing the same raw carnality for what seemed to be an eternity.

This realization helped me start the long process of walking away from the Confucian taboo against sex, to travel on the long road away from the idea that sex was an improper topic for "decent" persons. Because sex was an unspeakable subject in my family – and a subject that was whispered about among my friends and peers in Korea—I was in a state of denial about the sexual being in me. Pornography cracked open the door to the truth I wanted to acknowledge. It was a "backdoor" discovery, a truly unhealthy way of learning about the most human part of a human being. Because nobody had ever told me about sex and sexuality, I took the unspoken—and unspeakable to some—route to acquiring this knowledge. I put what I learned into practice, to find out how much of it could be carried into action.

In my affair with "Bob," I found him to be a much more satisfactory partner in bed than the callous Jonathan. Untainted by sex with prostitutes, Bob knew how to treat a woman with at least a minimal amount of courtesy, giving and taking pleasure at once in both a gentle and powerful manner. With him, I was no longer an insatiable woman, no longer accused of being a demanding American woman intent on emasculating her man. With him, sex could be enjoyable and reenergizing, an activity that replenished the very core of a man and a woman, and I thought I was ready to embrace it as such with any man who I thought was special enough to deserve that intimate connection with me.

I was determined to discard the shame attached to sex, although it took much longer for me to continue to manifest in action what lay in my mind. My sexual escapade with Bob, as instant and unhesitating as it was, came from my sudden impulse to test my ability to practice what I learned. But the one-time success couldn't be sustained long enough to eliminate the gap between theory and practice. Even today, over three decades after I initiated that very gratifying sexual adventure, I am not entirely certain that I am free. I am not at all certain, in fact, that I am totally divested of the cloak of coyness that a woman, regardless of her race, is supposed to put on—that false requirement to pretend to hesitate when she wishes to run to bed with a man, naked and shameless.

But because I was undoubtedly the one who led him along and because he so willingly came along, I at least learned how to get over the self-disparagement that a woman was supposed to feel as she initiated a sexual relationship with a man. I could honestly claim that I had the courage to declare, "Yes, I want you in bed now. Let's get to it." Although I was not brave enough to be entirely free from the fear of being branded as a loose woman, I became strong enough to disregard—or disown, if necessary—a man who felt that a sexually honest woman was less than desirable. "If he doesn't call me the next morning, I would feel disappointed because of the opportunities we'd miss," I would admit. "I would be sorry because we may lose the potential for a good time, not because I regret having gone to bed with him – not because I didn't play hard to get as a woman *should*."

For the first time in my life, I was capable of laughing at the way I used to be—at the woman I was in my early youth—and the women who in their more mature age still held on to the sexual norms that flourished a century ago. Perceiving their sexuality as cherished property to give away, these women chose to believe that a woman, once she had given in to a man sexually, was no longer a source of mystique. They feared that their bodily treasure had been robbed when their men didn't call them in the morning after the much-awaited initial sexual encounter. One may call these women victims of patriarchy, slaves of a culture that led the so-called second sex along with such a deceitful lie, but I refused to call them victims. Why give them the credit of being victims when they so willingly went along with a system that insisted they lie about the most natural human desire? Why feel compassion for them when they wished to buy the medieval dogma that objectifies a woman's body as a sanctuary not to be touched sexually? Why offer them the benefit of being the oppressed lot when they so readily cooperated with the institution that oppresses the female sex so one-sidedly?

Jonathan represented the multitude of men I had to fight against so fiercely, and thanks to him, I became freer than I used to be. Thanks to him, I became a bit wiser about my choices in men, a little more selective and discriminating in my judgments about those I was interested in. Ironically, it was my very bad relationship with Jonathan that helped me in my efforts to strike a fine balance between morality and pleasure – between the two ends that create a human relationship. I recognized the two conflicting forces that must be reconciled: the need to be honest about one's craving for pleasure and the need to be honest with the right person who is carefully chosen. I learned that the impulse to be pulled only by pleasure or morality must be resisted by all means. What a huge price I had to pay for a lesson so simple! Because my knowledge had been gained so brutally and through so many violent conflicts, I discovered that learning how to bridge the gap between one's actions and words doesn't happen without a prolonged and exhausting emotional battle.

I also came to understand the power of sex to cut—as well as make—the ties between human beings. I knew that unless something truly unthinkable happened, Jonathan would never leave me alone, and I knew that I had to create an unthinkable situation where he would have to come to the realization that there was no more hope for us. Having sex with another man was the only way I could force him to accept a breakup. Sex touches upon the most intimate parts of our body and mind, and sexual infidelity wreaks havoc unlike violations of any other rules in a relationship. A forbidden affair was the most effective way—the only way—out of my relationship.

Before coming to America, I had been in a very small emotional prison over relationships, where dim corners and dark turns led to lower pitfalls and narrower traps. The prison in America was much bigger, with floors full of bottomless holes and unfathomable snares. I seemed to serve long sentences in this huge prison during my first few years in America. My time there was hardly more than a series of falling and getting up, a vain succession of jumping and running in attempts to escape. Because desire without readiness governed my choices, I was gullible to theories sold without practices, which made me easy prey to men who had nothing to offer but hollow rhetoric.

I was unprepared to create a life different from that of the female masses I wished to leave behind in Korea. I possessed nothing but a zealous determination to avoid a man handpicked by my father and an unstoppable will to join the ranks of men and women—Americans—who I had heard were free from the tyrannies of dynastic norms and traditional mores. But then, I was truly disturbed by the degree of the fear of intimacy that most Americans were proud to exhibit in their relationships, and absolutely astonished by the caliber of the stinginess (emotional as well as monetary) they were so unabashed in displaying to one another. While they were reluctant to spend ten dollars to pick up the bar tab for their beloved friends, they had no reservations about purchasing a five-thousand-dollar stereo system that supposedly produced exquisite melodies they claimed could not be offered by a less expensive machine. So very generous in catering to their own consumerism, and yet so very stingy in investing on human beings, they were enslaved to what seemed to be an absurd materialism.

Because they moved so often and because there was so much change in human relationships, Americans were constantly afraid of losing their loved ones, wary of being attached to anyone but themselves. "They might go to California tomorrow morning," women said of their boyfriends in Boston and men said of their girlfriends in New York, "I don't want to wake up one day with an empty heart." Since opportunities in achieving one's career goals—

usually for the sake of making more money rather than for more opportunities to fulfill one's destiny – governed most Americans' choices, it was natural for them to spend an outrageous fortune on tangible objects they could keep. Spending ten dollars on someone they called a friend today but might become a stranger tomorrow didn't seem like a good investment. I was probably guilty of stereotyping a people. After sharing my observation with another American, she responded with a storm of disagreement. "Americans are just as different from each other as Koreans are," she said. "You shouldn't generalize."

I was willing to acknowledge a certain degree of fairness in her protest. At the risk of offending those who deserved to be separated from what I called a "plague of consumerism," I had to bring up one observation. "When it comes to over-trusting individual differences," I said, "nobody seems as incorrigibly mistaken as the majority of American citizens who like to live in the same houses and watch the same TV shows. They seem oblivious of the fact that two hundred different TV channels have nothing to do with two hundred different individual creations, the fact that three hundred different brands of white bread do not mean three hundred different kinds of individually baked breads."

None of those in my sight were blessed with the freedom and the riches I had thought were granted to all Americans. They were not free at all but enslaved by what they owned and what they feared. They zealously fought to keep what they called their selves when they actually didn't have much of their selves to begin with. I started to wonder why I had worked so hard to come to America, to a country with so little to offer to replace the rules I had tried to leave behind, and I felt something that could very well be called a sense of futility.

Without the life I discovered in academics, I would have gone back to Korea with what little I owned in a suitcase. In school, I found myself in a place where I thought I could belong, in an alcove where there was the least friction between my pictures of America and the reality of America. Academia was where there seemed to be the smallest amount of the vices I so instinctively dreaded in existence, racism and sexism. It seemed to be America's jewel, a haven where visions were safer and the gap between theory and practice wasn't wide enough to cause disillusionment. Although it was also an emotional prison where I had to deal with prejudices, it was dotted with lamps set up by the brightest minds, rid of the cancer eating away the dark centers and dim borders. Because it was a place where *ideas* were encouraged, I could be rather proud of my aloofness toward consumerism and ownership, shielded in an exciting way from the fear of human relationships that dominated so many Americans. By conversing with the minds that created worlds of ideas, I was often free from the craving to be with another human being physically. By studying the words these minds gathered to construct their own worlds, I could create my own routines that were much different from those of conventional lifestyles.

Being alone was a magical gift, not a sad state of existence as defined by popular songs and Hollywood movies. Reading and writing about Whitman's "Song of Myself" in solitude until dawn was far from madness but instead a visionary challenge against the day's diurnal routines. One could begin at the end of the day and finish at the beginning, overthrowing society's designated work time to adopt one's own. I preferred to work at night since words came to me more easily in the still of the night. I also enjoyed watching the sunrise, the first rays spreading on the trees to reveal the birds chirping on the branches. Dawn was a great time to tell a story, the kind of story worthy of remembering.

During my first few years in America, I didn't possess the writing skills that were up to par with the sophisticated concepts in my head. I would write in an overly redundant style, with sentences such as "Whitman's sense of self, although very God- and country-oriented, shows itself to be extremely egotistic and selfish in that it sings of nothing but the greatness of the soul in him that he believes resembles that of God and therefore is a divine entity." I so admired smart American academicians who were good with words. I was nearly frantic to be connected with people who seemed to embody what I wanted to achieve. I zealously tried to befriend individuals who proudly called themselves citizens of the world, individuals who defined themselves as members of a common humanity rather than as members of a nation. Because I deeply detested Americans of Jonathan's camp—those with little more than the ability to take advantage of their race and national origins—I was just as deeply compelled by the need to admire those in the opposite camp. In fact, the more I despised the former, the more I found myself in love with the latter. I wanted nothing more than to plunge into a world where people were free from the filthy banalities of the materialistic world. I created a la-la land that reflected my personal visions of America, and chose to be oblivious of the fact that the academia I constructed in my head was merely the other side of the dark place, the sunny area that showed the inescapable shadows of the other. It was simply another face of the same country that was made of all sorts of people. Although less infected by the vices I saw in the rest of America, it was a far cry from the mecca of justice and equality that I wanted to think it was.

But I owed my academic success to this illusion I created. As racecar drivers set their sights on the finish line, I set my sights on obtaining a master's degree and I passed. I passed the first gate to enter American academia because I had secluded myself for nearly half a year with a car racer's will to pass the exams. I could bring my almost decade-long race for a PhD to an end because I could so single-mindedly devote myself to the draining race. I could learn so many of the beautiful lines woven by my favorite authors by heart because I focused so zealously on learning their multiple meanings.

This fiercely devoted life of mine had its price. Because I fell so passionately in love with Vladimir Nabokov and James Joyce, whose lives as exiles reminded me of my own, I couldn't get close to living men. Since I spent so much time with my beloved authors, I couldn't take the time required to create intimate relationships with men around me. Living so ardently with people in books, I kept myself insulated from the reality in which I could have loved men in my life. I alienated myself from the routines in which I should have learned to tolerate the human shortcomings of the human beings around me – a very inevitable and necessary component of living. I knew that there was no way I could cohabit with living men in the same house where I lived with these authors and that there was a great deal of emotional cowardice in my choice to dwell in the world of words created by these authors. I was resolute to remain sheltered from the hurt that could be caused by a man with flesh and blood, to invest my energy on intellectual pursuits that seemed capable of yielding a visibly pronounced outcome. Love for a man seemed to me incapable of materializing into a concrete harvest, as momentary as bubbles dissolving into a hollow space. It could offer nothing but memories of inner torments and empty feelings, and it was void of the ultimate meaning I was seeking because a man could not provide *ideas.*

I fell into the very trap I dreaded, into the snare in which the tangible conquered the intangible. I became guilty of what I condemned, of surrendering to the fear of intimacy that I perceived as an emotional plague in American life, and I found my head spinning in an all-too-familiar confusion. Except that of materialism, I seemed to have allowed myself to adopt the worst of American vice, locked in the stubborn walls that kept me from reaching out to a member of the opposite sex. In my heart, I remained firmly detached from a man. In a way, I became the extreme opposite of Jonathan, of the man who was unable to stand being inside the lonely walls of an American life and had no second thoughts about trading his solitude for a relationship. I made myself into a casualty of the culture that was driven by the need to sacrifice relationships for lone achievements. My fear of intimacy wasn't born entirely of the need to adjust myself to an American-style life. It was carried in from Korea, where women were automatically required to give up work for love, where very few women were allowed to preserve a sense of self after being married, and where the act of loving a man was supposed to mean only one thing – giving herself up. But it was dramatically reinforced by the fear of finding myself with another man like Jonathan, by the terror—yes, terror—of having to face a man who expected me to be an Asian woman, not a woman.

I do not claim that I didn't have any man in my life after Jonathan. I was far from being a woman made of stone, to use a Korean metaphor, and I sought the company of men with the same intensity with which any young woman of my age sought them. Without a streak of narcissism, I confess that a number of men were passionately fond of me, that some of them would have been happy to share the rest of their lives with me had I granted them a chance to do so. Without a shred of arrogance, I also confess that I could afford to treat these men poorly because I could have a string of them at once. They somehow found me compelling, physically and mentally, and didn't hesitate to put themselves at my whim as they thought it was necessary to sustain my interest. Being university men with education and common sense, they were relatively untainted by the demoralizing cultural assumptions made about Asian women, uninfected by the particular brand of racism and sexism that characterized Jonathan. They were capable of intellectually resisting the racial stereotype, although they were not entirely free from it emotionally. They fought it because they knew they were not free from it.

I was ashamed of the egotism that governed my relationships with men. I recognized the fear of intimacy that motivated me to be so self-absorbed, the subconscious will in me to hurt men because I had been hurt by the system that empowered men at the cost of women. By the same token, I wanted to be bold enough to admit that I was not at all ashamed of having had a number of men in my life. I didn't see why female curiosity was something a woman ought to be shy about while male curiosity was something a man had the right to overtly brag about. Neither one was bad unless lying was involved. Having lied to Jonathan about my affair with Bob, I knew how bad lying was. But by no means did I feel I was disqualified from admitting the truth I believed in – that a woman's curiosity is just as natural and legitimate as a man's.

I was a so-called serial monogamist, the kind of woman who was often called "reckless," "rash," or even "brave"—a woman who had both the passion and the cold heart to plunge from one relationship to another without much vacillation. Or perhaps, I was a preacher's daughter, to use an American metaphor, who had just left her small hometown to discover a wide and wild world of sin. I was away from my home, a small country where women of "good" names obeyed the cultural injunctions for what was called chaste sexuality. It is entirely possible that I was trying to overcompensate, to make the statement that I could be just as sinful as anyone raised in a big bad city and to demonstrate to myself and to everyone else that I was courageous enough to break free of stifling sexual norms. But given the fact that so many men and women totally unrelated to preachers shamelessly choose to exhibit carefree behaviors, I have little doubt that under any circumstances, I probably would have exercised my female curiosity to the same extent that I did. Since I followed my own desire, I felt no need to be apologetic or boastful about it.

What makes me ashamed now is how I treated some people, including some of my dear friends who gave me more than I gave them, with callous indifference. So preoccupied with academics—my marathon for a brilliant career—I often neglected the most rudimentary rules of caring for others. I became a taker, a loud, self-absorbed receiver who very seldom exercised the virtue of giving. An incessant talker, I rarely practiced the quiet virtue of listening. "I think I can become as good as she," I would manifest suddenly in the middle of reading a book or even watching TV. I would declare: "She writes well, but her style could be a lot more polished," "She could smile more. I'm sure I could look better than that on TV news," "She needs a better plot," and "That woman isn't fit for that role. I think I could do better."

When a new graduate student from Korea called to seek my advice about which courses to take to fulfill the requirements for a master's, I was in a hurry to hang up on her, to tell her very impatiently to visit the English graduate adviser. When another friend called to ask if I could correct her one-page English composition, I very brashly told her to hire a tutor. But I called these women whenever I had something to complain about, and they listened as if I were entitled to their kindness.

Because failure was not an option, I worked myself to the brink of madness, always armed with a readiness to finish an exhausting task, but only if it was one that served my needs. My routines had nothing but deadlines, my days nothing but a succession of long stays at a library. Compared to my native-speaking colleagues, I had to devote twice as much time to writing a paper, and unlike the Korean male graduate students, I was a woman without a wife who was always there to absorb her husband's woes and to cook and clean for him. All I had was my own ego, and I had to put it up on a pedestal, perhaps unlike other single female graduate students from Korea.

Chapter 7
Butchering the English Language

While I was on my marathon for the America I was seeking, Big Brother was graduating from Harvard with a PhD in economics. After five years of hard work, he was ready to file his dissertation and go back to Korea with his wife and four-year-old son. With a bag full of credentials, he was returning to a family ecstatic about not only his achievement but also his wife's good job as his supporter. I was happy for the whole family, and I was proud enough to fly to Boston to attend his commencement ceremony to celebrate the glory the oldest son had brought to the Lee family. But I found myself in a protesting, ambivalent state of mind, which I tried to manifest with a deliberately poor appearance and a willfully pronounced demeanor. Whereas everyone on campus was dressed in their best for the grand occasion, I stood out, wearing a red t-shirt with a tight, round neckline, ridiculously baggy, faded jeans held up by a blue and white scarf around my waist, and ragged tennis shoes I had not bothered to wash for two years.

I was making a statement with my own fashion against Big Brother's splendid gown, and I was smiling a devilish grin inside as I stole the glory from him. In truth, that glory belonged to his wife, the woman who had nearly died during the two of their first five years of marriage, and I was declaring this loudly with my unsightly clothes. Because Big Brother and his wife missed my true motive, interpreting it as a sign of my usual disregard for appearance, I was all the more thrilled. I was delighted that I deceived them so well. To me, Big Brother's wife seemed weighed down by the emotional intensity that allowed him to immerse himself in work, and by the overwhelming mental load she carried as the spouse of a brilliant overachiever. Like a small tree shaded by a larger one, she seemed to have withered under Big Brother, succumbing to an illness that fell upon the smaller tree. Although her sunny disposition kept her unaware, her body knew, and her mind eventually learned what he should have done to make the shade a bit less dark. Suffering from tuberculosis for several months, from the same condition that had plagued him through his adolescence and early adulthood, she pleaded with him to change a few things in his daily routine. In her crisp, but firm voice, she told him to laugh a bit more, to blot out the sharp glow in his eyes with a touch of a smile—even a foolish one, if necessary—to walk without his frantic hurry, and to block out the tick of the clock while listening to the dings of their chopsticks on the rice bowls at dinner.

He probably never had the emotional leisure to slow down while at Harvard. But immediately after his graduate work, he started to show signs of change that I could only attribute to his wife's patient efforts. She softened him to the degree that he often stopped himself in search of milder words and less fierce hand gestures, to the degree that he could admit how much more effective he could be with a gentler expression of his well-intended tough love. She worked on him with the same degree of patience as raindrops that chipped away at the rocks on a mountain, thoroughly eschewing any manner of communication that could be called confrontational. No wonder she had fallen ill. Her marriage required so much self-oppression—which I would have called self-control under any other circumstances—that her body was robbed of the power to conquer the bacteria in her lungs. I shouldn't have been surprised to see her being whisked back to a hospital in an ambulance a second time during the first two years of their marriage, or to hear her receive no clear diagnosis this time from the same best doctors who had treated her for TB before.

"We can only guess," the doctors said cautiously. "We think she might be suffering from some of the transitional symptoms that may occur to patients who are recovering from TB."

I knew what the diagnosis was: RFSSO (Relapse from Severe Self-Oppression). But I kept it to myself. I knew I had no right to feel what Big Sister-in-Law didn't feel. I knew she was willing to pay the price for his success – and therefore for her success. Far from sad or angry, she quietly endured the illness that almost stole her life, envisioning the day he finished his studies, the day they returned home together to Korea with the results of his hard work and her devout support. Whatever happened to her would be worth it. She was going to be the wife of a Harvard PhD. As his glory was hers,

I thought that I ought to feel what she felt. If I felt anger, I was going beyond my boundaries.

I wouldn't be entirely honest if I didn't admit that I wore the ragged clothes because I was jealous of him for what he had achieved, for the unconditional self-sacrifice he took from his wife. Once again, I found myself wondering why a woman with his abilities wasn't entitled to the same degree of devotion from her spouse. For no other reason than being a man, he was granted the privileges that lay out of a woman's reach, reaping the harvest of not only a brilliant career but also a family. Although I was incredibly happy for him, I wasn't entirely successful in hiding my outrage. My contrasting emotions troubled me. I was celebrating a man's success that was made possible at the cost of a woman. I was feeling happy that Big Sister-in-Law had sacrificed herself for a man, exactly because she was one of those women of whom I didn't approve.

In protest against the injustice, to come to terms with my own hypocrisy, and then to laugh at myself, there was only one thing I could do. I had to keep writing. Only in printed words, could I envision a perfect world where I didn't have to face the contradictions in my mind. Only in printed words, could I create a republic where women like Big Sister-in-Law could at once keep herself and help her husband to succeed. Only in blank papers, could I describe women like us reaping the same degree of harvest in work and love.

During the two and a half years between receiving my master's degree and going back for a PhD, I led a double life. One life allowed me to pay the bills, the other gave me time to conjure a world where a morally perfect life was not only possible but also real. As exhausting as it was to live this way, it gave me a sense of self-sufficiency and an opportunity to be creative. I had a day job and was able to take advantage of the night in an effort to break away from the diurnal norm. For a while, I was even exhilarated by the fatigue, delighted by what seemed to be a combination of a true American dream and economic independence.

In the back of my head, I knew I was building a crude beginning that would serve as a bridge into what was to come decades later. It became clear that the book I was writing during those two and a half years was a loosely connected succession of moral statements. Too preoccupied to deliver a morally righteous message, I paid little attention to the most important task of literature—the complexities of human nature—and ended up with a four-hundred-page sermon that no one but its author could have tolerated to hear. The protagonist was motivated by nothing but a do-gooder's relentless will, a purist obeying the voice of his conscience. He was an illegitimate son of the richest power broker in Korea, a young medical doctor who his father had designated to inherit a flourishing economic empire, very likely one of the largest in the world. But the son chose to become a god rather than a tycoon and went to a leper colony off the south coast of Korea. By treating the abandoned and living with them, he attempted to wash away his sins, and by loving those whom only the gods could love, he endeavored to love himself, a bastard cursed by the country that was still swayed by the traditional mores of hating children born out of wedlock. With all that money and power under his thumb, he found himself unaccepted among the majority of people—the kinds of people whose acceptance he wanted—so he opted for suffering instead. He resolved to redeem himself by saving those who were damned, much like he was.

Obviously, the protagonist I called "Dr. Kim" was me. Out of the need to prove myself, I created a character who was uncannily close to me. I made him a man to make the story more acceptable to my audiences, who in my mind were both American and Korean, and I made him a medical doctor to endow upon him a certain professional glamour. Dr. Kim was a young man who chose to forsake the wealth he was born into in search of himself, a brilliant seeker who refused to tread on the easy road everyone else had paved for him. Much like my protagonist, I had left my society—the small circle of prestigious, well-educated youths in Korea for whom a comfortable middle-class life was virtually guaranteed—and much after my hero, I wished to return there to show who I truly was. The Korea I had left behind—the country I so loved—was the leper colony where Dr. Kim made a home for himself, where thousands of people lived in one natural environment and one man-made system, united by one hope and one vision. It was an island that the damned had made into a paradise, a small country sustained by the faith in its ability to beat overwhelming odds.

Back then, I didn't realize that if I had written about my life without disguising it as fiction, it would have been just as interesting or even more interesting. Nor could I have realized what is so obvious now. To prove myself as a Korean woman, I shouldn't have to create a male character suffering under Korean norms, a member of second-rank birth, and damned by his second-class citizenship. As fiercely as I rebelled against patriarchy, I allowed it to brainwash me to believe that I was unable to rise above its core precept – that to have any sort of significance, a protagonist has to be a man.

I laughed about the novel later and how I had handled the subject matter with so much naïve idealism. But I have absolutely no regrets about sitting up all night to crank it out, to conjure up very poorly constructed sentences so far removed from the English language. To avoid translating, as translation kills a story, I attempted to transliterate Korean into English—a phonetic Asian language into an alphabetic Western language—and came up with hundreds of pages of butchered writing, not knowing that they would be my best source of entertainment in the future. Instead of "I was sad, so I went home," I wrote "It was sad and I came home." In Korean sentence structure, the subject and predicate were mixed or the predicate was inconsistent with the subject, if there was even a subject at all. "It was so heavy that I couldn't pick it up by myself," would be in Korean "So heavy and couldn't pick it up alone." In an effort to achieve what was impossible—carrying one language over to another without the slightest damage to either—I created a bizarre hybrid of English and Korean, a language marked by its strange half meanings. This was another way I was being very Korean. I was trying to prove that being immersed in the English language didn't make me forget my mother tongue.

This novel, which I started writing more than thirty years ago, was the precursor to my memoir, *To Kill a Tiger*. I had all my protagonist's emotional characteristics—anger, frustration, competitive spirit, reckless behavior, relentless questioning, pettiness and cruelty, and unforgiving, yet forgiving mind eventually—and I took pride in displaying all of them with a ferociously consistent attitude. The only difference was that he ultimately became a man of greatness, an individual with moral perfection.

Butchering the English language proved to be a benefit to my subsequent writing. Failure is the mother of success, and my failure with this epic became the mother of the string of success I enjoyed with all my other writing. With an inspector's cunningly narrowed eyes, I started to discriminate against words of the same meaning that didn't fall snugly into the nuance I was looking for. With this effort, I became a micro-writer, measuring with pondering scrutiny the gap between Korean and English words of the same meanings, manipulating the distance between each word and phrase in an attempt to bring them as close together as possible.

A famous Korean saying serves as a good example here. Translated without micro-level manipulation, the saying would run as "When a woman has a knot to be unraveled in her heart, frost will rain on the fields in July and August." But translated with micro-level adjustment, the English version reads with natural smoothness as "When a woman is resolved to unravel the knot in her heart, she can blanket the sky in July with snow." Contrary to what I had believed about translations, I realized that by killing the original, I could make it live.

I became a better reader and writer by creating Dr. Kim. When reading, I found myself living in a writer's head, riding the emotional waves and steering the ways of the words. At times, I found that I could discern the forces that moved the writers along, and I could see what led them to choose the path their story took. As only an avid hiker can find the trails unseen by those who seldom get to the forest, only a writer with the experience of creating characters can see the paths another writer has chosen to keep and discard. In writing, decisions that seem to be made consciously are subconsciously driven, and having been a writer who made these decisions, I had far better clues as to what compelled another writer to make his or her decisions. This is why I have no regrets about having spent more than two years of my youth on what never became a published reality.

Chapter 8
John the Baptist

As I started to laugh about the novel a short time later, I laughed with a sense of humor and self-respect. Nor was I without laughter, meeting the man—the one man—who was poor enough in judgment to praise me for the "fine" English I commanded in the novel. I saw no malice in him, nothing resembling deliberate flattery or intentional deception in what seemed to be an honest audience's confidence in my writing. It pleased me, rather, to see how eager he was to believe in me, how zealous he was to endorse me. Although his emotional hypocrisy was soon proven to be as high as Jonathan's, I still had no reason to suspect him of intellectual dishonesty of any sort. In contrast to Jonathan, he was not only knowledgeable but also cogent in his reasoning. This man, my new boyfriend, had a sense of self that was tremendously solid in comparison to Jonathan's. Summarily, it would be fair to say that he had an authentic presence of self while Jonathan's was only a sham. Defining my grotesque English as being "beautiful," he wasn't trying to snake his way into my heart. He was being truthful, exercising his rather immature standards and thereby missing the strangeness in my English that was so laughably obvious.

Not surprisingly, however, a man who so adoringly looks up to a woman doesn't always find himself to be a winner. My new boyfriend, who so admiringly spoke of not only my talent as a writer but also my proven will to carve out my own destiny, failed to win me over eventually. I learned that he was short of honesty in matters of the heart. In his emotional life, theory wasn't practice, rhetoric was far from reality, and words totally divorced from action. He talked well in matters of intellect, so well indeed that I felt as though his tongue were often moving in the same direction as mine. Because he abstained from agreeing with me when he disagreed, such verbal aptitude seemed all the more valuable, and because he so often succeeded in backing up his points with solid reasoning, such a savvy communication style struck me to be a reflection of equally substantial content. Until I saw one day what lay beneath his very effective—and richly informed—tongue, I remained convinced that he might be the man for me. Before a watershed event came to turn me upside down emotionally and I reached the point where I decided to give him a new name— "John the Baptist"—I was nearly persuaded by the idea that he might be the one for me to marry. He and I even paid a visit to a Catholic priest to ask him if he could preside over our wedding in the near future. There is often that one decisive moment that divides a relationship into two disconnected periods, one before the moment and the other after the moment. My relationship with John the Baptist was similarly broken into two disconnected periods at that one decisive moment that crashed down upon us one night. Leaving the rest of the story blank to fill in later, I will leap into the part involving the watershed and tell you what and how it came about.

It started when I was throwing out a piece of paper, a page off a ruined manuscript of mine, into his trash can and saw a partly crumpled letter at the bottom. When I pulled it out, I saw that it seemed to be a love letter from a Korean woman. Naturally, I ironed it out with my fingers and started to read. I was immediately impressed by the profuse confession of love and the scorching anxiety of being separated. Obviously, she was a Korean woman waiting for an American lover to come and get her, a Korean version of Madam Butterfly who was pining her whole life away for a worthless Western man to whom she was nothing more than forgotten history. Her never-returning lover who broke the promise of marriage was none other than John, my current boyfriend who had recently asked for my hand. What disturbed me, however, was that her letter—burning with so much desperate love—was found at the bottom of a trashcan, crumpled and nearly torn in certain spots. "How could he treat something this precious so poorly? Why is he trashing his old girlfriend's heart like this?" I wondered.

It may sound strange that I was morally outraged by what he seemed to be doing to her because logically, I should have been rather glad. She still was my competition, although he claimed she was merely history. She was not only his most recent ex but also a provocatively nostalgic presence, having been the one who brought him close companionship when he was starved of it the most. She was a part of his past that could be his present in one vulnerable moment, possessed with the power to push me out at any given time. With one phone call from Korea, she could do it, I thought. He, in fact, was still proud of her, still missing her, reveling at times in the glow of the memory he had of her.

"My two-year service in Korea was like one day, thanks to her," he would reminisce. "You know how boring the military can be for someone who wants to go back to school as badly as I did. But she made it a lot shorter for me. She kept me from falling into the trap of an ignorant GI with a false sense of superiority by helping me to discover Korea. I fell in love with Korea through her."

I had known about her. The day I met him, I saw that he was wearing an engagement ring and I respected the engagement. Until he declared that he had terminated it, I had been no more than a friend to him, our activities strictly limited to dining together and talking and sometimes going to the movies. When we found ourselves being more than friends, I had every reason to believe that she was merely his history—at least on a conscious level—because he had told me so. In lengthy detail, he explained to me how he had reached that final decision. Until the night I happened to see her letters in his room, I realized I had been in the dark about how serious the whole affair had been and how he, while intimately involved with me, had been corresponding with her as well. Upon discovering her letters to him, which were her replies to his most recent promises to come and get her, I could hardly breathe from shock. I understood why he was still wearing the engagement ring. He wasn't wearing it out of sentimental memories as he had explained to me; he was wearing it to keep himself reminded of her. Physically shuddering, I recalled the conversation he and I had had several months before, during one of those days he, while still writing sweet words to her, had told me that she was no longer in his life.

"It's been too long," he concluded, "since we were together for the last time. She doesn't know how I've changed, and I no longer remember who she really is. She's just in my memory."

Characteristically of me, I challenged him by probing, "You've never tried. How can you tell?"

"If she comes to this country," he returned, "she'll be overwhelmed by the changes she'll have to make. She'll have to deal with a culture shock so deep that I'm afraid she may get physically sick."

It was his style to turn evasive when the subject strayed into an unpredictable direction, but I was bent on prodding further. I was not only curious but also troubled as to how he could have reached the decision to "dump" her after having spoon-fed her the dream of starting a new life in a promised land—after having instilled in her the cliché—the so-called American dream—that must have meant so much to her. Having been lured into it once myself, I knew how seductive it could be, and I knew how overwhelming it could be in its power to thwart a person when it was denied. I became more scornful of it than I was of deceit of any other kind, including blatantly obvious lies and transparently false propaganda. I had chances to witness it being propagated without a concrete plan to have it materialized into reality. John the Baptist—my own boyfriend—was guilty of such a scam. Regarding himself as a superior white male endowed with the heroic power to deliver a woman from what he defined as a pit of tradition—the Korean culture that he perceived as being so mean to women—he deliberately fed the American dream to her for half a decade, reveling in the visions of saving her that he had never planned to execute. He molded and then wielded her American dream as a power point, as a big hand he could lift over a vulnerable child in order to keep her frozen in one spot forever.

In that watershed moment, anger took instant possession of me, casting out anything else that might have put me in the sway of another emotion, including jealousy. My eyes fell on the chain of letters strewn on the floor in his room as if they were spilled beans waiting to be swept up by a broom. My anger grew into outrage and I stomped out into the living room.

"You'd better get in here right now," I yelled at the top of my lungs. "Right now!" As he came in, dazed, I pointed at a chair for him to sit, axing the air fiercely with my index finger. I ordered, "Sit down and listen to this." Then, I picked up a few of the letters from the floor and started to read, enunciating each word with the loud, deliberate slowness of a kindergarten teacher: "I bought a pair of gold rings for us, one for you and the other for me. I hope your finger size, as fat as it was, didn't change," "While I'm waiting for you, a day is as long as a month. I know you'll be back to Korea this summer," "Longing for you is as sweet as being with you. Anticipating what we once envisioned is the best part of it all," and "Dreaming of us being together keeps me going. You will return for me, I'm certain." I was rapidly translating her Korean words, skipping the long and many lines in each letter into short, pithy summaries, fighting my own voice that escalated until it just about cracked through the roof.

"You never planned to go back to get her, did you?" I growled. "You kept promising her, promising her, promising her, didn't you? You ruined a woman's chances at getting married and you enjoyed doing it," I steamrolled on as he sat, his shoulders slumped from the shock and his mouth twitching from shame. "It was a power trip and you loved it. Without your false promises, she wouldn't have wasted three years waiting for you—three marriageable years, at that. Actually, it was five years altogether because you were with her in Korea for two years before you came back to America three years ago. Now she's an old maid, with so much less going for her. You know as well as anyone who's been to that damn country that for a woman of marriageable age, just one year makes a difference. You put her on hold for five years—five long years! And yet, you laugh at abusive GIs who rape and beat up their Korean girlfriends. But you are just as bad. They rape women physically, and you do it emotionally."

In a way, he was more of a sham than Jonathan, who exploited his privileges as a white male in an Asian country to an appalling degree but who, as far as I could tell, had never made a false promise to a woman. While Jonathan was appalling, John the Baptist was being unconscionable. While Jonathan was physically violent to me, John the Baptist was being mentally—in a wickedly cerebral and tortuous way—brutal to another woman. He was a moral danger to me. If he had the wiles to toy with one woman's heart with such cunning, he would have the skills to play with another woman's heart as well, and I, as his second fiancée, would sooner or later find myself in her position.

John was then on army reserve, planning to go back to full-time military service after being commissioned as an officer in the near future. As it seemed that his plans were in order with no anticipated turbulence, I had all the more reason to be apprehensive. I became suspicious of the official reasoning he offered me – that he chose to remain on army reserve to support himself economically while he was attending graduate school. He would make a sweet promise to me and say, "Once I'm done with my master's degree, we'll both go to the same university to get our PhDs there. We'll have an equal marriage, I promise you." He knew just what to say to appeal to women like me, and he knew what to do to keep a conventional woman like his fiancée captive. He would use the rhetoric of women's equality to play up to my standards but make the vows of a traditional relationship to maintain the other woman's doting faith in him. Why else was he writing dream letters to her at the same time he was telling me he wanted a career woman as his wife? His hair was always short, shaved to the top with his scalp showing on the back, and he was spending half of his time in the military. Obviously, he was going to be a career soldier. He was playing mind games with me.

Habitually, he would make statements such as: “Women aren’t going to be the way they were before,” “Men can’t expect women to follow them one-sidedly any more. They have to compromise,” “A bunch of women are going to march on the campus to celebrate the women’s movement. You want to go with me to show our support?,” “Professor John Smith in Anthropology said so many sexist things in his classes that his female graduate students filed a complaint against him. He’s a jerk,” “Some men say women don’t have much math and science brain. They’re sexist,” “A guy on my army reserve unit uses vulgar language about women. I don’t respect men who don’t respect women,” and “It’s difficult for women to be honest. Men should understand that.”

Planning to go back to the military, seeking a wife to follow him around army bases, and hoping I would be the one, he would say he expected me to be a woman determined to carve out her own path. Claiming that a relationship was a compromise between a man and a woman, he wasn’t even prepared to consider a compromise. He was looking for a woman who would sacrifice her life for his, and to make me into such a woman, he kept telling lies. He worked hard to hide who he was, to condemn the men who harbored his sexism. Because he was one of them, he had to condemn them all the more fiercely than any man who wasn’t.

It occurred to me that he was probably warming up for another power trip, for the thrill of having under his thumb a woman whom he and others perceived as being much stronger and more independent than the previous one. I feared that I was part of another psychological stunt, one that would enable him to brag about how almighty he was because he was great enough to prevail upon a woman—a woman who was daring enough to come to America alone as a graduate student and was determined to build a home all by herself in a foreign country—and persuade her to surrender her hard-earned opportunities just to be with him. *He wanted to be a conqueror of the strong, not of the weak. He wanted to be a conqueror of a feminist woman, not just a woman.*

For the life of me, I couldn’t understand why he wanted to go back to the military. In my presence, he loved to show contempt for the men and women in uniform who, in his mind, were ignorant and incompetent enough to thrive on their American citizenship alone. He sneered at the former GIs who, according to him, couldn't stop being the same old miserable lot even after quitting the military, which he saw as the last resort for losers. Because the subject of his scorn included officers, of whom he was going to be one, his decision to go back to the army was all the more ironic.

"Some GIs think they speak good Korean just because they can impress the girls on the base," he would say with disdain. "You know, they don't need to speak much to have sex with the Korean girls who hang out there." He then would imitate the English spoken by these girls – who were usually called by the nickname, "Western Princesses," or sometimes by the vicious appellation, "Western Whores," by the title Korean patriarchy gave them. "Me no need beer. Me need money," he would chatter away in his well-practiced falsetto-soprano voice, diving into a GI's mangled Korean in that well-rehearsed fake baritone of his. "'Pali pali hapshida,' meaning, 'Let's do it fast.'"

His own Korean was just as butchered, his pronunciation incomprehensible for the most part. When he impersonated a GI with poor Korean, there rose to the surface an eerie resemblance I always suspected, a kinship that he so vigorously denied because it was so undeniable. He seemed to be protesting too much, constantly compelled by the need to be who he wasn't, to be a gentleman with the moral decorum to stay away from the Western Princesses whom he perceived as being beneath him.

"My girlfriend, Oksoon, was a high-school home economics teacher in a local city," he would emphasize. "She was a lady from a good family. I met her through an officer friend of mine who got to know her through the principal of her high school." With fierce pride, he would then go on about her moral character, "She was twenty-six years when we first met, and she was a virgin. I was three years younger than her, a horny young sergeant crazy for sex, but she wisely steered me away from it. She wanted to wait until we got married, and I had to obey to keep seeing her. Although I was frustrated, I respected her for that. I still do. I can't imagine a woman being a virgin after three years of such a serious, intense relationship with a man. I'll bet she's still a virgin, and she's over thirty."

So transparently, he was playing a messiah in Oksoon's life. He was in love with himself—not with her—in love with his own self-image as that of a deliverer, flirting with his own role as that of a liberator. John the Baptist—the name I gave him shortly after discovering her letters—suited him perfectly. He was a prophet to her, an American version of the savior who was expected to set a poor Asian woman free, to bring her to a long-awaited exodus into the promised land. Being a lady with a college education—not being one of those Western Princesses, those poor, uneducated, and unfortunate women who found themselves serving American GIs to make a living—Oksoon boosted his hungry male ego all the more, endowing him with the extra reward of a respectable appearance he so deeply coveted. He was about to save a woman from a decent background, about to wed a lady who was not only a self-sufficient professional but also a sexually pure Madonna. He was about to witness his power to mold her rebirth in America. To him, he was Marlon Brando in the movie, *Sayonara,* the famed star who rescues his geisha lover from economic bondage. But he seemed to himself even more heroic because his girlfriend was a respected school teacher, not a geisha. He was going to exhibit his unique power as an individual because in his mind he was far from one of those low-ranking GIs whose only leverage over their Korean wives was that of American citizenship. In addition to the collective might he believed he had the right to wield over her, he desired to create the appearance of a highly personalized marriage, a seemingly truthful union untainted by the hierarchy between the two nations.

In vanity, he well surpassed Jonathan, the vicarious one who seldom lost an opportunity to brag about my so-to-speak "ladylike" background – including the fact that my brother was going to Harvard. John the Baptist was so much more adept at concealing his peculiar brand of racism and sexism, so expert in hiding behind the mask of a kind, well-meaning gentleman. Because he was so successful in being known as a good man somehow, I couldn't make myself understood by those whom I considered to be my friends. I felt like I was screaming at a wall, "Didn't they see what I saw in his face? When I came upon it for the first time, it struck me to be an incarnation of hypocrisy. My first intuition was right."

For no reason I could explain, I was afraid that there was something about John that gave off an air of murkiness. I swear to the gods that this suspicion wasn't a product of my retrospective analysis. It was a vague, but powerful foreboding that kept me at bay for quite some time. For a year or so until we became, upon his persistence, more than friends, I found myself with none of the physical chemistry that a woman must feel for a man in order to be involved with him physically. He was, in essence, too yin and not enough yang, with an exceedingly large amount of graveness in his visage. Behind his glasses with a fake gold rim, there reeked an air of a dangerously subtle and effective duplicity, a mind that was in effortless harmony with conspiratorial silence. "Humid" was the adjective Koreans would pick to describe such a face, to get a glimpse into the shadowy depth of what lay beneath the surface of his deceptively kind personality. His seemingly shy warmth, which my friends saw as the sign of a nice guy, disturbed me as it enabled him to hide calculating schemes that a blatant unfriendliness could not. To my friends, I seemed to be the one spinning a cynical narrative about a good man, a harsh woman with a tendency to overinterpret a mistake that had been made by a young man a long time before.

In terms of the degree of his wrongdoing, John the Baptist was by no means one of those ugly American GIs in Korea who committed the all-too-familiar crimes. He didn't kill or beat or rape a Korean woman. Nor was he one of those military scum who drove drunk, hit a civilian, and took off. As far as I could tell, he had never misbehaved or abused anyone. But in *essence,* he was a liar. He was a deceiver, a manipulator who reveled in wielding an ungrounded sense of superiority.

He reminded me of the American GI who had a relationship with a relative of mine—my paternal grandmother's niece—and had a son with her during the Korean War. As this GI, whom my family called Mr. Gone, never kept his promise that he would bring her to America and marry her eventually, John the Baptist never kept the same promise he had made to Oksoon. It seemed that he never intended to make good on his word, never doing any more than writing sweet letters to her. "If he'd had a child with Oksoon because she wasn't so old-fashioned, would he have become another Mr. Gone?" I wondered. "Mr. Gone never rescued his lover from the ignominy of being left alone in Korea with a bastard—a bastard of mixed blood at that—and eventually married an American woman in California to have three children with her. John seems to be a prime candidate to do the same thing."

Aunt Myongsoon, the mother of the mixed-blood bastard, used to come to our house in Seoul to chat with Mother and Grandmother all day long. But during those seemingly endless hours, she rarely mentioned her son unless asked and seldom returned any more than a monosyllabic comment such as, "He's OK." She knew she was a war bride bringing shame to her family and clan. She knew that her son, Manho, didn't care to be a topic of conversation among his relatives. Manho didn't—and couldn't—see himself as a Korean because, although he was born and raised in Korea, Korean law didn't recognize him as a citizen. Korean law only granted citizenship to those who were fathered by Koreans. Being a war child with a half-white face, Manho was shunned by everyone except his mother. I could tell how ashamed he was of himself because even in pictures, he didn't look straight at the camera. He stared at the floor, his angular face somber and crestfallen. Like a Korean, he was sitting on the floor with his legs folded, but unlike a Korean, he didn't display that subtle, rarely visible camera-smile Koreans were so famous for. In the few pictures of him that were hidden in a drawer of Mother's chest of drawers, I couldn't see anything but the sad face of an abandoned lot.

"John's not a Mr. Gone," some of my American friends would insist, "and you're not a war bride. Nor is Oksoon. Oksoon made the conscious choice of waiting for him, of missing her marriageable age. She wasn't powerless."

"Oksoon *is* a war bride in a way," I would fling back fiercely. "John wouldn't have been in Korea had it not been for the Korean War. There is no combat as of now, but the Korean War lingers on. It could happen at any time. We have the DMZ because the war isn't over yet."

"Still, John's not Mr. Gone. Every individual is different."

How could I explain to my American friends—whose country has never been conquered by another—the wounded psyche of a woman created by a conquered country so distant from theirs? Never had the truth, "Every individual is different," seemed to be such tired cliché as it did at that moment. In my wounded historical psyche, I was Oksoon and Aunt Myongsoon. I was one of those countless Korean women who were destroyed by American GIs, one of those numerous women who, cursed by poverty and a lack of education, found themselves involved with soldiers from a powerful country, with a pack of men who couldn't show anything but reckless contempt for the women of a powerless country. That I, being more fortunate than they, came from a less poor family and therefore was equipped with more education, seemed only a superficial difference. Everything was irrelevant except the fact that we were women of a conquered country.

From my perspective, John the Baptist was worse than any of those physically violent GIs who mobilized their arms and legs to beat and kick the powerless women at their feet. With a highly cerebral tactic of stalling and manipulating, he killed Oksoon slowly, watching her languishing in vain. He secretly enjoyed killing her emotionally.

"It's like picking up a gun and shooting her for three straight years," I hurled at him. "Physical violence is visible, but emotional violence—of your type, particularly—is invisible. It doesn't even throw you into prison." In terms of the emotional state, he lived in, he was no different from the GIs who so often shocked the whole of Korea with their sometimes-unspeakable crimes.

In 1982, the year when John the Baptist asked me to marry him, Mother gave me an update on Aunt Myongsoon. After failing her repeated attempts to persuade Mr. Gone to take Manho to the U.S. and make him a U.S. citizen somehow, she gave up. She had to be resigned to watching her son settle in Korea, to send him to college in the country that discriminated against him as much as the U.S. Army discriminated against Korean women. She decided to open a bar with a friend of hers, also a war bride with a bastard son of mixed blood.

"After years of painstaking search, I managed to find out where Manho's father was living and wrote him letters," Aunt Myongsoon confided to Mother many years before I had left Korea. "If I pile up the letters I wrote to him over the years, they'd cover the whole floor of my room and reach the roof."

Aunt Myongsoon became partners with her friend, investing all the money she had made by waiting on the GIs just like Mr. Gone for a decade and half. Being one of the owners, she was spared most of the time from the brunt of the insult that fell upon her employees, but she couldn't entirely avoid being involved in the girls' bickering with their GI customers. One day, one of her girls was quarreling with her customer over the money he owed her for the drinks and tips. Aunt Myongsoon intervened on her behalf, trying to talk to him in her pidgin English. Confronting the drunk GI, who kept pounding on the table and accusing the girl of lying, she threatened to call the police and scrambled to the phone on the counter. But the GI got hold of her from the back and threw her to the floor, and she fell, landing on her left shoulder.

"If she'd landed on her head, she'd have had a concussion," Mother told me over the phone. "She was lucky only to have part of her shoulder bones cracked." When I asked her about the settlement, she said quietly and angrily, "Aunt Myongsoon knew it'd be no good to fight. She gave up."

As I began to picture John and Mr. Gone together—as John the Baptist's reddish-brown hair and pale blue eyes began to merge with Mr. Gone's dark hair and ebony eyes—it occurred to me that Mr. Gone had probably used some of the same "absurd" lines as John used. I could see John writing to Oksoon lines such as, "Connie Chung is an American of Chinese descent, but she's one of the highest-paid anchors in the U.S. If you are talented and hard-working, you can be at the top of your field in this country, even if you're a woman of color." I could picture Mr. Gone saying in a singsong voice to Aunt Myongsoon, "In America, you can be anything you want to be. You'll find yourself in a whole different world."

These two GIs offered their Korean girlfriends an outrageously rare opportunity and fed the American dream into their hungry ears. In my mind, John the Baptist was exactly the person he condemned: a GI he so contemptuously laughed at for perpetuating the American propaganda machine. I was afraid that if I married him, I would be one of those gullible, powerless women. I would be back in the emotional prison I was trying so hard to escape.

I would be a liar if I forgot to admit that there were moments I felt tempted to give in to the demands of the ancient patriarchy that had been bred in me. While detesting so intensely what John the Baptist had done to Oksoon, I couldn't entirely erase a voice pleading with me. More than once, I shocked myself. "Forgive him for what he did to Oksoon," I justified. "Love is unconditional, forgiving, and accepting. Be a woman." Fighting against the true woman in me, the one I had created, the one I had always listened to over everyone else, I went on. "You do love him, or you wouldn't be so angry at him. You don't want to be one of those pathetic women who don't have love in their lives, do you?" I went further to suppress my true feelings. "Don't think so badly of his self-absorbed attitude. He's a man, and a man has to stick with his career because he has to provide for his family. A woman's career is dispensable, after all, since she's not the one responsible for the livelihood of her husband and children. See him from another perspective and acknowledge he's a good man. Trust your friends. They all think he's a nice guy. They think you're unfair to him."

I tried to justify him by saying, "What he did to Oksoon wasn't a conscious, deliberately executed scheme but a result of the cultural instinct brought on a combination of factors, including the conventional male chauvinism that he so vociferously denied having, the sense of superiority he carried as a white male, and most disturbingly, the GI culture that fostered corrupt, manmade hierarchies. He was a product and a willing perpetrator of everything he condemned. Yes, he's a hypocrite, but he's a product of his environment."

In spite of everything I believed, I was afraid of the possibility, probability more likely at that point in my life, of being labeled a spinster. I heard myself blurting out the age-old injunctions for obedience and anonymity, the wishes to negate myself for a man and to be a happy slave for the rest of my life. I was opting to surrender all the opportunities I had fought so very hard for. The man I chose was a military officer who expected me to live on army bases, in the environment I absolutely abhorred, a soldier with whom I wasn't going to have even a vestige of myself. He wanted a stay-at-home wife who raised a houseful of children for him. I was in danger of disavowing myself – the self I had worked so hard to preserve. I could barely recognize myself in the words that came out of my mouth in just two months after his leaving. "Take me with you," I heard myself beg. "I want to go wherever you go." He called me from Arizona, where he was temporarily stationed for half a year or so before returning to Korea, to invite me to visit the Grand Canyon. As I kept begging, he returned a long silence, most likely stunned. I could tell how unexpected it must have been to him.

It took me several days to come to grips with what had happened in me. Recognizing the forces of the ancient patriarchy that had pushed me to lose myself, I let out laughter. I wasn't sad or disappointed; I was rather glad that I had created for myself the last chance to test myself. As there is always a surge of bad weather before good weather settles in, there was consistently a spell of backlash before progress was finally made. The unbelievable words of surrender I had blurted out were the last rush of the patriarchal command that ushered back the new, true woman and made her flourish permanently. They were the catharsis that kissed the old woman in me good-bye forever. After the last test of myself, I never looked back. I changed my phone number and had it unlisted to keep John the Baptist from calling. I never missed *him* although I missed some of the moments I had shared with him. I remembered the daisies I had picked with him on a field outside Lawrence, Kansas, and I remembered the pork ribs he had cooked in the charcoal grill on his backyard.

Chapter 9
Women Forgive Too Easily

No matter how many times I tried to tell myself that John the Baptist was in no way one of those physically violent GIs, I couldn't stop seeing the familiar scenes from my tragic historical memory as they rushed back to me. One by one, I counted the rape, murder, and sheer brutalities that had not been reported in Korean newspapers – the physical crimes that I wanted to think were less atrocious than the mental crimes committed by John the Baptist. Certainly, it would be hideous hyperbole if I compare what John the Baptist did to Oksoon to what the Nazis did to Jews. He wasn't a Nazi, nor did the US Army slaughter six-million Jews. But without this hyperbole, I would be lost as to how to describe the American soldiers' barbarism. In terms of the severity of the emotional hurt the Korean people and I had to experience, there is no other *metaphor* I can find. I am forced to resort to the most famous metaphor in history simply for the reason that there would be no other way I can convey the everlasting trauma the American soldiers brought to my people. How else could I explain to a people who have never been conquered by another country? The following includes only a few of the numerous incidents that brought living nightmares to my people:

In 1987, three women were raped by four American GIs while traveling on a train, and in 1954, a nineteen-year-old girl, who was passing by a US Army freight train, was gangraped by three GIs. Additionally, in 1953, a fourteen-year-old girl was raped and murdered while in 1961, a woman was raped and strangled to death by her GI boyfriend. In 1962 also, a woman was shot to death by a GI, to be followed in 1968 by a twenty-year-old woman whose body was found in a US Army bag in the overhead compartment of a train. The autopsy revealed that she had been strangled with a necktie, her body dumped in the feces in an outhouse, and then stuffed into the army bag with soy sauce all over her to prevent decay. As if these weren't enough, in 1969 a GI threw a woman to the concrete ground, causing a life-threatening concussion, and again in 1971, a twenty-year-old woman was stripped and murdered by a GI who then attempted suicide.

Because many incidents like these went unreported, these were probably only a fraction of the crimes committed by American GIs. It was whispered that in some cases, parents didn't report the statutory rape of their teenage daughters because they were afraid it would bring dishonor to the family. It was also rumored that some adult rape victims chose to remain silent for fear of being shamed.

But these victims and parents chose silence primarily because it was virtually impossible for them to bring the offenders to justice. Because of SOFA (The US-South Korean Status of Forces Agreement) signed in 1967, the Korean government couldn't present any of these crimes to the Korean court. Tasked with trying and sentencing these men, the US government either absolved them or gave them only minimal punishments ridiculously unfit for the caliber of their crimes. "Trash from the US weighs more than metal in Korea," some Koreans lamented. "After crying for justice for months and years, we won't even get the satisfaction of seeing the Americans locked up for a few years."

In the decades since I turned down John's proposal, I have continued to hear about American GIs' heinous crimes in Korea and have continued to realize how unjust SOFA was. I learned that ever since the US Army landed in South Korea in 1945, there have been at least 100,000 criminal incidents, including reported and unreported ones. I also learned that because so many atrocious felons haven't been brought to justice, most Koreans have learned to treat anything less than murder as if it were little more than a misdemeanor. A drunk driver who hit and paralyzed or killed an innocent citizen and ran from the scene was not even a noteworthy case. So used to the American GIs' dehumanizing behavior, most Koreans weren't even surprised to hear that a GI had poured trash into the Han River, the source of Seoul residents' tap water. Rather, Koreans deplored their status as a global underdog. They often lamented, "We're geographically right beneath China and across from Japan. Our small peninsula is doomed to be always invaded by superpowers. We're bound to be a globally marginal state." So fed up and demoralized, they were robbed of the energy to fight back until one truly heinous murder.

On October 28, 1992, a Korean woman named Yoon Kumi was found dead. She was naked, with two beer bottles stuck in her uterus and a cola bottle fixed into her vagina. Her rectum was pierced by an eleven-inch-long umbrella handle, her entire body was covered with bloody bruises, and white laundry detergent powder was spread over her in an attempt to eliminate evidence. An American GI had hit her on the head with a cola bottle, and while she was bleeding to death, he pushed it into her vagina and tore her rectum with the umbrella handle. From the fingerprints on the beer bottles in her uterus, the police identified a GI named Kenneth Markel as the killer, but because he was with the U.S. Army, it took a year and a half for the Korean government to be able to arrest him. Instead of a death sentence, he got fifteen years in prison after the victim's family received about 9,000 dollars in reparation from the U.S. government.

A people's pride was hurt. Suddenly and passionately, Koreans found themselves leaping into the strong sense of national autonomy they had succeeded in preserving for five-thousand long years. As the only nation in the vicinity of China that wasn't absorbed into that superpower, and as the only nation in the world that defeated the powerful Mongols in the thirteenth century, Korea was indeed unique. Once stirred up, the fierce strength they held that had protected their country against so many impossible odds was manifested in an energy that couldn't be suppressed by any outside forces. Upon hearing of Yoon Kumi's murder, Koreans instructed their children, "You are going to grow up to make your country heard by the rest of the world. You will go to school and pick up the tools to make your country strong and resilient. You will tell the world what happened to your country – *your* country." Enraged as they were by the Yoon Kumi tragedy, Korean adults didn't take to the streets. They knew that the next generation would do it for them, armed with a louder and more effective voice. The energy they passed on, along with their righteous wrath, to their young ones was *internal* and therefore irrepressible and lasting. It was as if they had concealed this fighter's face behind the mask of a people resigned to accepting the fate of their nation as a small, marginal state – as if they had disguised their unconquered and unconquerable will in the meek persona of a conquered people. Because they were locked up in an emotional prison for so long with so much pain, they ironically leapt up with so much spirit and volition. Out of the prison, they could make themselves into an unstoppable force. They could launch, to use a Korean metaphor, a stroke of fire on dry grass.

In fall 2002, when I was in Korea on sabbatical, I witnessed this fire spreading across the country. When a U.S. armored motorcar operator was acquitted after killing two teenage Korean girls on a sidewalk, hundreds of thousands of Korean citizens gathered in protest for nearly three months in the freezing winter. In perfect order and quiet, they held a series of candlelight vigils, standing in groups of hundreds in open arenas in Seoul and nearby cities, demanding that the United States apologize to the families of the two girls and to the Korean people. As expected, the vigils were organized by young men and women in Korean citizens' leagues, by the youths who inherited the righteous anger of their parents' generation and learned how to show it with a degree of composure remarkable for the extent of the anger that had accumulated during the decades of simmering silence. Crying in a calm, unanimous, but sonorous voice, they requested that President George W. Bush personally and directly apologize to the Korean people, not indirectly through the U.S. ambassador as he had tried to do immediately after the killing. Upon receiving the apology from President Bush, they then proceeded to encourage their fellow citizens to rise up peacefully against the U.S. Army's reckless disregard of a people's dignity. The protestors received passionate letters and signatures from ordinary people in every corner of the country. Moved by the youths' leadership, some grade-school children even cut their fingers with a knife to write a letter in blood to the Korean government, hoping to persuade the American government to do everything within its power to lower the U.S. Army's crimes in Korea and to change the unfair SOFA. Because the nationwide movement was so well-organized and carried out in such an orderly fashion, there was not one violent incident on the part of the protestors, not one unpleasant clash between the police and the citizens' leagues.

Spurred by the momentum, the Korean media—particularly the Korean internet that boasted its globally unprecedented speed and coverage—began to shine a light on the U.S. Army's crimes in Korea with more scrupulous attention to facts than ever before. One report I read was about a woman in 1999 who was strangled to death by an American GI because she refused to perform perverse sexual acts for him. Another report described a Korean man who was electrocuted by a high-tension wire, which a U.S. Army unit had refused to remove from a construction site despite repeated requests from the workers in 2001. Having lost both of his arms and legs, this man couldn't drink a glass of water by himself. His wife and children would have to take care of him twenty-four hours a day, seven days a week for the rest of his life. A third report was about a couple GIs who discharged sixty gallons of formaldehyde into the Han River, polluting the source of Seoul's drinking water. I also watched a news interview with a victim of a drunk driver who described how the GI who had hit him and made him a paraplegic paid only a fraction of the medical costs after destroying his life. What the U.S. Army committed upon Korean civilians was a string of personal terrorist acts, and SOFA was condoning this terrorism. If Koreans were caught pouring barrels of chemicals into the Hudson River, President Bush would declare it an act of terrorism. But somehow Korean lives weren't nearly as precious as American lives.

By 2002, South Korea had grown to be a global economic player, so the United States had to respond to its citizens' protest, but there was another factor that spurred the U.S.'s response. In 1995, three American GIs were charged for abduction and rape of a twelve-year-old Japanese girl on Okinawa and tried and convicted in Japanese court. Reported on TV worldwide, this incident played a role in informing Americans of their army's brutalities in other countries. The story of the two Korean girls killed in 2002 was reported on American television to the same intense degree, bringing the Korean people's protest to the world's eye. It is troubling to realize that it took an incident in a more powerful country to shed light on the issues in a less powerful country.

In 1995, watching the Okinawans' protest on TV, I thought of John the Baptist. *He's probably frothing in the mouth, ranting about those GIs*, I said to myself. He had ceased to be an individual to me. To me, he was nothing but a faceless member of the U.S. Army who had committed a crime against a Korean woman. I saw no difference between the American GIs who murdered Korean women in unspeakable manners and the ones who killed them through mental manipulation. My mind traveled back to 1984, the year I said goodbye to John the Baptist. Eleven years later, I had one more chance to realize that I had done absolutely the right thing by leaving him. I remembered my friends who had tried in vain to tell me to forgive him, and I remembered what I had told them, "Women forgive too easily. That's why they are seen as pushovers."

How proud I was that I had never forgiven him! Thirty-five years ago, forgiving him was synonymous with betraying myself. Watching the

Okinawans' protest on TV, I had one more opportunity to see that I wasn't a woman who forgave men at the cost of hers*elf. Women forgive too much—and too easily*—I thought. Perhaps if their forgiveness were less frequent and more difficult, there might be fewer men with John the Baptist's hypocrisy.

Without a shred of regret, I remembered the weapon I had used to punish John the Baptist. Soon after discovering Oksoon's letters in his room, I initiated an affair with another man, motivated by revenge for myself and all those Korean women whose lives the American GIs destroyed. I got even not only for myself but also for Oksoon and Aunt Myongsoon, and I felt justified. Only, I felt sorry for the man I chose as a pawn for my revenge. Not knowing that I was using him, he developed a genuine liking for me, and when I had to terminate the brief relationship, he was shattered. I hurt one human being to hurt another, and I was ashamed. But I quickly erased the guilt by validating my motive. "I used a man to teach a lesson to the man who had committed an unconscionable moral crime," I reasoned. "I did something bad to punish the man who did something far worse. He ruined another woman's life. What I did is nothing, compared to what John the Baptist did to Oksoon. At least I didn't ruin a person's life." Driven by the will to wreak vengeance upon him, I remained callously indifferent to the man I had picked. It wasn't until a year later that it occurred to me that I owed him an apology.

Though ashamed of having deceived an innocent man, I never felt any guilt toward John the Baptist. "He not only deserves the punishment but also asked for it," I continued to reason. "Without my revenge, he'll never suffer the way Oksoon suffers." I knew I was resorting to the only weapon in my possession to bring some justice for myself and Oksoon – no matter how small. I weaponized my sexuality to make him feel the pain he made Oksoon and I feel. Because I wasn't able to bring him to the Korean court where he ought to be tried, I exercised my sexual power to bring him the emotional sentence that I believed should be imposed on him. On behalf of the powerless Korean women, I made him feel *their* pain.

I was certain that a man far suitable for me than John the Baptist would show up someday, to work with me—not over me—and help me have it all—a brilliant career, a happy marriage, and lovely children. Now, I find myself thanking John the Baptist. He was the one who, by being who he was, empowered me to walk away from the trap of forgiveness that awaits so many women everywhere. As it became clear later, my relationship with him awakened me to the need to remain morally alert. Without the pain and humiliation of watching a woman being manipulated by a man so deceptively—without the emotional strength to resist—I might not have earned the insight and will power necessary to live a life free from the act of granting false forgiveness.

I also learned that women themselves must be leaders for their own lives. It started to occur to me that Oksoon herself must have been willing to be manipulated by John the Baptist. Certainly, she was smart enough to realize that after five years of unfulfilled promises, he wasn't coming to get her. She should have summoned up the courage to terminate the false relationship and look for another man. But she allowed herself to believe him over and over again, turning a blind eye to his power trip. I wanted to lecture her, "One who volunteers to be enslaved is just as bad as one who enslaves another. In a strict sense, you're not a victim to John's deception. You're a victim of your own deception. You victimized yourself." Well-educated and economically self-sufficient with a steady job, she was by no means one of those women who had no choice but to welcome their men's cheating hearts. Yet, she gave away her autonomy to a man. I thought that there were so many women like her everywhere and that they must share the blame. I believed that before they ask men to stop victimizing women, they should stop victimizing themselves. "If they lie to you once, shame on them," I concluded in my imaginary lecture on Oksoon. "If they lie to you twice, shame on you."

I went back to work with no love. With a sense of relief—and with a sense of loneliness—I redoubled my focus on my very amateurish writing, falling in love with Dr. Kim over and over again. Knowing how long it was going to take me to be able to raise the level of my composition to match the high concepts in my thinking, I labored on. I knew that if I kept writing a million poor sentences, a hundred good ones would eventually be born.

Upon finishing the very immature first draft, I decided to go home. Tired of living with the characters in my book, I wanted to be with living people, with my loved ones in Korea. Having by now formed the habit of engaging a lengthy dialogue with myself before making a decision, I said, "It's been five years since you left home. A lot of things have changed. Look at your country from another perspective and try to find out who you are. Rediscover your roots."

I was homeward bound for the first time in half a decade.

Chapter 10
Living on Crocodile Tears

Of all the snapshots of my time at home for the first six months of 1985, only one stands out in my memory like a skyscraper-sized tombstone on an endless, flat green field.

On a beautiful day in April, Less Big Brother married and made the whole family happy. But it didn't take more than an hour for me to feel utterly detached from the joys of my beloved family. I had a rude awakening—a bitterly humiliating realization that I was a damaged commodity. To my family and my country, I was a woman of indecent moral conduct—a woman of debauchery, to put it a bit more severely—who was justly deprived of her rights to appear on the marriage market. I had not only cohabited with a man for a brief while but also had had more than one boyfriend in my few years in America, all of whom were Americans with blue eyes and brown hair. When Big Uncle (Mother's elderly second cousin) started talking to me at the wedding reception and expressed his wishes to introduce to me a highly successful young Korean man who would soon graduate from MIT with a PhD in mathematics, Mother pleaded with me in whispers, "We're afraid that the young man and his father will investigate your life in America and dig up some of the things you did."

The result of the investigation was doomed to be known to Mother's second cousins and her third and fourth cousins, and to become public information owned and dissected in the clan's rumor mill. A thorough, secretive KGB-style investigation—the same that Big Brother and his wife had endured—was bound to fall on me. It was highly unlikely that the young man and his family would forgo the process, and in my case, the scrutiny would be much greater because I had lived alone in America for five years, during which time I could have done anything unfit for a decent single woman. Although it occurred to me that my family would also investigate the young man's past in America, I quickly buried the thought, well aware that a woman's right to exercise the same scrutiny was hardly more than a mere theory.

On the marriage market, a man and his family had an upper hand over a woman and her family. The former had the power to evaluate the woman's moral conduct and make the final decision. In principle, the woman's party could exercise the right to reject a man with a proven record in indecent conduct. I knew of a woman who said no to a man because it was discovered that he had lived with a "foreign" woman in America for three years. But one thing remained absolutely clear: A man who was found out suffered far less damage than a woman. For the supposedly loose lifestyle I had dared to exhibit in the big, decadent country, I was treated as a moral ex-con in my native country. Since the truth of my past in America was bound to serve as an inexhaustible subject of gossip among my relatives, my family and I were afraid. The possibility of being turned down by the man alone was rather inconsequential, compared to the emotional fallout that would affect my family.

In Korea, a man could claim ownership of a woman's past and hence exercise the right to deny her a future. As such a man, Less Big Brother became another reason why I never went back to Korea except for brief summer visits. Until he finally married a woman seven years younger than he, he was a self-professed, commonly acknowledged womanizer with a splendid track record in sexual conquests. But as Big Uncle brought up the subject of the young man at MIT, Less Big Brother was the first to put on a condescending frown, the first to contort his face with an expression of overt shame and disapproval. While the others were merely concerned and worried, afraid of the awkward and possibly hostile dynamic that might stain the good relationship between my family and Big Uncle's, Less Big brother was morally judging me, forgetting that he himself should be a recipient of such harsh blame. At thirty-two, he belonged in the category of an "old bachelor," but he was fortunate enough to have found a bride who was at once young, beautiful, and intelligent, though he didn't quite deserve her. Although there was no way for me to be certain, I had a feeling that she was one of those "undefiled" virgins whom Koreans praised as being fit to make ideal wives, ironically coveted by men with Less Big Brother's sexual past, innocent and inexperienced enough to make their husbands feel powerful.

I didn't blame my family for reacting out of fear of the consequences. Less Big Brother, however, was being a champion of hypocrisy, a mastermind of dishonesty and a downright dogmatist. Having never cohabited with a woman before getting married, he was "clean" without a proven record of indecency. One could argue that for this reason alone, he was entitled to the privileges I couldn't access. But from my perspective, he was a sexist bigot. Compared to him, Father and Big Brother, despite their attitude toward women being far from praiseworthy, seemed honorable. As far as I could tell, their wives were the only women they had ever been with.

I wasn't surprised to be faced by Less Big Brother's attitude in 1985. By then, Korea had changed to the degree that the young blood of the nation—both male and female—no longer condoned or accepted his sort of hypocrisy. Young men and women in their twenties laughed at it and branded it as an outdated mind-set that revealed a man's insecurities and weak machismo. But none of these changes that seized the youths of the nation had any impact on Less Big Brother and his generation. Although his womanizing stopped when he married, he remained the same as ever in his attitude. He revealed himself as one of the typical men of his generation who still held the moral mainstream in their hands. Even into the twenty-first century, Less Big Brother and his peers—all in their fifties—were still in control of the nation's dominant sexual mores. They stubbornly clung to the notion that a man's sexual blemishes were infinitely more forgivable than a woman's. Proud as I was of what the younger generation had accomplished, I felt no desire to return to my homeland. I didn't want to live in what I called a grave of glory, an emotional place where I, thriving with the professional honor of an English PhD, was to wither in the personal shame of being a morally tarnished woman.

But I learned that I couldn't escape patriarchal norms in America either. In a way, it was worse because men perceived me not just as a woman but as an Asian woman. In physical appearance, I was a member of a population known for making concessions to men and for being more "feminine" than American women. It angered men to find out I wasn't. It is no wonder I have never married, choosing instead to be a single woman whose only companions were long-haired tuxedo cats. I would rather be lonely alone than lonely with someone, and over the long, hard, but productive years spent with books and lovely felines, I eventually found myself quite content. I now say with humor that when I get home, the toilet seat is never up. It isn't having to live alone that bothers me, but the constant comments from those who insist that I still can—and should—find a man.

"You can go beyond the stereotype," they say. "A man worthy of your attention will see you for what's inside, not for the myth they project into you." But they are wrong. No matter how bright and self-analytical, an American man can't entirely free himself from the power of the myth that is so ubiquitous and deep-reaching. There are immense differences between individual men, but none of the men I have met were entirely free from the stereotype. The impulse to stereotype me would stir under the conscious attitude of the supposedly most open-minded, trustworthy, and honest men, and words they wouldn't say to an American woman would pop out of their mouths in my belittled presence. This preconception, however, that rises out of their subconscious isn't the only reason that has kept me unmarried. It is because their comments put me right back into a place for second-class citizens, reminding me why I left my native country. It wreaks emotional havoc upon me in a lethal, almost irreversible way. As far as my relationships with men are concerned, I use the term, a "center blank," because my emotional center still remains blank.

Despite how unhappy I was in Korea, it was impossible for me to leave my country without some sadness. If I ignored the volcanic rage that erupted when I bid farewell to my motherland, I would be a liar. If I didn't admit that the country I cherished so—my homeland that I wish to protect with fierce passion—betrayed me with an emotional sadism I couldn't condone, I would be dishonest and dim-witted with blind patriotism. I will admit that I was someone who never sacrificed her self-interests for anything larger than herself, but I was certain that I was entitled to claim that I had a genuine love for my native country. For the life of me, I couldn't understand why a people so courageous as to brave dictators' guns in an effort to realize their dreams of democracy could be so callous in crushing a woman's dream for equality. I could not grasp how a nation so fast in developing its economy could be so slow in acknowledging women's rights.

But as much as they suppressed a woman as an individual, they encouraged her discipline as an academician and admired her achievements. Absolutely ruthless in demanding that a woman be resigned to being a solitary spinster if she wished to be her own person, they wholeheartedly believed that an old maid was worthy of their support. While the idea of bringing a *woman* and an *individual* together in a woman's life was condemned, the choice of killing one for the other was heartily welcomed and even actively promoted. The check my parents gave me before I left Korea in 1985 was in recognition of such a choice on my part. It was a prize in appreciation of my decision to kill the woman in me to allow the academician to live. As grateful as I was to my parents, I was unable to see the money as anything other than the kindness of the very people who were cruel to me. It seemed that my country shed crocodile tears for me, and I was humiliated to have to accept the check in order to go back to graduate school because I had no financial resources of my own.

Once again, I turned my anger into a relentless drive. My country and my family's crocodile tears became a source of energy. I found myself redoubling my resolution to become a rare individual who lived proudly against the unfair norms. As painful as it was, being rejected by my country's norms made me the woman I am today: a woman who never stopped being a fighter.

Chapter 11
My Name Is Merry Lee

During the first semester of my doctoral work, I worked hard and earned As from the two most demanding professors in English at Kansas University. As the second semester came, I was ready to apply for a graduate teaching assistantship, hoping to gain my first chance to be financially independent. If I could describe the bleak emptiness I felt when this first chance was denied, I would be a modern-day Shakespeare immortalized for her words. I can only try to describe the scenes that threatened to engulf me in despair during those few months after I was rejected by the professors I trusted.

They told me, "You still make little mistakes rarely made by native speakers. To qualify as a graduate teaching assistant, you need to be able to write without errors." They spoke the pre-prepared words of professionals who were experts in being kind with their cruelty, using vocabulary that displayed extraordinary talents in being quiet and natural with their hypocrisy. They harbored no doubts at all about the European graduate student named Suzette, the one who was known to make more mistakes than I in her speaking as well as in her writing. But they wasted no time in showing grave reservations about my qualifications to teach English 101 – the same class she was teaching.

A part-time faculty member in the English Department told me how the department had hired her as a graduate teaching assistant in English without a shred of doubt.

"I know her. She's grossly unqualified. I read the first draft of her doctoral dissertation, and I don't understand how the department can hire someone like her and give you such a hard time. Her writing is hardly better than that of her freshman students." She shook her head in disbelief. "Your writing isn't perfect, but at least you write like a PhD candidate, not like a college freshman.

Besides, you're an English major. She's in Women's Studies. She doesn't know how to teach English."

"She told me the director of the Freshman and Sophomore English hired her five minutes after she showed up at his door with a CV," I said.

"And we don't know when they will hire you," she added. "They say you have to wait until you are ready. But if you aren't ready now, when will you be ready?"

I gave this colleague an honest list of my errors, which consisted of small mistakes, such as prepositional mix-ups between "on," "in," "to," and "for," confusions about definite and indefinite articles like "the" and "a," missing the plural *s* in words like Korean Airlines, reversing syntax in cases like "He embraced the place instantly," rather than "He instantly embraced the place," and mispronouncing words like "repetitive" and "develop" to make them sound like "repaetitive" and "davelop," though people had no problem understanding what I said. Her jaw dropped. She couldn't understand how any of those knowledgeable professors thought I would be unable to teach English 101 because of those tiny missteps.

"You're not applying to teach a graduate seminar in grammar," she raged. "You're asking to teach freshman composition, for God's sake."

"My complex sentences may sound a tiny bit awkward at times because I'm only a graduate student in my first year of PhD work," I said angrily. "I may write, 'My bad habits weren't corrected by my mother's repeated warnings,' instead of 'My bad habits weren't corrected despite my mother's repeated warnings.' When I don't know how to tell the subtle differences between these two sentences, they may sound slightly off the mark. But these professors seem to forget that their native-speaking graduate students are off just as often."

"I, myself, am one of those native speakers who makes the same mistakes as often as you do."

"Now, I'm auditing a freshman composition class to pick up freshman grammar." I laughed mirthlessly.

"Oh, God!" She couldn't help but laugh as well.

It was uncanny for them to ask me to attend a freshman composition class. What made it even harder was their inability to recognize their own hypocrisy.

“The European graduate student doesn’t make errors in her writing,” one professor said. “I’ve had her in my classes.” She dismissed the evidence-backed truth that had been proven time after time.

Another was bold enough to tell me, point blank, “We have international graduate teaching assistants in our department, but they’re of European descent.” As though their heritage made them more qualified than I was, another professor said, “You need to work on your mechanics. You need to attend the class for international students with grammar problems for a whole semester. I think highly of your thinking ability, but you have writing problems.”

I closed my eyes for a small reprieving second and imagined a world in which I replied, “You’re violating the very principle that you so loudly profess: meritocracy based on an individual’s qualifications. Statistically, yes, it’s true that Asians have more difficulties with English than Europeans do, but if you indeed are faithful to what you say, you should be able to differentiate between individuals, not ethnicities.”

Instead, I returned her gaze, famous for the icepick-sharp intellect, and defined by a total lack of emotional grace. I kept my silence. I was afraid that disagreeing with her would transform the look in her eyes into a series of knife-like words that would tear into me. I couldn’t say anything. All that was available to me in that professor’s windowless, boxlike office was a barrage of unspoken words that came to me in that imagined world behind my closed eyes. But when my eyes opened, that world ceased to exist. In that moment, I called to mind a Korean proverb that had never felt quite so poignant before: “She is the one holding the handle of the knife, and I’m the one facing the blade.”

Suddenly, I heard myself lying, “I accept your evaluation completely. I will do everything I can to improve my writing.” I knew that if I said anything else, I would appear to be making excuses for myself.

I had once failed a midterm exam in her class. I couldn’t afford to explain to her that I had botched the in-class essay because I was a much slower writer than most of my classmates and needed more time. I appreciated the second chance she had offered by returning the essay to me and asking me to rewrite it and bring it back to her in a week, but I couldn’t tell her that.

I wanted to say, “I’m forever grateful to you for having given me a blank grade on that lousy paper and for having given me the gift of a brand-new grade. But messing up an exam in a graduate class doesn't mean I'm not capable of teaching the most rudimentary English in the whole world." I fought to avoid repeating the statement that was now a cliché among the women in my department: "You cannot be a feminist and a racist at once." I bit my tongue to eschew the proclamation that was so universally accepted as the truth among the faculty, male and female alike, "You cannot preach the common humanity of everyone and be a racist at the same time."

I wouldn't be telling the whole story if I didn't fully disclose the nuanced dissimilarities in my professors' attitudes when they tried to tell me what to do. As there are good cops and bad cops working together in exacting confessions from a suspect, there are good racists who know how to couch their racism in kind words and kinder deeds, and bad racists who don't know how to bridge the gap between cruelty and kindness, between the bitter content and the sweet form that must be used together if they wish to be truly effective with their racism. Aside from the professor who very bluntly and sharply noted that all their international teaching assistants were of European descent, they all played good cop with me – good racists, kind enough to present their discrimination in the form of advice. They were trying to help me, they claimed, so that I could be an effective English professor someday.

"Maybe you're taking it too hard," a friend, a graduate student in another liberal arts department, said. "Maybe they're trying to help you. Look how much of their precious time they're spending to guide you. Or perhaps, they don't know they're being racist. I wouldn't be surprised if the only definition of racism in their minds is the KKK."

As I convinced myself that maybe she was right, I remarked, "Everyone makes mistakes," and I added quickly, "Hate the sin but not the sinner." I knew even then, as I was speaking, that I was absolutely incapable of practicing such a cliché. I also knew that I had no choice but to be hypocritical. I laughed, recalling another cliché that I had heard somewhere, that it is as impossible for human beings to live without hypocrisy as it is for fish to live without water. Again, I was marshaling words to persuade myself to believe in my professors' sincere intentions. "I'm vexed by what they're doing, but I'm not really mad," I said to my friend. "I'm not going to make any final conclusions about whether they're racist or not. I'll leave it as an unanswerable question, as an ambiguous query. After all, isn't ambiguity better than hate?"

Had I been spared the history of being struck over and over again by the same unfortunate curse in my professional life, even in my professional life as a full-time tenure-track and tenured faculty, I doubt I would be digging up my initial exposure with such a degree of burning ire. Because I had, over the span of so many years and decades, no choice but to repeatedly cope with the discrimination presented to me in the form of encouragements, I am robbed of the ability to soften the sharp edges of my vocabulary. Because I was awarded, over nearly half of my lifetime, nothing but a cheerful mask to hide my pain, I am deprived of the intellectual grace that would serve as a veil of warmth to cover my direct disclosure.

Upon close examination, any perceptive person would be able to pick up on the wrath glittering behind my jocose and more often mischievous eyes, as well as the grief peeking out of the inviting but equally biting humor I speak with. They would be able to tell what enormous energy I have had to exert to establish myself above the hostile environment. They would understand how I came to call myself Merry Lee, and they would see how nicely my laughter, the firearm I equipped myself with to combat adversity, becomes me. To escape the doom of seeing myself as a powerless victim and to free myself from the trap of being defined as a second-class citizen for the umpteenth time, I had to constantly work myself to the point of near death. I incessantly struggled to pretend to be who I was not, and in truly believing who I pretended to be, I was living yet another cliché: "If you pretend long enough, you will become what you pretend to be."

After I went to Affirmative Action to protest the rejection and my professors were consequently informed of my protest, Brad, the professor in charge of hiring graduate teaching assistants, called me in to his office. He told me, "My rejection letter was an administrative error. We circulated your folder from five years ago. We'll create a brand new one that's more attractive."

Hoping that the second chance would bring me the desired outcome of being hired, I eagerly repeated what he said to myself. I convinced myself that he had made an administrative error because I wanted to believe it wasn't racism. I had to have faith in him because without it, I couldn't go on.

I would remind myself that it was my fault, too. When I applied to be a PhD candidate five years earlier, I was childish enough to write personal handwritten letters, begging for consideration, and they were also placed in my folder. No wonder I was passed over. Ashamed of my own unprofessional endeavors, I avoided the question that I should have asked, "How could you circulate such an outdated folder?"

During the semester in which my professors had asked me to do the lengthy series of work to improve my writing—during the months before I went to Affirmative Action to force them to give me a second chance—I had paid half a dozen or so visits to Brad. I reported to him the feedback I received from the faculty members whose classes I audited and who corrected the problems in my writing that I was told were an area of concern. Brad told me that I didn't need to attend the junior grammar class another professor had suggested I take. He also told me that in terms of sentence complexity and structure, I was solid enough to be an effective teacher, but that I still made tiny idiomatic errors that may sound a bit off to my freshman students. He told me that the only thing I could and should do was to keep writing and have an expert correct my smaller errors. But he conveniently forgot to remind me of the deadline for application and failed to instruct me to update my folder with a new letter of application and the most recent letters of recommendation. He had sent a reminder to everyone whose application was incomplete—everyone except me—and he had signed and mailed the letter of rejection to me without another thought. "It *was* an administrative error because he made a mistake," I tried to surmise one more time. "He probably had too many applications to check." Still, I wondered why he had welcomed me back into his office so many times. He took the time to advise me on the classes I may want to take in the following semesters. He even engaged in a long conversation with me about my specialty and told me that literature by women of color was a promising, cutting-edge area.

After circulating my brand new application file among the selection committee, Brad started to avoid looking me in the eye, and not long after, his girlfriend, another English professor named Deborah, began to cast disturbing glances at me. She seemed uncomfortable with me, and I saw in her a combination of anxiety, jealousy, and even hints of anger and resentment. She didn't appear to be overtly hostile or hateful, but I could see the flicker of raw emotions in her eyes as she struggled to control them. As a see-through top would expose one's body parts, the transparent layer of civility she wore on her face only highlighted the boiling undercurrent of her indignation. She seemed to be fighting to suppress a sense of being affronted or trying to conceal an overwhelming sense of danger. I couldn't quite define the complicated feelings in her eyes, but I could tell that the sight of me aggravated her. It was as if she knew that I wasn't responsible for what she felt, but it also seemed as though she was unable to forgive me for being there.

It wasn't until several months later that I thought I could finally define the feelings in her eyes. I was able to pinpoint the one feeling that seemed to lie under her emotional mushroom. I became convinced that Deborah was threatened by my presence and the possibility of me becoming another one of the many female interests in her boyfriend's life. She was in extreme danger professionally. Having put all her eggs into the one book she had written and being uncertain about its publication, she was facing the imminent possibility of not getting tenure and therefore having to leave the university.

I didn't know what was going on between the two. But I was afraid that possibly, Brad found me attractive and was entertained by the conversations he and I shared in his office. I guessed that perhaps, in addition to the natural jealousy a woman feels toward another woman, she felt suspicious because her boyfriend chose to see me more often than strictly necessary. I even suspected that she was trying to cope with the thought that she was losing her place in his life, wondering what would happen to them if she had to leave the university because of her unstable professional standing. Since Brad was known to have been an active chaser of female graduate students before he met her, it seemed almost likely that she had a good reason to be concerned.

I was able to feel a certain amount of relief by reasoning that Deborah would have reacted in the same manner toward a woman of any race who threatened to steal her boyfriend's attention. As I realized this, I thought, *She'd have felt threatened if I were white or black. At least she isn't racist in her jealousy!*

Chapter 12
Inferior, yet Superior

Now, one may wonder why I am delving into these intimate details of my unwanted interaction with the pair. Perhaps, I am over-analyzing a situation any woman faces when she is erroneously perceived as a threat by another woman. My guesses and observations may be unwarranted because none of them could be substantiated. My experience with the couple was so short and superficial that it shouldn't be significant enough to take such a prominent place in my long-term memory. And yet, it stands out in my mind with the vividness of a tall tree in a desert, and I must explain the one simple reason why: I am an Asian female whose place in white-male-dominated America is precariously visible and invisible at once, and whose status is simultaneously elevated and lowered by the very factor that makes me recognized and ignored. I am a member of a group that is aggrandized for its gender and trivialized for its race.

From my memory, it was during my second or third visit to Brad's office in the spring of 1986, a month or so before the day in April when I received a letter of rejection from him. It was several months before the beginning of the fall semester in the same year, a couple months before he started to avoid making eye contact with me. In the middle of the conversation about my coming application for the teaching assistantship, I asked, "A friend of mine teaches Russian for the Russian Department. But before she was allowed to do so, she had to attend an intensive language school in Minnesota and be certified. She made a deal with her department and fulfilled it. I know there's no such institute for would-be English teachers, but if I go through an intensive tutoring process with an expert, and if this expert believes I'm ready to teach freshman composition, would you be able to vouch for me? Can I make a deal like the one my friend made with the Russian Department?"

“I can’t promise you anything,” he declared, his cheerful attitude suddenly hardening into a demeanor of white-hot austerity. He lifted his chin up, drawing a thin, flat line with his broad lips. His face seemed to weigh my fate with deliberate indifference, his eyes fiercely but obliquely directed at the wall beside my chair. My future was in his control, a control he exercised with an inflated sense of self-importance. Instantly, I noticed that he wasn’t aware of what he was doing. The power trip he was pulling on me came to him in spite of himself, provoked by my less-than-wise request. It was simply a reflex reaction triggered by my unrealistic suggestion. Out of desperation, I asked him if he could consider my hypothetical qualification after weeks of constant pestering, which ultimately had failed to lead into a more conducive prospect for my teaching assistantship.

It took me half a second to realize that I had made a mistake. I put myself in a position to be the mouse to his cat. I was ashamed. Immediately, I corrected myself, trying to float a disarmed smile across my face, “I’m not foolish enough to ask anyone to promise anything. I was just exploring options.”

In a wink, his eyes regained their jolly shimmers and his mouth settled back into a slight curve of contentment. He came back to being the man he normally was, the professor known for putting his students at ease, the popular one whose classes were almost always full. I could tell why I had never heard a mixed opinion about him or his teaching. Brad was at once jovial and competent, capable of being buddies with his students and yet maintaining a firm sense of authority over them. I thought it was something in his face that made him so approachable and yet pleasantly dignified, the expression traversing miles of emotional distance in a second that simultaneously inspired and entertained his students and friends. As he laughed jocosely in a low, soft voice and abruptly flew into a serious, high-pitched tone, he showed himself to be a very smart person with a talent for comedy, a man whose genuine anger and frustration came with an equally natural humor and wit. In fact, the grave look in his face rather accentuated the charm of his smile, being a sure sign that the lighthearted expression was coming back in an instant. Not exactly handsome in a conventional sense, Brad could be called handsome because of his ability to combine rigor and ease. Together with his tall, slender body, his face presented a man who was sufficiently hard and mellow at once.

But that day in his office, I felt as though he was a cat enjoying his mouse. He was in a place to dole out his power, and I was reaching for a very emotionally expensive chance to exact a small benefit from it. It was an unspoken reality between the two of us. Although this unspoken reality may take place in any relationship involving professional hierarchies, there was something else between us that wasn't at all typical to such relationships. What I saw between him and I came from a pattern I had experienced for many years in my interaction with white males, a pattern I knew I was going to see for decades to come. As aware as I am of the truth that every man is as different as every woman, there is a certain paradigm that I believe is established—and perpetuated—when it comes to the power dynamic between white males and Asian females. As an Asian female, I can't tell how many times I was perceived as being less as an *individual* while being elevated to a higher status as a *woman*. I so often failed to be perceived as a person equal to white males—or females—in terms of intellectual and professional qualifications, but I was hugely successful in being perceived as more desirable in terms of the ability to entice members of the opposite sex. I was superior as a partner for romance, but inferior as an individual with the right to be independent.

To a large degree, this pattern of gender conception is universally applied by men and women of any race. A romantic relationship tends to imply a hierarchy in which the man leads from a higher position and the woman follows from a lower position, and a professional relationship, to the contrary, dictates an exchange in accordance with the individuals' qualifications regardless of the male-female role division. When a man and a woman go out on a date, it is the man who is tacitly required to pick up the bill and the woman to quietly acquiesce. When a man and a woman go out for a friendly outing, however, it is usually a Dutch pay that is expected. Is it a mere assumption that a man is expected to own and drive a car if he wants a woman for a romantic relationship, but not the other way around?

Is it a mere coincidence that the inability to drive is a much more serious shame for a man than it is for a woman? It seems that only friendship without romance would allow a pair to be equally in charge. In an age when men and women are being constantly urged to find ways of being equal in all areas possible, it still is taken for granted that women follow men's lead. To make it worse, it is women who, loving to complain about gender inequality, still deeply wish for their men to be on higher planes than themselves. Many women refuse to pick up the bill even once because their men have picked it up a dozen times in a row. Still, more women automatically expect their men to drive and are inclined to think much less of those who don't, but not of other women who don't. They will not take the steps to solve the problem which they so vehemently protest against.

If I were a white female, Brad still might have ignored me professionally. He probably would have found himself sliding into the pattern of interaction a man would pursue with a woman he saw fit for a romantic relationship. In his mind, I very seriously doubt that he contemplated any kind of liaison with me that wasn't strictly professional. But his actions made an indelible impression upon my mind of the prototype of the white male so hauntingly familiar to me. He loved to pay attention to me because of my ability to elicit his male curiosity, but he so callously disregarded me because of my seeming inability to be his equal as an individual, as a human being, and as a fellow academician. Why else could he have failed to take the very first administrative step of making a candidate's application file complete after so many visits from her that he seemed to so thoroughly enjoy?

Given my experience with him, and with every white male whom I had more than a one-time contact with, I couldn't help thinking that his failure to see me as a job candidate came ultimately from his perception of me as an Asian female. Being an amateur myself, I was partly responsible for the initial rejection I had received from him. I realized that I should have been the one to make sure that all the documents had been turned in to make my application file complete. I was sorely reminded of the painful fact that being an international student from Asia, not from Europe, I was more exposed to doubts about my qualifications to teach English. But inevitably, I couldn't avoid the thought that the so-called administrative error wouldn't have happened if I were white. I couldn't avoid speculating that I came to receive the brunt of an administrator's careless attitude because of the racial stereotypes stacked against the Asian female. I came to the conclusion that I was good enough to be an object of beauty, but not good enough to be the subject of one's respect. I wasn't perceived by Brad as a person who could professionally excel. I can't explain how degrading that was. I left my country only to face the same pattern of objectification in another country. It seemed that I had come so far just to end up in a place where I was made even more invisible by racial stereotypes.

There was nothing, nothing I wanted more than the opportunity to become an American. I was determined to work hard to prove I was one of those immigrants who helped their adopted country become a melting pot in theory and practice. In fact, I believed the United States was my husband while Korea was my motherland. I was eager to do my husband right by doing the utmost I could to spread the *idea* of American democracy for every demographic. But the members of my husband-country—especially the majority of those who were in charge of running it—treated me like an aggressive beggar who deserved little more than pity or casual charity. Because of my skin color and my accent, the American in me had to not only ask but also yell and scream to earn an opportunity to be accepted as an American.

I must acknowledge that in the end, Brad proved himself to be a far more advanced breed than Jonathan or John the Baptist. He wasn't the sort to make false promises to a woman like John the Baptist, nor was he akin to Jonathan, the Asia bum who expected me to be a superwoman and subservient at once. Brad was a conscientious academic capable of analyzing himself, a man who finally saw the individual in me and didn't hesitate to make a series of endeavors on my behalf. Determined to make it up to me, he, after kindly instructing me what to do to make my application complete, took the trouble of seeking each member of the GTA selection committee to explain to them why my new application file was being circulated after the initial screening was over. I acknowledge that I saw a good man despite his flaws, and I am aware that one may find it unbelievable that I could so easily let go of my deep-seated resentment against his stereotyping.

I was overwhelmed by the need to be recognized as a candidate with equal opportunity, to be accepted by my department, and simply be granted an opportunity to be considered as one of those worthy of the membership. Having left my motherland not only physically but also emotionally, because she so ruthlessly judged that I was a moral ex-con with the record of having co-habited with an American man, I had no choice but to make my life in America. For me, failure was not an option. Success was tantamount to life and failure equal to death. To be able to live, I had to succeed. Anyone who helped me succeed in America was no less than a savior to me, no matter his past conduct or mistakes. I didn't have the emotional leisure to hold a grudge, so I forgave him instantly. I couldn't afford to feel anything about him that wasn't positive. Impressed by his serious efforts on my behalf, I came to a conclusion. I eagerly rationalized with the woman in me who had been resentful, “You know how powerful the forces of stereotype are. They’re as pervasive as the air we breathe, and you know we can’t live without breathing the air. What you hate is the power of the preconception that is deeply ingrained in him, not him. Now he sees it. He’s given you a second chance. You need to give him a second chance, too.”

I sincerely congratulated Deborah on receiving tenure. In my second or third year as a graduate teaching assistant, she finally got the verdict from the State of Kansas that she was going to be a permanent faculty at the university. She had no more reason to doubt the future of her relationship with Brad. I thought I would have a second chance with her and hoped that she would gain some degree of friendlessness toward me. The raw “mess” in her eyes was diluted into a milder, less intense stare, and she started to look at me without the same fierce anxiety that used to resemble hostility, so I had reasons to feel my hope was well-grounded. A year or so after she had received tenure, we came to the point where I could walk into her office to borrow a cigarette and be asked if I had matches. Asking her for a cigarette was a deliberate attempt on my part to let her know that in my mind, she was a friend. Asking me if I had matches was a sincere gesture on her part to tell me she was fine with me.

As our interactions became less strained, I began to find her attractive. Without the severe stress that used to bring a contorted frown between her eyes, she had regained the usual equanimity that restored the bright, appealing features of her face. She was sexy in a conventional sense, but her sexiness was made all the more compelling because of the shine emanating from a highly intellectual mind. As the serious glow in Brad’s dark eyes was rather inviting, a sure sign that his wit and humor was coming back in a wink, the flames of heavy thoughts in her blue eyes were rather enticing because they were reflections of the cheerful expression she could don in a moment. Her face was squarely shaped, with a round chin descending from slightly tapering contours, conjuring a peculiar charm that suggested both logic and emotion. Her short, lustrous light blond hair showed a female beauty tempered by an academic discipline. Although petite and of medium height, she was striking. The balanced blending of femininity and rigor she exuded seemed to add a few invisible inches to her slight build. I liked to watch her because she was so visually pleasant.

Her sense of discomfort with me, however, didn't entirely disappear. Although she had learned how to keep her feelings toward me under the surface, she had not yet conquered them, and I was afraid she would never overcome them completely. Every now and then. I saw flashes of the mess leaping out of her eyes, to be quickly diffused by a forced effort to be civil, and I found myself flinching momentarily in an attempt to marshal a smile in return. My smile seemed phony to her, I suspected, being awkwardly improvised, as hers looked equally reluctant to me. She betrayed her raw feelings in spite of herself, and I, halted by the need to cope with the uneasy emotional situation, immediately sought my own way to mend it. Without hesitation, I secretly declared myself above her, throwing silent, but kind words at her. "I know how you feel," I said to her in a mute monologue. "Once threatened, forever threatened. Although it's not my fault, you have a reason to be uncomfortable with me. I understand." In my mind, I treated her as a child who was once scared by a traumatic incident and was unable to forget it. I saw myself as a forgiving, tolerant, and noble adult with a big enough heart to embrace a child suffering from the yoke of the memory, as a wise old woman dealing with an immature youngster. I created a version of myself in my imagination that was probably far from true. By constructing a morally superior person in myself, I tried to build a defense mechanism that enabled me to survive and ultimately rise above the treatments I didn't deserve from anyone. I wore a mask. To foster the generosity of the oppressed, I practiced a look for my face. I opened my closet door and took out a paper box Big Brother had given me shortly before my coming back to America after the half-year-long visit in Korea.

"It's not just for a young bride," he suggested. "It's for anyone who has to make adjustments for a new life. When you return to Kansas, you'll probably find some inspiration in these masks."

The masks he insisted on me packing into my suitcase were a set of three different faces of the same woman, carved in three different pieces of the same square-shaped, dark brown wood panel. Connected by small metal rings attached to the holes drilled on the edges of the wood pieces, these faces—these masks—could be folded together, topped by the smiling one hiding the two others that were respectively sad and angry. Laying all three of them flat on my desk, I preached to myself, "I'm married to America, and the Americans I have to work and live with are my husband and his relatives. As a newly married woman has to wear a smiling face in front of her in-laws, I will put on a cheerful face in front of these Americans. I will hide the sad and angry faces, pushing them far into a tiny corner in the back of my head, only to bring them to the surface when I have a chance to 'grab the handle of a knife,' to use a Korean metaphor, and expose the hypocrisy they backed me into. I will wait for the day when I can tell the world about the prejudices and racism they subconsciously projected onto me."

Eventually, this happy, wooden face came to me so effortlessly that I didn't have to make any emotional attempt to keep the others suppressed. My face and mask were made inseparable. They fused into each other through years of consistent use.

It was this union of the face and mask that made me so spontaneous with my merry greetings to Brad as he barely uttered the monosyllabic word of hi to me, keeping a physical distance from me by at least seven feet. These greetings showed him that he no longer needed to be embarrassed by what he had done to me once, that he no longer had to avoid making eye contact with me or be self-conscious about having harbored a feeling toward me that wasn't strictly professional. For the remaining eight years of my graduate work in Kansas, every time I ran into him in the hallway and saw him deliberately averting his eyes from me, I opened the closet door in my apartment and took out the three faces of the young wife.

Convinced as I was that my smile was genuine, I wondered. I was amused by how artificial the bride's first face was, with both ends of her mouth turned up in the shape of a perfect crescent moon, and her eyes betraying a flash of rage that failed to be blunted out by enough time. Hers was a cartoonish smile with no human complexity. Having consciously modeled my smile after hers, I couldn't help thinking mine, too, might be as artificial as hers, lacking the genuine look of a person untouched by suppressed ambivalence. I imagined my brows without a curve, as sharply formed as hers, and my jaws as firmly clenched without any space for contentment or honesty. It would cancel out the humor and good will floating in my eyes.

A perceptive observer could not miss the layering of merry austerity in my face that was actually the mask of the young bride. The faces of sadness and anger were also visibly one-dimensional, with their foreheads wrinkled by thick lines of unspoken agonies, and their cheeks elongated by the emaciating forces of muted indignation. Akin to the smiling face, they were void of the tempering power of complex human emotions. I almost knew that those who were close to me could detect the rawness of the bride's facial expressions in mine. "They perhaps see through me," I said to myself, "how hard I work to soften the jagged edges of the bride's look of sadness and anger. I bet they can see her un-tempered faces in mine."

It would hardly be an exaggeration to say that my life in America—so far over three decades and a half—has been an effort to make the three faces of the bride as touched by humanity as possible. To be accepted by my husband, who in his subconscious racism constantly reminded me of how I had to prove myself over and over again to be treated as an American, I had to spend every available moment honing my feelings toward those in-laws of mine. In order to accept them as human beings with as many faults as mine, in order to be accepted by them as such, and in order to be able to consider them as my family whom I was destined to live with, for better or worse, until the end of my life, I had to make it my habit to re-carve the young bride's masks into time-honored faces of a complex human being. I had to be a traditional Korean woman who believed that once married, a woman should live and die in her husband's house, to be the "ghost" of his family, no matter what. My three faces had to be tempered to be rid of the crudely pronounced expressions, to be mixed with looks of understanding accompanied by compassion and respect. They were to be toned down by a sense of pity toward all human beings because all human beings were to be pitied for their shortcomings and for their failed efforts to overcome. My smile had to be genuine rather than phony. My sad and angry looks had to be mitigated by other emotions. The three faces had to stop looking so contrary to one another.

"I choose love over hate," I declared. "Until my face stops going back and forth between the genuine and phony, until the mask of the simple-minded young bride becomes one with the face of the complex young Korean woman who longs to be an American, I will not cease making the effort. Yes, indeed, my smile may betray cracks in my mask occasionally, and my love may not be entirely sincere sometimes. But there's one thing I'm absolutely certain of, and that is my need and desire to *love human beings*. Doesn't ambiguity—or even phoniness—come from this heartfelt need and desire to love instead of hate, after all?" I talked to the young bride in me incessantly, just as she talked incessantly to me. During the rest of my graduate school days, I had so many monologues that they became part of my life, as common as eating or sleeping.

If I could put together all the words I shared in my dialogue with myself in a single line, they would be long enough to reach the sky.

I was becoming a person who knew how to practice the *art* of loving. As the emotional repercussions from the faculty's united racism fell on me, and as I started to notice overt changes in their attitude toward me, I once again felt my hands touching the invisible mask on my face. I remembered the heated conversation I had exchanged with Suzette, the European graduate teaching assistant who had been hired on the spot. Recollecting the words that we had flung back and forth on the phone, I thought about how I had tried to conjure a smile untouched by hate. I tried to effectively display the young bride's crude smile filtered into a more complex expression of humanity. It was a smile defined by a human being's wish not to lose love for another human being.

Immediately after I had received a letter of rejection from Brad, I called her to tell her, "I just wanted to know if you had received a renewal of the annual contract for your graduate teaching assistantship from the English Department."

"Why do you ask?" Suzette replied, pretending to be nonchalant despite the severe anxiety leaking through her raspy voice.

"I got a letter of rejection from Brad today. I was wondering why. I thought maybe the department didn't have enough money to hire new graduate teaching assistants or maybe not even enough to renew the current GTAs' positions. If you got yours renewed, I thought that might be a sign they have enough money to retain the current ones and perhaps hire a few new ones." I struggled to clamp down the high-pitched intensity creeping out of my deep, husky voice.

"I think I know why they turned you down," she returned, her own mask slipping. "You probably didn't make enough progress in your writing."

If I had the ability to form the right words to throw at her in that moment, I could very well surpass Shakespeare with my prose. I heard myself sneering back at her with an outspoken fury, "You know my writing is as good as anyone else's. It's at least as good as yours. And I know how to teach."

"Are you saying I don't know how to teach?" She was getting as overt with her anger as I was. The painful insecurity was seeping out of our falsely composed attitudes.

"I didn't say that. Why are you twisting my words?"

"Yes, you are. Just because you came to my class once to observe my teaching and give me honest feedback, you have no right to be condescending to me."

"You invited me," I reminded her. "I ran into you on campus, and you gave me an instant invitation to come and see you teach. You asked me to do it for you."

I drew in a long, loud breath to restrain myself as the scenes of her class rushed back to me. It was by far the most pathetic class I had ever seen, with students only physically present, and the teacher rambling on with words irrelevant to the topic for the day. It was a class without a purpose, made of a series of random readings from the text and a succession of casually picked concepts with no connection to each other. I couldn't tell what she was talking about. All I could hear was a string of mispronounced words such as "gesture," which was pronounced with a *g* sound instead of a *j*. The class had started without an announcement of the main topic, and it went on aimlessly as if steered by a driver spinning her wheels in a circle. Since there was nothing of the class that stayed in my memory, I was unable to give her any feedback. When she wouldn't stop asking, I just told her that her students were relaxed in class and that it was a good sign. It was painfully obvious that she wasn't looking for honest feedback. She was longing to hear what she wanted to hear: that her teaching was OK.

"Did you call me to criticize my teaching?"

"I just wanted to find out if you got your contract renewed."

"It's none of your business."

"I'll ask the English Department why they rehired you and turned me down."

"If you ask them why they rehired me, that'll put me on the spot."

"Why would that put you on the spot? I'm not going to tell them anything about your teaching."

"If you ask them, that'll make me look bad."

"Why?"

"There's no point in continuing this conversation."

She hung up on me and I let out a loud falsetto laugh to silence the beating of my heart. I was shocked by her paranoia, astounded by my own foolishness. I shouldn't have called her. I should have known how insecure she was and should have understood why she would panic at the mere possibility of me mentioning her name to the English Department. She knew she was far from qualified, but she was in dire need for an on-campus job. Being an international student, she was forbidden to work outside the university. In order to graduate with an advanced degree in Women's Studies, a field that didn't offer any financial opportunities to its graduate students, she had to retain her teaching job in the English Department. It was impossible for her to think that I was merely trying to find out whether she had received a renewed contract. She was the only GTA in the English Department I personally knew well enough to call on the phone, but the call appeared to her as an attempt to report on her to the department. She felt her survival was in jeopardy. Or if I use a cruel cynicism, she probably felt "her own feet itching as a thief would feel his own feet itching from a guilty conscience," as Koreans would say. My phone call did nothing but create a situation in which one international student was pitted against another.

As weeks and months passed, there were several instances in which I found myself to be the object of intense hostility from some peers of mine close to Suzette. I finally saw the worst consequences of my professors' racism. What I had dreaded more than anything else was taking place. I was being hated and despised by my peers who labeled me as a backstabbing "bitch." The ripple effect made me nearly sick as I received a series of ugly glances from a number of Suzette's friends, who among others were her former boyfriend and two fellow graduate students in English who had a chance to hear what I guessed to be Suzette's grossly exaggerated and distorted interpretation of my phone conversation with her. Believing her side of the story and thinking that I had threatened to expose her incompetence to the English Department, these three individuals stared at me as if I were a snake. I even thought I saw a pair of a shark's eyes in her boyfriend's face. As they refused to return a smile to mine, to the merry bride's smile, I could hear the words they were throwing at me in silence, "You're so phony, so two-faced!"

The young bride in me silently persevered. She played her role well enough, her face made a bit more opaque by my human touch and a little harder to read. It was she I wished to please more than anyone else in the world, she I was afraid of crossing more than anyone else in my life. If I lost her support, I knew I would be back to being the Korean woman without a mask, upon whom the curse of racism would fall with a much stronger force. A young bride who hesitated to bear any of the burdens her in-laws placed upon her was doomed to be unwelcomed, and I couldn't afford to be unwelcomed. I was to be what *they*—my professors and peers—expected me to be. I was to be inferior and superior to *them,* not to be an equal. I was never going to be one of *them,* but I was going to be the one working for *them.* Self-censorship to an ultimate degree was going to be my professional life. Self-negation to an extreme degree was going to be my emotional life.

And yet, I must reiterate here what I said before – that not all of my face was a mask. Not every emotion I expressed was phony. Not everything I said was a lie. Like any other human being, I couldn't live without a mask, and I couldn't live with a mask alone. I became used to making the mask part of me, and me part of the mask. "If you wear a mask long enough," I now say, "it becomes you." Thanking Brad and everyone who helped me embark on my teaching career as a graduate teaching assistant, I wasn't entirely without true feelings of gratitude. "Even if you weren't nearly as desperate to succeed," I heard my mask speak to me, "you'd still be grateful. Under any circumstances, feeling grateful would be far better than feeling resentful. You won't make yourself into a bitter person, no matter how bad the situation is."

My mask and I became part of each other, and together, we created this definition of myself that was going to be an absolute emotional necessity for decades to come. Placed time and time again under the yoke of adversities that threatened my mental health, I was to find myself falling back on this positive self-definition over and over again. For three decades and a half, I kept myself from falling into an embittered emotional life. I struggled to keep up my smile—my mask that became me—in the face of all odds.

As a tenure-track faculty member, and eventually even as a tenured faculty member, I probably came across as being phony. Sometimes I suspected I was indeed phony. This real and projected phoniness came from severe chronic fatigue syndrome, an illness I developed as a result of the constant burden of having to work on myself. My illness was the physical manifestation of the emotional war I fought with myself, an accumulated by-product of the everlasting battle with my colleagues and my environment.

"Are you sure you're still grateful for this life you've got?" I ask myself even now. "You have to sleep half of your life away because of your illness. Aren't you miserable inside? Aren't you lying to yourself?" I may be lying, I answer myself. But having to lie to myself in this manner is far better than making myself into a sour old woman. If this is a lie, and if this lie is what keeps me going in the human world, I will embrace it for years to come.

Chapter 13
Dying to Live

My mask and my true self began to fuse together, but I reserved a corner in my heart that existed apart from the young bride's influence. "We're all human beings," I repeated my mantra. "We all have emotional sanctuaries in our hearts untouched by masks." I realized I must not be the only person donning a mask. In fact, I began to recognize that the English professor I admired so much must also be divided into her mask and her true self. This professor was the one who made the absurd suggestion that I attend an English 101 class to fix the errors I made occasionally. She was the one who had shown enough hypocrisy to defend Suzette's composition for being free of errors. But she was also the one who helped me eventually receive the desired graduate teaching assistantship. After persuading Brad to recirculate my newly made folder among the judges who had already finished deliberating, she wrote a glowing letter of recommendation for me, going out of her way to personally spread good words on my behalf among the faculty she could influence. Her name was Jane, and she became my chief mentor who guided and inspired me through the nine-year-long doctoral work.

It occurred to me that Jane, too, had to wear a mask for me, maybe that of the young bride's mother-in-law. Slowly, it dawned on me that she had to pretend to accept me as who I seemed to be with my smiling bride's mask, just as I had to do for her. We both had to navigate our relationship in the grey spaces invented by our personae, in the realm that was neither a mask entirely nor a true face totally. In my desperate effort to create a close relationship with a person—an American—who could help *me* become an American, I clung to her as if she were my savior, making her an object of an overwhelming and sometimes blind admiration. Because I saw her as the best of Americans, because I saw in her an unreserved sense of justice and an unhesitating courage to manifest her mind, I placed her on a pedestal, nearly worshiping her. She became a role model I wished to emulate in the smallest details of her conduct, even in her appearance and fashion trivia. I wanted to wear the same elegant skirts she wore and the same discreetly flamboyant blouses she put on. I decided to try bright colors toned down by subdued hues and prominent pitches refined by receding shades. I wanted to cultivate the same glamorous air tempered by an intellectual aura.

Unlike Jane, I wore red. Red went better with my dark black hair than lighter colors such as the soft pink that highlighted her beach-white face. Jane had silky brownish-blond hair, a long swath that I suspected came down to cover half of her back. Fine and straight, it was far from wiry like mine, and it was always bunched up by a rubber string into a neat, flat knot on the back of her head, its smooth texture almost entirely concealed. It seemed that in order to cultivate a look of severe austerity, she had divested herself of anything that could strike one to be potentially sensual. She thoroughly erased the appearance of a woman who still entertained the hope of living a *woman's* life and a highly accomplished academician's.

To me, she was a woman who had arrived at her lifelong destination, a place where she was determined and finally content to be a scholar dedicated to spreading her social ideas and helping those who sought the same. She was one of those single women who found satisfaction in work and sought primary comfort in the companionship of her cats and the faithful friendship of the few she deeply cherished. In her personal and professional demeanor, I saw a woman who gladly made herself into the embodiment of what so many young idealistic women wished to be – a model of a woman who had created and earned a life in which the hard work of realizing one's talent in words came with the highest level of personal happiness achievable. To condemn the bad of the world, of which she had seen a lot, she used her words. To praise the good in human beings, of which she had seen plenty, she exercised her art of loving human beings. It looked as if the severe austerity of her appearance was there to ironically reveal her remarkably tender heart. From the fresh bread she personally baked for her friends, I smelled the aroma of the warmth hidden behind her glasses, and in the oranges and apples she brought for her colleagues and students in her office, I saw an enveloping affection exuding from behind her eyes. Always in demand by everyone in the department, she still found time to bake several loafs of bread to give to others. Constantly wanted by many on the campus, she still had time to buy fruits to encourage the people who came to seek her advice. When I received the occasional orange or apple she bought and the piece of the loaf she baked, I smiled happily, getting a glimpse into the loving woman in the industrious scholar.

I knew what a burden I was placing on her by making her into an idol in my mind. I was depriving her of her humanity. I was setting myself up for a situation in which I would find myself disappointed by the smallest faults in her, even by the very typical shortcomings universal to all human beings such as shying away from conversing about one's painful memories. Once, she vaguely mentioned to me that she had failed in love, hastily precluding the details of her experience that I very much wanted to hear.

"Most people fail in love at least once in their lives," I said. "You're not the only one."

"But when it happens to you, the failure looks like the worst thing that could ever happen," she returned. "You forget it happens to almost everyone."

"How long did you date him?"

"For about 5 years. I knew it wasn't going to work from the beginning, but I couldn't stop seeing him."

"When was that?"

"It was when I was a beginning assistant professor here."

"Was he a professor here?"

"Yes."

"What did he teach? How old was he and how old were you? Tell me about him," I inquired, my eyes shining with curiosity.

"It was a long time ago," she said and then dropped the conversation by changing the subject in a subtle way. "I don't think about it anymore. It was in the past." There was a soft, but firm finality in her voice and I stopped asking. She wasn't offended by my question, but the topic brought back the pain that she had buried for many years. It seemed that it was something she talked about in specific detail only with someone close to her.

As much as I admired her as my mentor, I liked her as a friend, but she never—almost never—bared her innermost feelings to me. I knew I was the reason it was nearly impossible for her to be anything other than an emblem of a superhuman in my presence. Sometimes I felt sorry she chose to be so guarded with me. I was demanding something impossible of her – to be both a bosom friend with well-known failures and an impeccable role model without any at all. I wanted her to wear the mask of a mother-in-law and be her true self at the same time, the perfect synthesis of an entirely human person and of a totally divine, inspiring presence. She knew she couldn't be both, so she elected to be the latter.

As an American and as one of my figurative mothers-in-law, Jane guided me with her usual combination of rigor and warmth. Most of the time, she was gracious enough to let me see nothing but a mother-in-law's patience, carefully concealing the less than positive expressions she must have kept to herself. Sometimes, these expressions came through a slip in the mask and, in spite of her best efforts, she made an emotionally distancing gesture. At times, she made a slight frown, deepening the furrow between her brows, blinking her pale blue eyes, and betraying a quiet, but nervous anxiety that caused me to internally flinch. I thought I could almost touch the sharpness of the piercing gaze behind her glasses. More than once, Jane told me to see her as nothing but a human being. Perhaps, she knew that I saw her as a human being, but she sensed that I chose to erase what I saw. Afraid that I may lose the idol I created, I stubbornly ignored the human being in her. I only beheld the idol, and she was probably aware of this.

Sometimes, I let my bare faces peek out of the bride's smiling mask. These were the sad and angry faces that escaped the grip of the young wife's discipline, betraying their raw expressions. Jane understood why they were so raw. In the place where she was divested of her masks, she probably empathized with me. She saw a woman raging at the injustices of the world, at the sexism in her native country and at the racism in her adopted country. She admired the young woman that I was, the bold spirit that had leaped across the Pacific to live a brand new life in her chosen country. She wanted to help me succeed in my adopted country, to create a niche of my own in the promised land by spreading the words of the individuals who fought to carry ideals into reality. There still was an *idea* of America in these individuals' written words as there still was room for more scholars to be added to extend this *idea* for those who had been excluded in the past.

Under her guidance, I chose multicultural literature of the United States as my area of specialization. In addition to the canon of American and British literature, including major authors such as Herman Melville, Nathaniel Hawthorne, William Faulkner, Ernest Hemingway, and F. Scott Fitzgerald, whom I had to study because they were required to earn a PhD in English, I chose to discover a spectrum of lesser-known authors yet waiting to be picked up by scholars eager to make them visible. I wanted to be as good as Jane, whose reputation for diversity in scholarship was unmatched by anyone on campus. She was not only tremendously well-versed in all periods of traditional American literature established by white male and female authors but also amazingly knowledgeable in numerous areas of literature constructed by anonymous minority male and female authors. She had started with Herman Melville and Nathaniel Hawthorne, the white male pair whom she called her old friends, but she had extended her research efforts to include groups who had been left out by her old friends, by *them* as she called them. She was one of those Americans who wanted *democracy,* not just democracy by and for *them.*

Having to diversify my courses to fulfill the requirement, I could only take two of her classes, but in these two classes, I learned more than I ever did from five different classes I had to take from other professors. In "Hawthorne and Melville," the 900-level seminar about the two greatest authors of the 19th-century, I found that she was not only highly knowledgeable but also talented in presenting information in ways in which modern audiences could relate. While Hawthorne was a representative author of the 19th century, she explained, Melville was a prophetic one. Melville could demonstrate the loss of America's democracy through Captain Ahab's choices, while Hawthorne was limited to pointing at the dangers of puritanism in his time. According to her, Melville was open about the fact that *Moby Dick* was based on his experience as a sailor, while Hawthorne was shy about the origins of *The Scarlet Letter*, claiming that he discovered the story in the Custom House. Lacking the honesty and courage that enabled Melville to admit that the novel was his experience, Hawthorne had to pretend that the Custom House, not he, was responsible for the novel. She was definitely more partial to Melville, but in her coverage of the two, she was equally thorough and fair in acknowledging their merits and faults. Although Melville was her idol, she never hesitated to acknowledge that he, despite his prophetic visions, was still a nineteenth-century white man not entirely free from racism. She relentlessly criticized him for having created Fedallah, the Filipino character playing the shadows of Captain Ahab. She said, "Fedallah is the white male's stereotype of an Asian male. He's far from a fully developed character. He only functions as Ahab's shadow, into whom Ahab projects his dark side. He's the East into which the West projects the other."

It was refreshing to have a chance to compare her to another professor who offered a 900-level seminar about William Faulkner and Ernest Hemingway. In contrast to her, this professor lacked the courage to be honest with Faulkner's shortcomings. He would keep justifying him as a product of his time and defend him for his racism. He would say, "Faulkner was a white Southerner and he did have racism, but he consciously fought it. He deserves credit."

Unlike Jane, who condemned Melville for failing to overcome his racism, he conveniently condoned Faulkner for the same failure. He refused to treat Hemingway, one of the two authors in the seminar, equally to Faulkner. Eager to call Hemingway a petty man with a score-settling vendetta, he never mentioned any of Faulkner's deficiencies. He worshipped Faulkner and expected his students to do the same.

The Faulkner professor was unprepared. His seminar was disorganized, loosely constructed without a definite number of textbooks and a list of items for discussion. His students could tell that he had not read the books before coming to class, but because he taught traditional authors such as Hemingway and Faulkner, part of the required PhD coursework, they had to take him. Despite his negligence, he enjoyed the benefit of large enrollments and could avoid the consequences of such poor work. His students couldn't afford to complain when he returned their 20-page-long papers with zero comments and nothing but letter grades. They were glad that they had to take him only once, and I was, too.

Extremely well-organized with maximum coverage possible in one semester, Jane's seminar was the opposite. She was perceptive and thorough when grading her students' papers. Although many professors were diligent enough to make specific, detailed comments in their students' papers, Jane was exceptional in that she saw a concrete person behind each paper and treated it as such. To her, a paper wasn't just a paper, it was a person. It is no wonder that she always had large enrollments with students petitioning to get into her already full classes. Although notorious for being demanding and rigorous, she was in constant demand because students knew she cared about them. To her, teaching was a vocation, not just a job. To her students, taking her class wasn't just work, it was an inspirational journey. I saw how inspired they were when one of them brought to class a huge pot of duff she had made at home. Even while she was reading one novel a week and teaching two classes as a graduate teaching assistant, this student found time to cook duff, the food the sailors ate on the ship in Melville's *The White Jacket.* Dipping into the duff, we all pretended we were the sailors, reciting lines from the novel.

In "American Women Novelists," the second class I took from her, she continued to ask her students to explore the same theme she had asked them to pursue in the Hawthorne and Melville seminar. This time, she introduced a spectrum of women authors from all ethnic backgrounds, including white, black, Asian, and Hispanic ones.

On the first day of class, she said, "I hope you've read *Moby Dick.* If you haven't, you can buy a used copy for a dollar fifty at Town Hall Bookstore in downtown Lawrence." Over the broad peal of laughter, she continued, "If he lived today, in 1987, Starbuck would be a helpless liberal unable to bring his emotional revolt against Captain Ahab into action. He knew Ahab would sink the ship and kill the whole crew, but he ultimately failed to prevent him. He would be one of those meek Americans Martin Luther King described in his 'Letter from Birmingham Jail,' one of those white moderates who just talk but do nothing to help promote the civil rights of minorities. I confess to you that I'm one of those meek white liberals." She paused to hear her students roar into laughter. "I hope you don't mind if I guess that you, too, might be those indecisive liberals, whatever your background may be." Waiting for another peal of laughter to be over, she resumed, "But as liberal academicians, we do the job of circulating information necessary to promote democracy for every group, not just for one group. We study Toni Morrison along with Edith Wharton. We study Alice Walker along with Joan Didion. We understand commonalities and differences between these women and try to figure out how to help their communities become equal to each other. In terms of action, we may fall short of Dr. King's standards, but in our words, we can get close."

In her "American Women Novelists," I picked up not only some of the most famous names in the history of American women's literature but also the healthy cynicism that kept a perspective about life in general.

"Don't carry what you learn from this class into your personal life," she would warn her students. "Forget it when you go home and fix something good for dinner." Believing that literature had the power to change the world, she believed that one should ignore it for living itself. Demanding that her students read one novel a week, she told them to relax. *She's so full of contradictions*, I thought, laughing. *But life is full of contradictions and she's one of those human examples.* As a graduate student, I couldn't practice her advice, driven to excel. But I kept it in the back of my mind and found myself using it later – much later when I earned tenure and began to try to live in the present.

It was Jane who inspired my dedication to authors, such as Zora Neale Hurston, Maxine Hong Kingston, Maya Angelou, Anne Petry, Gloria Naylor, and many other women of color who were renowned among scholars interested in multicultural literature but were little known in the mainstream in the 1980s. It was she who also led me to be interested in global literature such as African and Middle Eastern literature, Asian literature in English translation, and Latin American literature in Spanish and English, and it was she who suggested that I write a doctoral dissertation in women's autobiography. The topic allowed me to combine my all-consuming preoccupation with finding a way to help democracy reach American women of color, and my interest in exploring how women manifest themselves in the very self-conscious genre. Emulating her spirit of extending democracy for women of color, I refused to call my area of specialization "off the canon." I called it the "extended canon of American literature," convinced that there was no such thing as established or non-established American literature.

What was called the canon was what had been subjectively or arbitrarily selected by the majority of audiences, who were mostly white male and sometimes white female and were either led or misled by their white male and female critics. What was called the non-canon was the body of writings that lay unseen by white male and female critics, often a tradition of literature that wasn't blessed by theories connecting them together into a coherent historical presence. There were white male and female authors who were not included in the canon as there were minority male and female authors who were included, but I thought it was fundamentally unfair that one group of audiences, largely white, had the exclusive power to determine their place in history. It was characteristic of me to specialize in multicultural literature. I had come to America to seek another America. Upon discovering that the America I had envisioned—the home of democracy for everyone—wasn't really there, I began to try to find the America that was elsewhere, and I felt as if I found it. I found this America in my work, in my commitment to help extend democracy for women of color, for the last group of people that America had failed to reach. I was going to become one of the voices by, of, and for these women.

In "Autobiography and Fiction," the course I created and taught in 1988 after taking "American Women Novelists," I mobilized my professional and personal expertise with utmost enthusiasm and passion. I made the class a balanced blending of authors from all backgrounds, including male and female, white and black, Asian American, Hispanic, and Native American. Ranging from *The Education of Henry Adams*, to Ralph Ellison's *Invisible Man,* to John Niehardt's *Black Elk Speaks,* to Sandra Sisneros' *The House on Mango Street,* to Maya Angelou's *I Know Why a Caged Bird Sings,* and to Hisaye Yamamoto's *Seventeen Syllables and Other Stories,* my selections spoke to my longing for an inclusive America, for the America I was looking for. Because I was so engaged in the topic, my students were equally engaged. They knew where I was coming from, and they responded personally as well as professionally. Surprisingly open and honest, they often volunteered to reveal their own racism and prejudices. Because I refused to pass judgments on them, they were at ease and felt free to show who they were inside. Because I told them that racism is a human impulse to which everyone is vulnerable, they had a chance to realize that they weren't necessarily evil just because they harbored racist feelings sometimes.

"Racism isn't just KKK-style evil," I explained. "It's an impulse embedded in a human being. When we admit it as a natural part of us, we can be honest about it, and it's a lot easier for us to work on it. When we condemn it as a hideous evil, we hide it out of fear." As the class fell into absolute silence, astonished by my revealing comments, I continued, "I condemn one's lack of effort to overcome and one's failure to overcome. I don't condemn one's natural feeling."

A student spoke up, and I could have danced in front of the whole class. "I might be one of those racist people," he said. "I always thought having a token black in a workplace is a cool idea." Over the laughter that broke the awe-inspiring silence, this student went on, "Having grown up in an all-white small town in Kansas, I'm afraid I instinctively want to avoid black people. Believing on an intellectual level that we must treat black people equally, I embrace the idea of working and living with them. But emotionally, I'm not ready. I don't want to see more than one black person in my workplace because if there's more, I'd feel uncomfortable. I guess I believe in a token black system." As I praised him for being honest, the class echoed me with approving laughter.

"I was born and raised in a Chicago suburb," another student spoke, "and I wouldn't be surprised if I prefer a token black system." Laughter—the kind of laughter that comes from learning something new in an honest, pleasant way—was the hallmark of my class. I may be flattering myself, but I feel entitled because I could put my students at ease with such a sensitive topic as race. Jane was proud of me, having heard about the class from a colleague of his who observed my teaching.

How ironic it was that Jane, the very person who had once betrayed my trust, gladly took the burden of ushering me into constructing *my* America! Intellectually, she had transcended her skin color, having devoted her life to realizing the very best of what it means to be an American, and yet emotionally, she wasn't entirely free from racism. I was at times tempted to think of her as a hypocrite who failed to practice what she preached. Because I expected her—and thought I had the privilege to expect her—to be more than an ordinary American, I felt all the more disappointed in her. But I always tried to keep in mind the truth that no human being was entirely free from racism and that she was only human. I had no right to expect her to be above human. In everyone, there is a gap between an intellectual consciousness and a subconscious racism, and she was no exception. I decided to focus on the things that drew us together, the fact that we were both determined women fighting for our place in a world we both resented and adored. If we wanted to create the America, we both envisioned, we needed to keep the good in it and the good in each other. I wanted to fill the divide with the endeavors we made together to make America reach every American, and in this effort, I came to see her as a great American and myself as her disciple.

Whether it was rationalization or glorification—or a true feeling—that I chose in order to make the effort to dispel my sometimes confusing feelings toward Jane, I don't know to this day. All that I am absolutely certain of is that I came to see her as an embodiment of the best American because there was nobody else in my life who embodied the best American as well as she did. I had no one else to emulate, and no greater ally. I couldn't live in a country where premarital cohabitation with a man made a woman a moral ex-con. I had to make a life in America. Jane herself knew that I still had—and had to have—faith in the academic system even though she had caused me to question its integrity. She knew that I saw an honest person behind her mother-in-law mask. She was ready to *be* the great American I saw in her, to remain that American for me for many years to come.

Gratitude became one of my most constant companions in graduate school. As a graduate teaching assistant exercising new-found authority over my students, I grew to sympathize with my professors. I found myself recalling the petty mistakes I myself had made in the early stages of my academic career. I remembered how, during my first year of PhD work at my beloved alma mater, I rushed to one professor to protest in tears after receiving a grade I had thought unfair from another! In retrospect, I realized I had deserved an even worse grade and looking back, I had to laugh at myself. I also knew I had to laugh at my experience with those professors who were small-minded enough to pick on me for trivial mistakes. Some of them downgraded me for using the wrong preposition such as "on" instead of "in," for missing the plural "s" in words such as Korean Airlines, and for making an extremely subtle agreement error between a noun and a verb. They constantly penalized me for making errors that were beyond my ability to avoid at that point in my career because of the nature of Asian languages. Knowing only too well that there was very little distinction between plural and singular nouns and subject and verb agreement in any of the Asian languages, they seemed to enjoy punishing me.

But there were professors who, although rigorous in evaluating the content of my papers and the overall quality of my writing, generously forgave me for these errors and rewarded me for my fluency and high level of sentence complexity. They made careful, painstaking comments in my papers, admiring me for my ability to write in a language so different from my native tongue. In an attempt to admire them in return, I worked hard. They were aware of how hard I had been forced to lobby to receive a graduate teaching assistantship, and they made every effort they could to help me. It was as if they had felt some sort of collective guilt over what had happened to me, and I was determined to set them free from this guilt by becoming a success.

I worked until I brought myself to the point where I was so exhausted that I had to watch the news with my eyes closed. At the end of the day, which often was made of sixteen hours in a row of reading, writing, and grading papers, I was unable to keep my eyes open. They felt as sore and wasted as a pair of giant spiders that were dried up in a blazing sun until their bodies and spindly limbs desiccated. Wholeheartedly, I believed I could please the gods by achieving what everyone told me was impossible, by using words in English with the same beauty and power commanded by the authors I studied. "You came to America at the age of twenty-four, with ten hours of experience in writing and speaking English," I reminded myself. "It's been only five years since you came to this country. You have to reduce your peers' twenty-five years into your five. You have to work twice as hard because while they write two pages in a certain amount of time, you can write only one. Your dreams aren't going to come true without an incredible amount of nightmares. Don't you forget." I snapped my eyes open in the dark, forcing myself to laugh so I didn't cry, listening to my maniacal laugh in the night air as if from a distance, as if it was coming from someone else.

I cried, too. Every night, I massaged my arms and legs to diffuse the aching soreness I had gained from too much prolonged sitting, finding myself in a usual spasm of rage. "I know how long it takes to get a PhD in English, for native as well as non-native speakers," I screamed internally. "But my native-speaker colleagues don't have to waste their time combating racism. They don't have to teach students who discriminate against foreign teachers who speak with an accent. They don't have to be disturbed by ludicrous comments in their student evaluations such as: 'Why should we learn English from a non-native speaker?', 'She speaks broken English', 'She doesn't speak English, but she teaches it', 'She shouldn't criticize Americans in America, as I wouldn't criticize Koreans in Korea', and 'I failed English because my teacher is a foreigner.'"

I hoped that with more experience, I would be able to gain more trust from my students, but I was mistaken. Although my teaching skills improved, their attitude toward me didn't. Because they never stopped seeing me as being unqualified to teach English, my performance was largely irrelevant to them. Each semester, I had to face a new group of students who didn't know me, and each semester, I had to make twice as much effort as anyone else to earn the same level of confidence from them. Not everyone was prejudiced, but there were always some individuals who distrusted me because of my background. With just a couple students marking me down in a class of fifteen, my student evaluations could go down significantly. It was no wonder my numbers were always lower than those of my colleagues.

Pushing my temples in with my middle fingers to erase the pounding headache, I heard myself shouting in mute anger about sexism as well as racism, "Women have to combat patriarchy, but some women have to do it more than others. I have to spend so much more energy than most white female colleagues of mine on exorcising the male voices internalized in me. On a daily basis, I'm forced to fight what was constantly instilled in me by many of my former friends in Korea. I know they were wrong when they said, 'Women professors at my university are bitches. They don't know how to respect men. They're full of themselves. I bet they imitate men because they're insecure as women. Who would be attracted to them anyway?' And yet, I still hear their deriding voices in my head, 'imitator, insecure, bitches.' Sometimes, I still believe them."

I still heard them after having been away from the country for nearly a decade. I was still worried that I was turning into one of those "bitches." Several years of teaching in a less sexist country didn't assuage my fear. I found myself going back to the scene embedded in my memory. I saw men and women sitting separately at parties, women in the kitchen and men in the living room. It was the same style of segregation I had seen among the Korean graduate students at Harvard and their wives, but it was in Korea. The men discussed world affairs, the economy, politics, and international relations while the women talked about domestic matters like the curtains in their apartments and their children's piano lessons. Eating the food served by their women, the men stayed on big issues concerning the nation's welfare and its goal of becoming a global player while the women chiefly gossiped about other women. In this setting, there was no place for women like me. No words were necessary to have them ostracized because the hierarchy itself so visibly excluded them. Until I was professionally more secure with a PhD and tenure, I was unable to put an end to the torments caused by these kinds of scenes I had seen so many times in my adolescence and youth. Although I couldn't kick them out of my memory, I could eventually ignore them when I gained enough self-confidence to laugh at them.

I persevered. Even now, I shake my head in disbelief as I recall the endless strings of mistakes I made during the first couple years of my teaching. Yelling at my students in a soprano high enough to fly beyond the roof of the building, and afterward berating myself emotionally in an alto deep enough to dig a hole in the ground, I embodied a pendulum of extreme emotions. I always tried to put on a smiling façade to appear relaxed, but in a wink I lapsed back into a hostile grimace, pushed beyond my own range of tolerance by acute performance anxiety. A look of affection would be in my eyes for a split second until it suddenly turned cold, drilling into my listeners with an iron sting. In less than a moment, I traversed a distance of a thousand miles emotionally, covering one end of my self-expression to the other. I was so insecure and so confused by the conflicting and condemning voices in me, I lost the most rudimentary level of classroom composure.

Sometimes, I was so lost that I couldn't believe I was the one who was screaming. Once, I saw a student eating a hamburger in class because she was hungry with no break between three different classes, and I flared up. I pointed my finger at her and screamed at her for being disrespectful toward me. But as she stood up to leave the room, ashamed and terrified, I was suddenly overcome with regret and apologized to her. I told her to stay, my eyes regaining a smile in a fleeting second. At another time, I found myself enjoying a power trip over a student, making exactly the same facial expression Brad had made in his office when he said he couldn't promise me anything. I was a cat and the student my mouse, thrilled to deny him an opportunity to earn extra credits to pull up his final grade. With my chin lifted and my lips in a thin, straight line, I said I couldn't give him the opportunity because it wasn't fair for everyone else. As the student quickly apologized, I flew back into the same affirmative smile Brad had doled upon me, my fragile ego sufficiently gratified. After the student left, I broke into a spell of laughter, realizing how Brad-like I was and how everyone was guilty of what they condemned.

In my second year of teaching, I learned how to avoid using a high-pitched voice to warn a student and use instead soft eyes diffusing a menacing baritone. For my students, I put on the same mask that I was certain my professors put on for me. When a student told me she was going to send one of her essays to *Time* magazine, I encouraged her to do so. She didn't yet know it was far from qualified for the magazine, but I donned a mother's nurturing mask on my face to help her take the chance. She was entitled to find out on her own, I believed. I had given her essay a full A because it was well-written with solid research and a coherent organization, but the topic was a cliché. It was about how fast food threatened children's physical and mental health, sending them the dangerous message that speed was the single most important thing in life. With a teacher's mask, I successfully hid my prediction that it would be rejected. With the same mask my professors wore when they congratulated me about the high GPA I earned as a doctoral candidate, I congratulated her on the "good" essay. My professors knew I was only one of the many doctoral candidates with high GPAs and that I had a long way to go to be able to compete with superior candidates on the job market, but they still praised me as if I were the only candidate made for the best position in my areas of expertise. They wore a teacher's mask for me as I wore a teacher's mask for my students. In my second year of teaching, I began to exercise the soft power of the mask and drop the loud manifestation of power coming from a lack of power. Although I failed more than I succeeded, I kept polishing the mask until it eventually became inextricable from my face.

Another thing that made me work so hard on my mask was the high-level performance I believed I owed to my professors. I was constantly aware of the way my students viewed me because of my race, as well as a deep scrutiny from my professors who watched my teaching more carefully than they did my peers. Being an Asian, a female, and a non-native speaker teaching English, I inevitably drew unwanted attention like a red mark on a piece of black and white paper. My professors were only human after all, and they could only treat me as life had taught them. They couldn't help noticing me more than anyone else who was white and a native-speaker. I had to teach well not only for my students but also for my professors. I had to impress them to the point where I could erase the inevitable curiosity a human being feels toward a member of another group. Maybe then, I could vanquish the often unfair evaluations and judgments their human nature subsequently placed upon me. I worked until I thought I could almost hear my bones crumbling apart on my chair.

As teachers and students, we were caught in a very human circle of doing wrong and then doing right, in a cycle of unwittingly abusing the dignity of those who fall under our authority and then of consciously trying to make it up to them. As a graduate teaching assistant, I often made the same mistakes and corrections that were made by my professors whom I worked closely with. I failed to treat my students as they deserved to be treated, and in an attempt to show my repentance, I went back to treating them in an overly kind manner.

In the eight or so years of my work as a graduate teaching assistant, I constantly realized that one's prejudices couldn't be seen by members of one's own demographic, that they could be seen only by members of another. My students were incapable of seeing racism in themselves as they raised doubts about my qualifications and credibility as an English teacher, and I, for the first couple years, was unable to see racism in myself. In disbelief of my students' poor writing, I didn't hesitate to call them by adjectives such as "stupid," "idiotic," or, in less abysmal cases, "horrible." How could native speakers of the English language write such terrible English? I wondered. But as the years went by and as I became a more mature teacher, I started to realize that my students had received very little training in writing in high school, not at all prepared to make the quantum leap into the college-level writing I was trained to teach.

I eventually realized that when I called them "stupid" and "idiotic," I was as unfair to them as they were to me when they raised doubts about my ability to teach English. "I shouldn't ever stereotype them as stupid American students," I admonished myself. "If I do, I'd be just as racist as they are." As there were parts of my professors that they themselves couldn't see, there were parts of me that I myself couldn't see, and by witnessing this commonality among all of us, I understood why all human beings, teachers and students alike, carry habitual prejudices with themselves. All that any human being can do is to try to overcome, and all that I could do was to help *myself* to overcome. I wanted to live a life defined by love for human beings, not judgment.

To live, I had to kill myself over and over again. I had nightmares during which I saw myself dead in a beautiful large house, in a bed covered with colorful cemetery flowers seen by few. Over and over again in my sleep, I walked to the room farthest in the back. There, a tall, long-haired Korean woman was curled up in a fetal position. Segregated from the rest of the house, from the plenitude of the living daylight that filled me with a sense of being alive, the body—my body—was lying alone in the heart of the darkness. Sometimes, it stirred, staring at me in pitch-black shadows, pointing at me with her fingers in the utterly abandoned corner of the richly adorned space. It was telling of the poverty in its own splendid home, in all of its luxurious furniture and sunny windows and celestially high ceilings. Waking up, I heard myself let out a smothered scream.

But there was another dream of mine, and I had it just as often as the nightmares of my dead body. As if to cancel out the death in the luxurious room, this dream of mine brought me back to life, taking me to the land that was far away from where I was dying to live. I was living without dying, in an imaginary country that was located between California and Oregon and had no name. It was a country that I had built in my mind during my most recent years in America, a modified version of the utopia I had constructed in Korea in my naïve American dreams. I still called it No Name State and I still believed it was achievable. But now, it was rid of what was humanly impossible, of what was possible only in pure theory. More earthly than celestial, it allowed for human dirt, the inevitable shadows that came from the process of living in the sunlight and the unavoidable darkness following the journey toward brighter destinations.

Living in America, I found myself laughing at the pictures of the No Name State I had built in Korea. I saw the child I had been, the child who had envisioned living in a cozy hut in a forest that was surrounded with tall trees and clear water, with people walking peacefully alongside animals. Because there was no hunting in this land, deer galloped toward human beings, following them to their huts where they could share human food with the children of the happy parents. In this land, animals were equal to human beings. Plants were equal to animals. Insects were equal to birds. Trees were equal to grass. Sauntering in the forest, I didn't have to be afraid of anything, not even tigers and snakes and bears. Nobody, nothing, was predatory, with enough food and shelter. To the child I had been, this country—this No Name State—was perennially green everywhere.

After several years of living in America, I came to realize that this country I had imagined as a child was no longer green. It was nothing but icy white, reigned by death that came in the form of a relentless, year-round snow freezing every living being. Because it was governed by a perfect and hence lifeless *logic*, nobody could live in it. It couldn't exist.

In 1988, during the height of my graduate school years, I wanted to make this country livable, to have it materialized into a reality that lay firmly within the human reach. In my dreams now, the snow came only in Winter, to be replaced by the greens in Spring, and to be beaten by the life-raising heat in Summer. In it, nothing was perfect except in people's efforts to reduce the gap between theory and practice and their endeavors to combine rigor and compassion. Its people were just like me and my professors. They were honest, but forgiving, recognizing and yet embracing each other for the shortcomings inherent in human nature. There was racism, but this racism was restricted in one's subconscious, kept safely away from the conscious level, but when it happened to rise to the surface, it was justly condemned and if necessary, punished. Citizens of No Name State were realistic enough to acknowledge that racism could not be eradicated because it lived in one's subconscious, but they were wise enough to believe that it was possible to keep it under control. They accepted human flaws as they were because to be human is to be flawed. Applying rigor to point at the flaws, they exercised the compassion that was necessary to generate chances for self-correction.

Perfection was required only in one thing – in one's willingness to do all that one could do to help create a society that was just and fair for all. Failure was forgiven as long as one was intentionally dedicated to the journey toward the goal of achieving equality for all citizens, toward the purpose of arriving at the final destination at which democracy was complete enough to reach all citizens living in it. In the state between California and Oregon, one's commitment to democracy was perfect, but the outcome could very well be imperfect. Because perfection was required only in one's readiness, its citizens were preoccupied with being prepared, not with what was to come about in the end. When they, for example, practiced the habit of saving trees, they didn't necessarily expect there would be enough supply of trees waiting for them. None of them forgot to use scrap paper and write on the empty backs of the printed pages, but every one of them knew that such a habit couldn't save all the trees in the land, let alone guarantee a sufficient production of paper. Perfect in their attitude to save trees, they minimized consuming paper. They minimized killing animals, knowing that they couldn't live if they didn't kill some animals. They ate as little meat as possible, so that they could kill as few cows and pigs and chickens and lambs. They not only knew how to minimize needless consumption but also constantly carried what they knew into action. Crimes, too, were minimal. The vast majority of crimes were accidental rather than premeditated because most of the citizens were law-abiding and only a few were bad enough to do otherwise. Most crimes were mistakes rather than intentional, and only a fraction of them were products of deliberate plans. Unlike the rest of the United States, which was the most violent peacetime country in the world, No Name State was the most peaceful peacetime country one had ever seen on the planet Earth.

To beat the nightmare in which I saw my dead body, I envisioned myself walking in a forest in No Name State. I dreamed a dream in which I was no longer an outsider, no longer an immigrant and a woman of color dying to live in her adopted country. I was just a citizen trying to be perfect in my intentions to spread American democracy for all Americans, perfect in my readiness to make the earthly utopia reachable for all Americans like me. To overcome the nightmare, I practiced lucid dreaming in which the sumptuous, but dark house of mine became a birthplace for the country I created in my imagination. It didn't exist geographically, but I was certain that it *was* in the American mind, a place stronger than any geographically real place. To help Americans realize that it *was* in their collective conscious, I was working until I had to die to live, on a journey that was a succession of the nightmares and dreams. I was living a life in which my dreams were made possible by my nightmares.

To sustain my dreams, I let myself seized by an impulse to reenact such telltale nightmares of mine in my living routines. As often as I could, I made the half-hour walk to reach the cemetery at the edge of town, to pay a visit to the dead who must have witnessed a series of deaths in themselves while struggling to live. *Did they see their own bodies in their nightmares?* I pondered. *Were they successful in converting their nightmares into their dreams?* I thought they could hear my thoughts and tell me, "If you want to achieve your dreams, you'll have to continue to see your dead body in your nightmares. Stay healthy, so that you can endure as many nightmares as you must in order to achieve your dreams. Come here often and breathe deep."

To let my stomach breathe, I drew in the fresh dawn air, making a laborious, deep sound. I wanted to swallow the smell from the green trees and the lawn, the scent of the dews evaporating from the ground. The pretty colors of the flowers, which made a striking contrast with the drab, black and white tones of the tombstones, juxtaposed the beauty of life and the somberness of death, the opposites the cemetery celebrated as no other place did. Was life beautiful because it was ephemeral and was death to be revered because it made life so beautiful? I thought I could hear the sounds from the dead telling me how great death was because it inspired the living to live intensely before it took away everything. Listening to the swishes of the breeze, I wanted to live my life fiercely because death was going to steal it from me soon enough. I didn't have much time.

On the mornings that followed the nights I didn't sleep, I was sharper than ever. I was awakened ever more by the pre-dawn chills, alerted ever more by the dews of the morning that I imagined settled on me exclusively. No wonder I could smile back so easily to those early-bird strangers. I was going to be working for eight hours straight, as they were. Only I'd been up for sixteen hours in a row while they had been resting.

On these mornings, I was seized by an eerie, almost morbid sense of exhilaration, busy with making a fascinating observation. In Korea, graves were built in the shape of small, but pointed hills, covered with round mounds of soil with grass on top, while in America they were constructed to be flat on the surface, to lie long and narrow on the ground level. Tombstones were carved differently. In Korea, they were much thinner and higher than they were in America, with their tops uniformly shaped in the form of a broad-rimmed fedora hat and their bottoms invariably attached with a square rock to be used as a table. While Americans took only flowers to the buried, Koreans carried light foods and drinks to be placed on the table, to serve meals to their long-gone ancestors. Sometimes, little children liked to climb up to the top of the grave, jumping up and down like elves playing a forbidden game, forcing the adults to enjoy the sanctified part of laughing and shooing them away. As the urchins scampered off, thinking of stealing another chance to "insult" the buried elders, the adults looked away, secretly waiting for another chance to go through the same round of hearty laughter. Having watched the children and the adults enjoying themselves, I thought I could understand why Koreans built a dome over the homes of their loved ones. It was because they wanted to create a place where the living and the dead could laugh together at the sight of their impish little ones. They wanted, just for a moment, to teach themselves how to laugh at the rules violated.

And yet, according to a Korean myth, graveyards in the night were the home of horror and black magic, the refuge of unresolved problems that could be defined only by an absolute lack of humor. As ghouls and zombies are fabled to hang out in American cemeteries, banshee-style ghosts were supposed to roam graves in Korea, to split open the round domes of hard dirt in the thickest of the night. These wailing ghosts called "kwishin" were, without a single exception, female and were, without a single exception, deadly determined. They were not going back to the other world until they finished what they had come to this world to start, until they, without a shred of hesitation, accomplished the purpose they had returned to the living to carry out. The dead came back to avenge themselves, to ruin the lives of the ones who had victimized them, to destroy the homes of the families who had dehumanized them, and then to warn the living of the consequences of evil deeds. Some were crueler than others while some were more furious than others. Many were hurried enough to kill their foes instantly, several were leisured enough to drag them through a gradual, terrifying death, and a few were slow enough to drive them into a miserable suicide. But there was one thing that all of these ghosts had in common, and it was the fact that they had hearts hardened by untold stories. Once they had a chance to tell their stories by means of either atrocious deeds or hairsplitting words—once they were given a chance to be understood and to receive sincere apologies from those who had wronged them—they were willing in time to go away, to promise the living never to return.

In the cemetery in Kansas, I found myself rewinding a ghost movie that I thought was particularly more haunting. It was about a woman who was raped, maimed physically, and killed by an old man to cover his crimes. The woman came back as a ghost to murder his three sons overnight. She put them to sleep one by one, made little holes in their chests with her long fingernails, and sucked all of the blood from their bodies. She then waited until the morning came, until she could watch their father wail as he woke up.

"How can I face my ancestors when I die?" he cried. "I don't have a son to continue our lineage. I failed the most important duty I was born to fulfill." Leaving him alone to a wretched life, the ghost victoriously walked away, her long, disheveled black hair waving down to her waist and her broad, thin lips smeared with the blood from the three young men's bodies. Always wide open, her eyes never blinked, and perpetually unmoving, her large, cold irises remained resolute with a deadly focus, observing everything, including what was trailing behind her. The immaculately ironed, snow-white costume contrasted starkly with the black hair and red blood, increasing the onlookers' terror, as it covered her from the neck to foot. Her socks were also white, and her feet, removed from the land by an inch or so, slid over the ground as if on a pair of invisible skates traveling on ice. She wasn't flying high in the air, but running at the speed of slow wind, she could pass through anything in the way.

As far as ghosts were concerned, I wasn't capable of being scared by anything but these female Korean wraiths. Ghouls and zombies in black couldn't frighten me, so I wasn't afraid to visit cemeteries in America when it was dark. Like a taste for food, images of horror are cultivated, and I knew I wasn't going to be frightened by the spirits who never had a place in my cultural memory. On some insomnia-plagued nights, I even wished for a chance to test my daring, entertaining a wild hope of running into goblins. But the possibility of being hit by a drunk driver concerned me more. "People will hurt you. Ghosts will not," Koreans say. The pale-faced Americans who knew how to hide their racism were far more frightening to me, even though drug addicts roaming the streets had many more concrete chances to hurt me. "*They* are the spooks I have to watch out for," I repeated to myself. Equally as often, I thought in an attempt to reinforce my self-justification for living in such a dangerous country, "I'm lucky enough to live in a country where we have as many tales of male ghosts as we do of female ghosts. In Korea, we don't even have one male ghost story because it's only women who have untold stories. But in America, men also wish to be heard after death. The female ghosts in America aren't nearly as venomous as they are in Korea. The more patriarchal a country is, the more female ghost stories it spawns, and the more violent men are, the more unforgiving their female ghosts become."

I was desperate to escape the doom of becoming one of those venomous female ghosts. I was afraid that I would turn into a living "kwishin," if I were forced to return to Korea after failing to achieve the degree of academic success I demanded of myself. I was nearly throttled by anxiety. As I put myself on a combination of Prozac and Klonopin in order to keep my crying spells under control, I was even tempted to doubt the worthiness of my goal. Whatever it was, it seemed undeserving of my emotional sanity, of such a grueling process that threatened me both mentally and physically. I had to fight to the marrow of my being for an opportunity to make a life in America – to the point of being raped by a man who had claimed ownership over me through a green card marriage. I had to fight clinical depression with two different anti-depressants. Succeeding professionally had become a matter of life or death to me. If I wanted to choose life over death, I was to choose success over failure. I was to die over and over again to be able to live eventually.

Chapter 14
The Divine and the Human*

It would be a lie for me to say that there was absolutely nothing but work in my eight years as a graduate teaching assistant. Although I never had anything even remotely close to a balanced combination of work and love during these years, I often made strides, awkward and unsuccessful, in an attempt to take a break from my monotonous work-driven routines. Sometimes, I was desperate to have my days and nights of studying hijacked by events totally free from anything pertaining to academic pursuit. I craved an antidote. I believed I found such an antidote in a man I met, who resembled a woman from an ancient Korean tribal kingdom that existed a millennium and a half ago. This woman took a devoted painter away from the life that was ordained for him by the gods and brought him a human life that gave him the name, Cry-Smile. As I looked at the Cry-Smile mask on the wall in my apartment, I went back in my mind to the legend Father had told me.

Cry-Smile swore to the gods that until he finished painting the picture of the Buddhist utopia he had repeatedly seen in his dreams, he wouldn't allow himself any worldly activities, such as eating meat, looking at the face of a woman, using profanity, or going to any place of pleasure including bars, dance halls, geisha quarters, or even a teahouse. Even one look at a brothel would trigger the gods to damn him to an eternal hell, where he would have to live with hands and fingers stripped of their skill. A life deprived of painting would be awaiting him if he dared to allow an iota of impure action to enter his life.

---

* The legend of the painter, Cry-Smile, was initially published in my essay, "The Cry-Smile Mask: A Korean-American Woman's System of Resistance," in *This Bridge We Call Home,* edited by Gloria Anzaldua and Analouise Keating and published by Routledge in 2002.

He did everything he could to obey the gods. He secluded himself in his house for one-hundred days in a row. His routines were restricted to two rice and vegetable meals, sipping drops of the cold water from the well in his front yard, and dipping his brush into the black ink gathered in the little stone by the thin slab.

Sadly, on the ninety-ninth day, just one day before completing the painting, he happened to see the face of a smiling woman, and he smiled back at her. Not knowing he was in seclusion, she came to his house to peek at his studio and opened the door stealthily, her head tilted between the wall and the side of the door. As he raised his face from the painting, she said her greetings, and he found himself greeting her in return, his hands lifted from the ink slab, his arms arrested in the air in pleasant surprise. The perfect beauty of the utopia he was constructing on the paper was suddenly paled by the rapture of the vernal glances between the young man and woman. Like ice in fire, the need to finish the utopia painting was gone in a moment. The utopia was pallid. The world of human beings was colorful.

For the rest of his life, Cry-Smile wore a face manifesting his name. He cried, missing the celestial home he had wanted to create, but he smiled, having found the happiness of a man on earth. Forever disabled from painting, but blessed to mingle with human beings, he fell into limbo. He remained in a place between heaven and earth, where he happily painted the various worlds of humans but sadly regretted his inability to bring the gods' world into fruition. Until his death, Cry-Smile kept going back and forth between joy and pain, living in a succession of eternally conflicting moments.

It was probably my need, so urgent and overwhelming, to move toward the human side in the painter, as far away from the celestial as possible, that made me fall into a liaison with a man who turned out to be a loser. It started with a casual, sudden jump into sexual activity, developed into what seemed to be a serious, mutually beneficial relationship, and finally trailed into a friendship that came quietly as the fire of the romance gradually went out. Michael was a high-school graduate with a ninth grader's vocabulary, the muscles of an amateur weight lifter, and the energy of a marathon runner. I was instantly attracted to him because, having never seen a man with so much physical prowess, I felt as though he was the one who could help me to discover the woman in me. In the presence of his body, I could feel my own surging above my always preoccupied mind, finding a much-needed relief from the relentless habit of complete discipline.

He appeared to be an incarnation of the simplicity I was looking for, a refuge where I could seek a life of abandon away from the complicated questions in an academic's life. He was the one with whom I could enjoy a primitive release, with whom I could share a naked physical passion free from the paraphernalia of a civilized world. I knew I was creating a fantasy figure out of him, out of a person as complicated as anyone else I had ever known, but I couldn't help myself. To me, Michael was the one who took me to the human side. He was the one who whisked the painter in me away from the work of painting a utopia, to usher her into the pleasure of loving this earthly world. He was the one to induct the painter away from work and into love, to complete the smile over the cry in her face.

Michael was an alcoholic. I watched him making X marks in his calendar on the days he didn't drink, and I noticed there were far more blank days than there were marked days.

"To forget pain, I drink," he said. "I know I'm a loser." I was amused, far from alarmed or disappointed. As long as he fulfilled my fantasy by being a physical man, I couldn't care less where he was in his own life. "I have a very high IQ, but I couldn't go to college," he continued, taking my amused face for a non-judgmental attitude. "Since I was little, I've suffered from severe social anxiety and I couldn't interact with anyone outside my family. I had a problem making eye contact with anyone I didn't know, so I was teased by my peers, isolated from everyone. I didn't want to go to school. I couldn't concentrate, so I couldn't learn much." He wanted to date girls, to go to parties with his friends, to be good in academics, to be talented in athletics, and to be respected by his teachers and peers alike. Rejected by the chemicals in his own brain and consequently by the people surrounding him, he traveled through the spectrum of emotions essential to being human with his deficiencies. He felt what everyone felt—anger, frustration, despair, love, hate, jealousy, envy, respect and contempt—being as complicated as anyone else. But unable to find the vocabulary to express himself, he resorted to alcohol. He drank daily. He became an alcoholic—and eventually a loser bereft of the high mind that could have been achieved with his IQ.

What drew me to him was what I saw in him rather than who he truly was. The antithesis of me, Michael wasn't an achiever. He lived totally in the present, mindlessly and recklessly removed from the past and the future. He spent in a day all the money he had earned in a day. He made over twenty dollars an hour driving a delivery truck for Pepsi in 1988, but not a penny of his previous paycheck was seen in his bank book when he deposited a new one. He had never read a book of any substance in his entire life of thirty-two years. Instead, he had permanently replaced books with movies filled with action, sex, and violence. I once showed him a magazine article about King Kong, finding the author's analysis of the beauty and the beast interesting, but he chucked it away after glancing at the headlines. It was of no interest to him although he had watched the movie three times. He only liked the special effects that powered the hairy monster.

In an attempt to move from the celestial to the human side, I not only leapt to a distant place but also dove into a bottomless pit from which I struggled to get out for a long time. For many years to come, I had to fight the sense—the pang—of shame I felt about having involved myself with an alcoholic loser. Although I don't claim to be entirely free from a sense of class snobbery, it isn't that I feel embarrassed about having been with a truck driver. Had he been a truck driver with a sense of direction about his future and with a solid middle-class instinct to save for rainy days, I would have been proud of being with him. If he by any chance had liked to read and had been willing to discuss with me the magazine article about King Kong, I indeed might have been happy enough to show him off to all my friends and family. But he wasn't the kind of man you would want to bring home to your parents, and our connection was bound to fail. I went too far in my effort to find a man who could help me bring a smile over the painter's cry. Characteristically, I had to go all the way to the opposite end to be able to come back to myself. I didn't realize that the smile could come from me only when I was alone.

Knowing how lost he was, I kept him for five years. I had met him in a city in Southern California, where I had walked into a store to get directions to a house I was trying to find. As he volunteered to walk with me to the house, I told him I was staying there for three weeks or so before going back to the fall semester at my university in Kansas. He told me he would like to visit me, if my friend, the owner of the house, didn't mind. I said she wouldn't mind at all. So, he came and I went out with him, cruising all over the semi-tropical town in his old Toyota. In less than three days, we checked into a motel room on our way to San Francisco, jumped on the bed and instantly plunged into the joy of the bottomless sexual passion. It was a raw, highly charged, and prolonged sex, and it brought out the long-awaited smile from the crying painter in me. Being on vacation from several severely draining semesters, I was engulfed by an explosive sexual appetite as a starving child would be overwhelmed by the sight of a loaf of bread. I was a woman with a man, a human regaining an awareness of her body after a long time. Finally, I was a woman and the artist both.

Over the five years during which Michael and I gradually became more friends than lovers, the sexual fire faded away. Who he was to *me* was so different from who he truly was, and the fever couldn't last. Painlessly, we parted and re-met as friends, complementing each other without demanding too much of each other. I thought I could tell why so many people esteemed friendship more than romance. The nature of a romantic relationship itself is bound to raise the level of expectations because it inevitably comes with a hunger for what people can't get from each other and from themselves. In a romantic relationship, the lovers seek fantasy, a state of feeling that is necessary to place them in an emotional world where the objective reality can be replaced by an internal home of their own construction. They crave magic, and as they discover the sad truth—that magic is no more than a temporary suspension of a disappointing reality—they face a series of frustrations and eventually have to force themselves to redefine who they are and who they ask each other to be. The lovers have to lower their expectations, relinquish the person they met in their fantasy, and accept the person they encountered in their fantasy-less routines.

Naturally, a sense of shame accompanies these readjustments, since the lovers suddenly realize they were cheated by themselves as well as by each other. During the many years of my friendship with Michael, I often recalled what I had heard on the radio when I was in college in Korea. It was a talk show during which a marriage counselor advised newly married couples on topics such as how to cope with post-honeymoon blues or what they should do to preserve the feelings of excitement. She said, "A client of mine confessed to me that in just about a week after her wedding, she had a moment of a terrible awakening. She saw her husband squeezing toothpaste out of the tube and putting it on his toothbrush, and the sight made her almost cry. When they were dating, he was so tender and kind that she couldn't even imagine him handling a tube of toothpaste roughly. But immediately after they got married, as he carelessly pushed the middle of the tube in with his thumb and let two inches of the toothpaste drop down in the wash basin, she felt disillusioned. She felt terribly vulnerable because she knew she'd have moments such as this one for decades to come."

"You'd be amazed by how many women come to me, feeling letdown like this. They say these mundane moments nearly ruin their beautiful memories of their husbands. Men who come to me also confess a similar experience. Some of them say they were grossed out when they heard their wives making a loud noise slurping noodles. These wives ate everything so gingerly while they were dating. They in fact ate so gingerly that even their lipstick stayed on."

As Michael and I stopped being lovers, he was no longer the man in my fantasy and I didn't have to be vulnerable. I was still ashamed of having been his lover, an alcoholic loser's lover, but I could bury this shame because I no longer needed him in order to be the woman who overcame the artist in me. I wasn't a woman to him, and he wasn't a man to me. We were two people who shared good times—and memories of the good times—who could move away from each other without separation anxiety. By being the opposite of me and by being so far away from the world of books in which the painter in me was secluded, he could help me to restore my human side.

I remember the two of us going for a boat ride on Truman Lake and him paddling in a zigzag fashion to hear me scream and laugh at once on the spinning boat. I remember us watching UFO movies and agreeing about the existence of aliens and going to comedy clubs in Kansas City to listen to local standup comedians. It has been more than twenty years since I last saw him, but I have very little doubt about where I believe he is in his life. Most likely, he still is who he used to be, an alcoholic with few *X*s on his calendar because he drinks almost every day. Still an underachiever, he probably spends all his spare time watching Hollywood action movies and listening to audio tapes made by con-artists selling hypnotic instructions about making big money in a short time. I can envision his face, prematurely old with long, deep, and straight lines digging into his cheeks and forehead. I can picture him picking up a bottle of vodka and gulping it down in one short night, his eyes bloodshot around the clock. I can also see his once elastic skin sagging to look like an old cow's lean, wizened udders, all of its nearly translucent sheen lost.

When I met him for the first time thirty years ago, it was easy for me to see that in his younger days, he had been an exceedingly handsome man with a perfectly symmetrical face. His profile was breathtakingly beautiful, with a nose of exquisitely high shape and a mouth following a straight line that displayed sensuously thick lips, outlined clearly by light pink in harmony with his alabaster-like skin. I had never seen in a man's face a pair of lips with such subtle color and vivid outlines. The front of his face was dazzling, marked by an aura of smoldering masculinity. Going up slowly and sloping down at the ends in gentle curves, his brows followed the pattern of a bird's outstretched wings tipping slightly on the edges. They were a pair of beelines bent tastefully by mild ups and downs, placed in parallel to the large green eyes exuding the childlike energy and simplicity I once so desperately read into him.

Many years later, I realized that I could establish a balance in my life only in a relationship with myself. I put an end to seeking a companion to help me restore the human side in me from the utopia-painter. I only wanted to preserve my memories of Michael, the owner of the muscular, well-proportioned body with broad shoulders and a large chest, of the slim waist and the slightly wider hips parting into the long legs of which the shapely beauty was enhanced by much rigorous exercise. He drank often. He exercised often. He was so preoccupied with his physical appearance. I wished to envision him as he was before he was ruined by alcoholism.

I kept two remembrances of him – one of the few months we initially spent together in the towering flames of sex, and the other of the following four years defined by a quietly declared affection. With my eyes closed, I re-created what Michael and I shared in Southern California. In my memory, it began in the initial three weeks of the summer of 1988, passed into another three weeks of the winter holidays, and then ended in the summer of 1990. These were the weeks and months during which I flew from Kansas to Southern California to be with him, the intense periods during which I was engaged in climbing the tower of sexual fire with him. Then, I remembered the other part, the four-year-long friendship that began to bloom in the second year during which he moved from California to Kansas City to be with his family and to work as a long-distance truck driver. In Kansas, where I was working on my PhD in English, Michael continued to be the friend who helped me to be in touch with the human in me, instead of the artist always on the point of sinking under the weight of her visions of a utopia.

It occurred to me that my father had sent me the Cry-Smile mask, probably aware of my need to be human and divine at once. After having treated me as a moral ex-con, he felt guilty about sabotaging the smiling person in me and wanted to make amends. By sending me the mask, he was suggesting that I do whatever necessary to be both, to be a *woman* indulging her flesh and to be an academician conjuring a utopia. The mask was his way of telling me that I had every right to be both. It also was his way of showing me that I was going to be forever proud of being a Korean. He knew that I was going to learn much wisdom from the many stories told to me by my motherland, to be led right by the very country from which I had tried to run all my life. He had the foresight to see that the more American I became, the more Korean I was to remain.

Chapter 15
Theory Is Practice

With the Korean in me intact, I became a U.S. citizen. In April 1989, after a series of short interviews with a good-humored civil servant who told me more than once how astonished he was by my ability to teach English to native speakers at an American university, I was finally sworn in at a ceremony in a federal building in Kansas City. Of the excruciatingly long and boring rituals that lasted longer than two hours, I remembered only three things afterward: that I dozed off occasionally, that I was dumfounded by the incredibly drawn-out speech by an attorney, and that I couldn't avoid feeling a spasm of cynicism at the national anthem sung by three African-American students recruited from a high school in the city. Even the judge, who took his seat after a few brief words of congratulations to the newly born U.S. citizens, seemed to be working hard to hide the same boredom that fell upon everyone in the hall. Being the honorable presider at the center of the stage, he couldn't doze off like the rest of us. All he could do was smile sheepishly under heavy-lidded eyes.

"You have all the rights of a U.S. citizen," the attorney went on and on with feverish zealotry. "You'll be able to vote, to be tried in a court of law, to work hard and earn a decent living. You can be as rich as you want to be. You have the freedom of speech, the freedom of thought. Your properties are protected by the same US laws that protect every American citizen. Your police will take care of you in the same way they take care of every American citizen. You're entitled to all the privileges in the US Constitution. You can bear arms to protect yourself and your family…"

Was she instructed by someone higher up to regurgitate the lines from a government pamphlet or was it her own decision? I wondered about this several times during the intervals of my wakeful nap. I concluded that nobody could have told her what to say. This is a free country as she claims. She was free to exercise her freedom to repeat the government brochure.

As the attorney's passionate sermon finally ended forty-five minutes later, the three African-American high school students began to sing the national anthem at the podium. From their well-rehearsed voices, I could tell they had probably sung the same song several times in the past at similar ceremonies. I thought it was so ironic that the country didn't treat African Americans like US citizens but used them for ceremonial occasions to celebrate the glory of US citizenship. The whole thing was for appearance, designed to show how good the country was – even to black people. The entire performance caused me to fidget uncomfortably in my seat.

The civil servant gave a certificate of citizenship to each person in the audience, and as he walked toward me and handed me mine, he announced in a loud enough voice for everyone to hear, "This one is special for me. She's from Korea, but she teaches English to native-born US citizens at a university."

We shook hands as I replied, "Thank you very much. I will do my best to teach my fellow US citizens the importance of avoiding a comma splice."

Not knowing what a comma splice was, my fellow US citizens laughed, glancing at me with unusual curiosity. Most of them barely spoke what was necessary to communicate the simplest daily routines and seemed amazed by how I could do what they couldn't imagine. I thought of a Korean woman who had failed her citizenship test three times, unable to say the most rudimentary things like "I went to go to a grocery store to buy a carton of milk." She was smart as a whip, but because English was such a hard language for Koreans, she couldn't say more than three words in one sentence.

Many Asians were perceived as being silent or dumb simply because they couldn't speak much English. They were made fun of and sometimes denigrated because they sounded incoherent or strange. I remembered a Chinese man working at the food section at a grocery store whose English was so funny that it elicited laughter from the shoppers. One day, I overheard two teenage boys mocking him behind his back, imitating his English in a manner that made him sound like an imbecile, and I walked over to them and warned them in a menacing, low voice. I whispered, "If you go to China and speak poor Chinese because it's not your language, you wouldn't like to hear the things you say about this Chinese man. You'd be humiliated. I know his English is funny, but you can laugh with sympathy and respect, without your humiliating attitude." Staring at the dumb look in their faces, I continued, "He may be a lot smarter than he sounds. Just because he's not lucky enough to speak your language—your language, not his—well, that doesn't mean he's stupid." Going back to shopping, I sighed, realizing how often Asian immigrants like the Chinese man were treated poorly because of their poor English.

Later that evening, I had nothing to stem the flow of mixed emotions. As a cow sends the food in her stomach back into her mouth, I found myself returning to the discomfort that took hold of me during the performance of the National Anthem. *Maybe, not everything was a show*, I thought. *What disturbed me was the huge gap between the theory of the American democracy and its practice. The attorney who promoted the theory so eagerly bought my scorn because she failed to acknowledge the nation's miserable failure to practice it. If she can bridge the gap, she might make a hell of a lawyer. She may deserve the benefit of the doubt.* In another one of those numerous dialogues with myself, I went on, *There are reasons why people from all over the world flock to this country. They know at least there is a pretense of equal opportunity and they want to test it out. They stay in this country to see if the day will come when the theory accords with the practice. They're waiting to find out if the gap that makes this country look so hypocritical will eventually be bridged. They want to have a chance to realize that it's a gap to be closed instead of just a sign of hypocrisy.*

In Korea, nobody except a Korean could become a citizen. I had to admit the sad fact that in my home country, there was no hypocrisy about including other races or nationalities because there was no theory and hence no practice. A person born of a Korean father and a foreign mother was eligible because of the patrilineal tradition, but everyone else was excluded from the possibility of obtaining Korean citizenship. A Chinese national with a Korean mother and a Chinese father would be permanently barred from Korean citizenship. Any individual with a Korean mother and a foreign father was ineligible, and anyone whose parents were both foreign was eliminated. Some of these people were born and raised in Korea, but they could not become citizens. There were occasional exceptions made for foreign individuals who proved themselves to be indispensable for the benefits of the country, but these individuals were rare. The same was true in Japan, where everyone except those fathered by Japanese men was barred from becoming Japanese citizens. Unlike Americans who at least in theory tried to practice democracy for every race and nationality, Japanese and Koreans practiced it only for Japanese and Koreans.

I heard sad stories about the Koreans who were born and raised in Japan and could not become citizens and who therefore were forced to identify themselves as Koreans—not as Japanese—and equally sad stories about the Chinese who were born and raised in Korea and could not become citizens and who therefore were forced to call themselves Chinese—not Korean. Had I been given a chance to talk to members of other ethnic groups in Japan and Korea, I was certain I would have heard the same woe. In America, however, every ethnic American I had ever met was happy to define themselves as being American.

They said: "My parents are Chinese," "My parents are French," "My parents are African," or "My parents are Arabic." It was sure proof that as long as they were born and raised in the United States, they were allowed to name themselves as U.S. citizens, no matter how foreign their parents were.

"Japanese and Koreans don't even have room for hypocrisy," I continued. "They don't even have the theory of a melting pot. But Americans do."

I put my certificate of citizenship in a file and placed it under the masks of the young bride in the closet. Trying to inject an element of complexity into the simple, artificial smile of the newly married wife, I again said to myself, "I will help my husband country, my in-laws, to make their theory coincide with their practice. Haven't I been doing it all these years? I've made so much effort, and the dead woman in my dreams is a witness. To those who love to say the United States is the best country in the world because it's better than any other country, I'll have the courage to say, 'If we're satisfied with our country just because it's better than any other country, that means we have rather low standards. We mustn't be content with being comparatively better. We must be content with being absolutely better. Our standards should be higher.'" I paused to proclaim to the loud silence, "I will do everything I can to do my share in helping my husband country achieve such absolute standards. I won't stop until I have dedicated every ounce of my energy to help my adopted country bring its theory in accordance with its practice."

About two years after the citizenship ceremony, during which I spent many days dying to live, I found myself nearing the doctoral exams. Having heard horror stories about those who failed their doctoral exams twice and were permanently dis-enrolled from PhD candidacy, I was frantic. Frantic was my usual state of mind during all those graduate school years, but the panic that continued to engulf me for two years before the final gate couldn't be compared to anything I had ever felt before. If I failed once, there would be another chance, but there was a time limit for this second and last chance, and I was afraid there may not be enough days for me to prepare for a second time. I had to pass on the first try. I had to.

Everyone facing their doctoral exams panicked. But as always, there was an extra layer in my anxiety-stricken routines. In order to avoid being downgraded for trivial idiomatic errors in my writing, I had to demonstrate a high level of conceptual thinking, high enough to compensate for the problems unrelated to my ability to demonstrate such thought. It was the fact—and my obsessive awareness of the fact—that if I wasn't good enough to surpass my native-speaking peers with my content, my merits would be questioned. Although I wasn't going to receive a letter grade as I had during my coursework, I was going to be evaluated by five different members of my committee, not all of whom may forgive me for my ignorable grammatical mistakes. I steeled myself to be the old grade-monger I had been throughout my coursework. I didn't like that side of me, but I did what I had to, to be the best. I had to be more than just a grade-collector. I had to inspire enough genuine praise from my professors to know that my work had substance as much as, if not more than, my peers.'

As more days passed to bring me closer to the exams—as my thoughts ventured beyond Kansas to a place where I envisioned myself being called Dr. Lee—I felt my face opening into a touch of a smile. Again, I said to myself, "I've been a grade-monger, but it'll pay off. My future colleagues will be impressed. Wherever they are, they'll have my transcripts to dispel their doubts about my ability to teach English." I had to hold fast to my hopes for such a time, or my nightmares of failure would consume me.

I read one novel a week for the doctoral coms and graded ten freshman papers in the same amount of time. It didn't take long before I found myself going to bed every night with half-dead eyes. Still slower than most of my native-speaking colleagues in terms of reading and writing speed, I had to put twice as much time into finishing the same quantity and quality of work they delivered. I was also still in the stage where the subtle nuances of the new vocabulary I discovered had to be picked up with deliberately conscious, repeated applications. I spent an unquantifiable amount of time learning the very delicate differences between a series of words with meanings that seemed identical. When I came across nouns such as 'argument', 'dispute', 'debate', 'polemic', and 'contention', I composed multiple sentences using each of these words. In order to master the shades that made so much difference to the eyes and ears of well-trained English professors, I had to be able to tell what lay under the surface of the language. I had to learn how a simple choice of a word could dramatically change the feeling of a sentence, to absorb a spectrum of variations created by hardly noticeable dissimilarities.

I found myself having to devote extra hours and energy every day to the process of language acquisition itself. I knew that my native-speaking peers had to struggle with the same process because it was a natural part of writing. But none of them had to make the same extremely laborious effort. To deliver a paper in which the content and form were equal to each other, they didn't have to go nearly as far as I did. They didn't have to write and re-write the same sentence a dozen times in a row. I thought I could almost understand the rage of a mute person whose mind, so vividly alive and alert, was locked in an immobile tongue. I wondered if such a person tried nearly as hard as I in an effort to find the vocabulary that could successfully pin down the string of insightful concepts conjured by his unusually active brain.

I set aside a whole month before my doctoral exams to lessen the gap between my content and language. Altogether, the exams were made of three written parts and one oral, and each of these three written parts contained two essays to be completed in four hours. All of them were to be taken in three weeks, and during these three weeks, the professors on my committee evaluated my essays in the order they came in, marking their points and preparing questions to ask me on separate pieces of paper. If they decided to pass me, then I was to go straight ahead toward the oral exams that were set up to test me on my areas of specialization. I wasn't as worried about the orals because I could speak as fast as any of my native-speaking colleagues, and none of the five professors on my committee were as familiar as I was with my areas of specialization, literature by women of color, particularly Asian-American women. What I was worried about was my written exams.

Every day for a month, I sat at a desk for twelve hours straight, taking a one-hour break between each of the four-hour writing parts. I improvised topics such as: "Discuss the specific ways in which five authors from the American Renaissance envision democracy," "Make a case for continuity through a discussion of five different authors from both the 19th-century and 20th-century American literature," "Please illuminate the most strikingly common narrative features among modern women's autobiographies," and "How do the authors of personal essays use their selves to be voices for the larger communities? Choose five of them to compare and contrast."

Every day for a month, breakfast started at about 9:00 a.m., lunch was finished by 2:00 p.m., dinner was on the table around 6:00 p.m., and the pretzels and banana nut bread for a night snack were gobbled up by 11:00 p.m. or so. As I lay on my futon, my eyes screamed as usual, but I didn't rub them. In my imagination, I used a pair of tiny tweezers to pull out what felt like dried spider's legs sprawled across my irises. I then gently poked the tweezers into the center of my eyes, lifting what felt like the desiccated torso of the arachnid stuck on the outer layers of the pupils. Then, I dropped artificial tears onto the wide surfaces, tilting my head up to let them wash out what looked like the broken residue of the spider's body.

When I heard I had passed the written parts of the exam, I apologized to my eyes, and I promised that I will pass the oral exams due in one week, so that they could have a three-week-long break during the winter recess. I swore that they would be free from feeling the dried spider for a whole semester because I wouldn't be nearly as frantic as I had been. All that I had to read in the following semester were the books to be discussed in my doctoral dissertation, all of which combined would be a fraction of the writings I had had to read to prepare for the doctoral exams. There wasn't going to be anymore writing twelve hours a day for a month.

And indeed, I kept my promise to my eyes and passed the orals with what I thought was distinction. It wasn't because I was so brilliant as to make my professors speechless. It was because, as I had known, none of them were nearly as familiar as I was with the books in my areas of specialization. Although there were two professors on my committee whose knowledge on African-American women's literature was impressive and whose efforts to bring to the center the lesser known writings by women of color were consistent, neither one of them knew the authors on my list as deeply and broadly as I did. Not having studied any of these authors in specific detail, even Jane possessed little of the information I had to offer. None of the five members on my committee knew much of my dissertation topic, Asian-American women's autobiographies. It was easy for me to impress them. Within the first ten minutes of the exams, listening to the long, intense silence displayed by my professors and the sounds of the notes hastily made on their papers, I knew I was going to pass.

"I'd like to study American literature from the perspective of an Asian-American woman such as Hisaye Yamamoto, the one who, in her autobiographical story, 'Life among the Oil Fields,' describes a white couple who hit and killed a Japanese-American boy with their car and ran, later refusing to take responsibility for what they did. This couple is reminiscent of Zelda and F. Scott Fitzgerald in their manners and appearances, and Yamamoto raises questions about the racial hierarchies not only in the United States as a country but also in American literature as a field of study. She shows how, as America has been partly shaped and defined by people like this white couple, American literature has also been partly defined by them. The truth is, Zelda and F. Scott Fitzgerald were a pair of drunks with little concern for anyone but themselves. Because Fitzgerald produced great writings and deserves a prominent place in the history of American literature, he has been studied more than any other author. But it's time to study other authors. It's time that literature created by white males like him stopped being perceived as superior to all other American literature. It's time to define American literature by and for all the different Americas."

As my professors tried to draw me closer to the canon in their questions and comments, I tried to draw them closer to my expertise in my answers and responses. In a way, it was a seesaw game during which both parties tried to outdo each other in a harmless manner. I kept the conversation going as they took turns in falling back on the contents of my written essays to form more concrete ideas about my topics. Not knowing what to ask about my subjects, they kept going back to the titles in the canon, to the interpretations of the famous authors I had offered in my written exams.

"You wrote in one of your essays, Jid," one of them remarked, "that Whitman treated women as machines for biological procreation. I rather think he respected women, particularly old women."

"Whitman," I answered, "respected women a lot more than most men of his days did, but a close reading of his poem, 'A Woman Waits for Me,' reveals his true conception of women. Women for him existed ultimately to become mothers, not to become themselves. They weren't supposed to live as individuals with their own goals and purposes. They were supposed to live only to raise children. I wish he had sung motherhood as one of the many functions to be fulfilled by women, not as the only function."

"Between Mary McCarthy and Lillian Hellman," another began, "you prefer Mary McCarthy because she does a better job separating what she thinks is memory from what she thinks is fact. How reliable or unreliable is this separation?"

I explained, "I don't know how reliable or unreliable it is, but I do know that Mary McCarthy rigorously tries to separate fiction from autobiography. While she knows that these two genres are inseparable because autobiography must use fiction in order to create and sustain narrative logic and integrity, she wants to sharply demonstrate that there are clear differences between the two genres. Autobiography *is* based on fact while fiction is not. This is why at the end of each chapter, she adds those italicized annotations in which she voluntarily chooses to explain what she deleted, added, created, or interpreted. By confessing how she used fiction to tell the truth, she ironically proves how truthful she is to fact. By admitting what she possibly made up, she keeps the credibility of what actually happened."

I used my own answers as a stepping stone to lead the committee into my areas of expertise. I added, "The blending of fact and fiction will forever exist in autobiography, but the separation of the two will always be there, too. One look at *The Woman Warrior* will tell you this. In *The Woman Warrior,* Maxine Hong Kingston deliberately and spontaneously mixes fact and fiction to describe her life because she can't tell one from the other. Because so much of her life as she remembers it is told to her by her mother, and because her mother's memory in turn is embellished and exaggerated by the stories she herself created, she is unable to tell her own story from her mother's. But as a matter of fact, her mother lived in rural China until she grew old enough to be defined by ancient Chinese norms, while Kingston, born and raised in America, lived in another country. Growing up in a Californian Chinatown, her mother's outdated injunctions for women were ingrained in her, but as she was bombarded with American culture every day, she longed to be a liberated American woman with education and professional success."

"To be an American woman, to be a citizen of her country, not of her mother's, Kingston learned how to tell her mother's stories from her own, how to separate fact from fiction in her mother's autobiography and her own, and how to create her own story with events in her own life. She had to define herself against her mother who possibly committed a series of female infanticides in China. With no means to verify whether her mother indeed killed girl babies or not, she has to weave her own story, that of an American woman who condemns the Chinese custom of female infanticide. She clearly separates China from America to declare that *The Woman Warrior* is an autobiography, but she also mixes the two countries in her memory to show how difficult it is to tell the two apart in her imagination, and hence how much fiction there still is in her narrative that is supposedly about facts."

"It was well done," Jane said when she gave me the verdict for my performance as the other professors filed out of the exam room to congratulate me.

I was overwhelmed with a sense of relief, shaking hands with each one of them, thanking them. Thirty-five years old by then, I had learned that the best avenue into a successful human relationship was humility untouched by a false sense of modesty. I was no longer the egotistic youngster who I once had been in my twenties, no longer the arrogant, condescending breed who had enjoyed wielding an upper hand in a debate with individuals who I perceived as being less knowledgeable than I. From an academic perspective, there was no point in being condescending to any of my professors, who were so tremendously well-versed in many areas of American literature and were strangers only to my specialized subjects. Realistically also, they were the ones who were to write letters of recommendation for me to my prospective colleagues at other colleges and universities, to help me to find a long-term livelihood in my adopted country. One of them, who I later invited to serve as one of the three faculty on my dissertation committee, enjoyed a national reputation in his area, and the other, being Jane, was by far one of the most influential faculty not only in the department but also on the campus. The last thing I wanted to do was to jeopardize my amicable relationship with either one of these two professors or with anyone else on my doctoral exams committee. They held my career in their hands.

By the day Jane's verdict on my exams came, I had had too many nights during which the nightmare of seeing my own dead body forced me to wake up in sweat. I realized I would have to change my lifestyle in the near future. I asked of myself, "Why am I losing my humanity? I don't give more than five minutes to my friends on the phone. When they call, I hang up like a hurried machine. Is there any way I can turn my nightmares into dreams and be both successful and a human being?"

I found myself to be one of those people unable to give, and I was ashamed. *I want to be human again, but there's no way I can be human until I finish my PhD*, I said to myself. "After passing my doctoral exams, I'll have my dissertation coming, and after finishing my dissertation, I'll have time to practice the humanity I want to practice. Meanwhile, I'll be able to keep in mind the humanity I'm unable to practice. I'll be able to imagine the kind of person I'd have become had it not been for my nightmares and dreams. Without my nightmares and dreams, I'd be one of those so-to-speak 'ordinary people.' I'd be a kinder, more giving person. I'd give more time to my friends on the phone. I'd be less of an achiever, but happier." I wanted to have more ability to *create happiness* and to live more in the present. I wanted to live more to *be* than to *become,* and I wanted to be defined more by *living* than by *achieving.* Writing twelve hours a day to prepare for the coms, I had made a decision. In my attitude at least, if not in my action, I achieved a level of modesty, and I was able to show it to the professors examining me.

Chapter 16
Marriage of Heaven and Hell

During the three weeks of winter recess, which coincidentally fell immediately after the day of my oral exams, I offered myself a reprieve. I gave myself a chance to *be,* to *create happiness*, and to live in the *present.* Now that I was an ABD (all but dissertation), I had joined the ranks of those handful of graduate students who had passed all the gates but the final one, the doctoral dissertation. It was flattering to receive the esteem given to those who finally came near the finishing point after the long, hard marathon, to begin to see the light at the end from the penultimate stage. Now, I had no worries concerning uncertainties, with no more exams and no more papers or deadlines. Although there was a tentative deadline for the dissertation, it wasn't strictly enforced. As long as I finished it in a reasonable number of years such as two or three, including the time necessary to do the reading, research, and the actual writing, there was very little possibility for me to fear anything unexpected. I felt certain that I could be done with everything before I had to renew the time limit for graduate work for the second time. As many doctoral students did, I would have to renew it only once, and it would be sometime after the first year of my dissertation.

At the beginning of the three-week-long recess, I called Michael in Kansas City. After helping me buy a cheap used car, he kindly took a week off from his truck-driving work at a moving company and moved into the extra room in my apartment to help me learn how to drive. Every morning for a week, he and I drank Starbuck's coffee and ate croissants for breakfast. Then, he drove us to an empty lot on the edge of town, parked the car, handed the key to me, and moved over to the passenger seat. Before lunch, which was steamed rice and stir-fried vegetables for both of us at a fast-food Chinese restaurant, I thought I had overcome the cold feeling I received from the wheel. The morning hours enabled me to see the wheel as something warmer, as a helping hand rather than an alien instrument that could get me into trouble. The afternoon hours empowered me to feel even more comfortable with the wheel, bringing me to a point where I could almost envision being friends with the car. And the evening hours, which began after a hamburger for Michael and a ham sandwich for me at a local restaurant, gave me time to reflect on the day's lesson and to visualize the driving habits I wanted to acquire.

In the evening, Michael summarized the various instructions he had given me from the passenger seat during the day. He showed me how to move my hands on the wheel when turning to another direction, and I imitated his movements like an eager child.

"When you change the direction of the car," he advised, "you have the habit of keeping your hands in the same direction on different spots of the wheel. But you have to keep your hands in two different directions. When you turn right, you want to use your left hand to turn the wheel to the right and move your right hand to the left side of the wheel. Then you rapidly rotate your hands until the car makes its turn, keeping one hand under the other and making them take turns in going up and down."

"I've spent all my life reading books and writing papers, but my IQ turns into a single-digit figure on the road," I said, roaring into laughter. "I'd better practice."

I made exaggerated motions with my arms, slicing the air into wide, huge circles, my hands clenched into a pair of tight fists and my wrists hardened into little rocks. So intense in everything I tried, I was ready to break the invisible wheel into pieces.

"Tomorrow, you'll learn how to reverse and go back and forth in zigzag lines," Michael said.

You're beginning to drive at the age of thirty-five, I said to myself. "You have to practice a lot more than any of those Americans who started to drive at the age of fourteen or fifteen. Some of them started to sit behind the wheel at the age of twelve because they grew up on a farm. You're behind them by twenty or more years. It would take you days and weeks to get to the same point where most American teenagers could reach in just a few hours of training." I paused and went on, "You naturally want to complain, 'Why do I have to start everything twenty years later than everyone else? I started to speak English twenty-four years later than any of my native-speaking colleagues. As this handicap runs my life at the desk, it runs my life on the road. Even in driving, I have to work twice as hard as anyone else. But there's nothing you can do about it. You can't go back and change the past.'"

In my dream, I watched myself making giant motions with my hands, my arms intensely circling around the invisible wheel as if it were made of long, thick steel bars. I was ready to bend the steel with my bare hands, my hands almost digging into the hard metal. As I started to turn it rapidly after several tries, my hands finally moving as fast as if they were spinning atop, I remarked, amused, "To *be* an American, I have to *become* an American. I have to *become* a driver. I'll never stop *becoming* to *be.*" As I turned the invisible wheel for what seemed to be the hundredth time, I decided to wake up, having seen enough. I knew I wasn't sweating.

Knowing how ephemeral my dreams were without my nightmares, I wanted to make maximum use of the week Michael could afford. On the second day, we went to another edge of town that was sparsely populated, where I, under Michael's vigilant supervision, practiced driving in reverse in zigzag lines and changing lanes without slowing down.

"Before you go on an interstate and have to change lanes while driving seventy-five miles an hour, you'd better practice it on an empty country road," he said. "Tomorrow then, you'll be able to change lanes in more crowded parts of town." By mid-afternoon on the second day, I believed I was over my fear of the wheel. I had to believe so because if I didn't believe I was in a better place after a dozen hours of straight practice, I wouldn't be able to go anywhere. So much of my life was dependent on what I thought I could achieve, on the power of positive self-suggestion. Without strong faith in myself, I couldn't succeed in what I started twenty or more years later than anyone else. Self-confidence was all I had.

On the third day, as I arrived to the point where I could change lanes in a busy section of town, I could even tell a story behind the wheel. "When I came to America in 1980, some Korean students told me a funny story," I said. "They said when they were lost, they saw the name of the street and tried to find it on a map. They didn't want to ask anyone, embarrassed about their poor English. One day, one of them called a friend at home, seriously lost. Without a map in his car, he couldn't find his way back home, and he wanted his friend to come to where he was, so that he could follow him. He said he was at a street named 'One Way.' Boy, was he lost!" Michael and I burst out laughing at the poor student's credulity, and I realized I was driving in a forty-five miles per hour zone.

The third and fourth day were spent on the busiest intersections in town, including several blocks downtown, and the long, wide street along the shopping malls called 23rd Street. Having gained enough comfort being surrounded by vehicles moving in all directions, I could park in a vacant spot, pull back out onto the road, watch the ones coming toward me, and keep enough distance from the one in front of me. Once, however, I stood still for a prolonged period of time, failing to turn left to allow all the cars coming from the opposite direction to make their turns, and I was afraid. Having heard about the highway shootings in California, I nearly expected the driver behind me to take out a gun and aim at me.

"Oh, no," I screamed in a low voice. "The guy behind me may get mad at me. He may want to beat me up."

"This is Kansas," Michael returned, "not California. He's not coming to get you." Relieved, I lifted my hand and waved at the driver behind me, and to my pleasant surprise, he waved back at me, smiling. "Left turn is going to be a bit of a challenge for you," Michael said. "You just wait until all the cars make their turns and then as the light changes into red, you take your car out to the middle of the intersection with your turn signal on. Most people will wait for you."

Leaving the downtown area and turning right to enter 23rd Street, I suddenly felt scared by the traffic volume. But Michael warned me about the danger of slowing down, urging me to keep at the speed.

"You can get hit if you slow down on a busy street like this," he said.

Driving back home on 23rd Street on those two days would have been an uneventful experience had it not been for the mistake I made on the second day that was so reminiscent of the lost Korean graduate students' misadventure. Turning right to go home, I found myself going the wrong direction on a one way street, facing a truck coming from the opposite direction. Seeing how upset the truck driver was, I quickly drove reverse, entering a parking lot in front of a gas station. Letting out a sigh of relief, I said, "Those Korean graduate students who thought One Way was the name of a street probably drove in the wrong direction, too."

"Are you going to call your friend to come and get you?" Michael asked.

"I wish I could, but I left my phone book at home." We both laughed, standing in the cold as we filled the tank in my car.

After the fifth and sixth day, I thought I had earned some level of comfort with higher speeds. Going over the minimum speed of forty-five miles an hour, I found myself driving back and forth twice in the same day on the interstate between Lawrence and Kansas City. I sang to myself, "I'm not an American until I'm used to speed," pepping myself up to drive fifty-five miles an hour in the same speed zone. By now, Michael was also more confident in my driving. His vigilant instructions became limited to occasional remarks such as: "Go a little faster," "Now, you're going too fast," or "Don't slow down." It was a few days after Christmas, which gave me an advantage because the roads were nearly empty. I didn't have to start on a busy interstate. I could start by driving slowly on a wide-open highway, gradually build up the speed to enter more populated areas, and finally move with relative ease into the most crowded sections and stay on for a while. I was so proud, watching myself make it through downtown Kansas City to I-670 and then cutting into I-70 to Lawrence, my home away from home!

I did make a couple mistakes. One time, on busy I-670, I failed to change lanes on time, thinking the car sufficiently far away from me was too close. Another time, on I-70, I panicked at the sight of a huge truck turning into my lane and nearly stopped the car, causing the driver behind me to angrily honk the horn. But I made it by myself, and I couldn't find words to express my pride at my accomplishment.

On the seventh and final day of training, I continued to be speechless. I was ecstatic as I drove down I-670 in the rain, with Michael sitting beside me, his arms leisurely folded. All he had to do was assure me that I wasn't going to skid because of my speed and that I should get used to going a bit faster than I was going.

"You'll be driving in all kinds of weather," he said. "You can't slow down just because of the rain or snow."

"By the time I reach the point, if I ever do, where I can drive as fast as you on a snow-covered interstate, I'll have a cocktail party," I sang.

I never had a cocktail party to celebrate my fast driving. I never *became* American enough to drive as fast as Michael or any American who began to touch the wheel at the age of fourteen or fifteen. To this day, driving on an interstate remains to be a serious challenge for me, a daring feat I prefer to avoid if possible. Still, it is a struggle for me to drive even slightly over the speed limit, and an effort to stop the temptation to slow down on an interstate.

Now I live in Murfreesboro, Tennessee, a small college town thirty miles away from Nashville, and I need to carefully plan for a trip into the city, just to mentally gear myself up for the relatively short drive on I-24. I have driven on I-24 a hundred times at least for the past twenty-five years, but I still miss an exit, unable to change lanes on time. Sometimes, I panic at the sight of the cars behind me and wait for a whole minute or so to change lanes. I can almost hear the sound of my heart beating in my chest. I am still in the process of *becoming* an American. I have never been one. I'm afraid I never will *be.*

For the remaining two weeks of winter break, I was lucky enough not to have snow in Kansas. For eight hours every day, I alone drove the big old clunker, venturing beyond the city limits and winding through the vast wheat fields that comprised the center of the Midwest. I couldn't go far because the car couldn't hold out any longer than a couple hours at a time, but I was thrilled to have the two weeks as an opportunity to discover the country in another way.

"You're an American as long as you can drive a car," Jane said with humor upon hearing that I had bought one. "At the wheel, you'll see your adopted country from a whole different perspective." Used to seeing America only from the viewpoint of the books I had read, I wished to see America on the road. I craved to encounter, with my own hands on the wheel, the vastness of the land that impressed so many Korean tourists, the endless highways that lay stretched forever without another person in sight, and the frightening, sometimes terrifying, sense of isolation one experiences on the wide-open roads.

"On an American interstate," several Koreans had told me, "you can go on and on and see nothing but machines and concrete grounds, and you may have to wait for half an hour to get from one exit to another."

An eerie sense of exhilaration enveloped me as I found myself lost in a place surrounded with limestone hills, rolling into slow slopes where the long, broad strips of concrete grounds lay in stark contrast with the low stone walls flanking the road. It was a spooky place to be lost, a menacing landscape to watch, and it gave me a chilling sense of danger. I drove on, wanting to stay lost in fearful mirth. In a bizarre way, I was seized by the same sense of adventure that had engulfed me during those winter breaks during which I was left alone in my apartment while everyone else was gone home to celebrate the winter holidays. I was being me, sad but jubilant. I was alive, being totally by and with myself. Alone and menaced by where I was, I squarely enjoyed facing the scene that was the essence of my life, the series of snapshots that showed myself and my environment on a never-ending duel course in another country.

So, I took books into my car. If I wanted to preserve the newly discovered joy of confronting my environment, I had to make my car into a semi-home where I could read and write. I had to adopt the new habit of keeping books and pens and notepads in the machine that was going to make me an American. Whenever I purposefully lost my sense of direction on the road, I could park the car, open a book to make notes about it, and re-create the scene in which the essence of my life was again fostered.

"Americans keep all kinds of junk in their cars," Koreans said. "They almost live in their cars." Instead of soda and beer, I packed my icebox with purified water, apple juice and sometimes a potato sandwich. *I really am being Americanized*, I thought proudly. "I know how to do what Americans do." I went one step further, "If I want to understand American writers, I'd better behave like an American writer. If I'm going to study Hemingway, I'd better act like Hemingway." To imitate Hemingway, I opened the bottled apple juice, pretending it was beer. I remembered what I had heard on NPR several years before, a book reviewer's interview with a Russian scholar who said, "Some modern Russian writers drank a lot in an attempt to emulate Hemingway. They thought they'd be as good as him if they drank as much as he did." Although I never entertained the hope that I would ever be as good as Hemingway, I thought it might be worthwhile to make the effort of imitating him. Only, I tried with non-alcoholic beverages, afraid I would get really drunk at the wheel. To be an American, I also made the car a bit grungy, placing a large brown bag in the trunk filled with inorganic garbage, scattering some of it on the floor under the front seat and on top of the backseats. Covered with torn pieces of paper and beer cans and empty plastic bottles, the car indeed looked like one of those owned by a young American adult whose life took place in her car.

Driving on the gently rolling roads through the vast wheat fields of Kansas, I couldn't help marveling again and again at how big America was. "Big ideas come from big countries," Koreans said. "America is a huge country. No wonder they built an empire with their big ideas." I was a mesmerized beholder, riding with the continued ritual of deliberately getting lost and finding my way back. "No wonder Koreans are so impressed by this country!" I exclaimed. "They see greatness everywhere. Look at its infrastructure, for one thing. There's hardly a town without a public library, no matter how small, and there's scarcely a street that is not neatly paved, no matter how remote. In this country, it's not uncommon to meet a postal delivery man familiar with Whitman's *Leaves of Grass*, a cashier with lines from Nabokov's *Lolita.* Didn't I have a conversation the other day with a waitress at a restaurant who could quote Sylvia Plath?"

There were as many ignorant people in America as there were in other countries, but America was unique and special in that the chances of being surprised by an ordinary person were remarkably higher. In a small town in Kansas with a population of two hundred, I once met a farmer on a tractor who had read Irving Howe's books on the history of American communism. He actually enjoyed telling me about the alliance between American communism, the labor movement, and the farmers' coop. America was so unlike Korea, where it was nearly impossible to run into a farmer on a tractor who could talk about the history of Korean communism, let alone its roots in peasant farms and its joint movement with the labor force. In Korea, such knowledge was a monopoly of the intellectual population in big cities, mainly in the capital city of Seoul. All the prestigious institutions of higher education were concentrated in Seoul, and the lack of a solid infrastructure made it difficult for intelligent rural people to have access to the information that was available to residents of Seoul with the benefits of public and university libraries. Nor were there enough well-equipped secondary schools for farmers and their children, making it extremely hard for them to obtain printed sources of information aside from newspapers. Seoul was to Korea as Paris was to France, as London was to England, or Tokyo was to Japan. Coastal states such as New York and California certainly had a concentration of the most prestigious institutions of higher education, but in a small Midwestern town such as Lawrence, Kansas, one could easily find a decent library where a farmer could get hold of Irving Howe's books on the history of American communism. In America, Lawrence, Kansas was just as much of America as New York or San Francisco.

Some Koreans marveled that America was indeed geographically big enough to absorb half of the world's population. America was also emotionally big enough to welcome people from all over the world, to create large-scale unity out of so much diversity. My adopted country was a giant beauty born of an infinite spectrum of beasts, a furnace of opposites burnt into one consistent system, a home that was at once fluid and immobile. In the places in Kansas where I was thrilled to get lost and drive on the everlasting strips of the concrete roads, I saw a monolithic country of the most variegated composition. I heard a solo in a chorus. How else could an immigrant woman such as myself, whose voice simultaneously sang of Hisaye Yamamoto's "Life among the Oil Fields" and F. Scott Fitzgerald's *The Great Gatsby,* drive around with a purposefully aimless attitude in the middle of nowhere in Kansas? How else could I celebrate the ever-changing definitions of American literature, driving on the roads that were so unchanging because they were so solidly built?

Perhaps I picked Michael as a lover and then as a friend, thirsty for the other side of the country unseen by those Koreans who had told tales about the greatness of the huge country. I wouldn't summarily call him ignorant, but I certainly would hesitate to categorize him as being knowledgeable. Reading every line and word in a local newspaper, he could absorb information extremely fast, to the degree that he could effortlessly memorize names and events and report shocking news in the most precise details.

"Kansas City police arrested a guy who kept fifty-one dead cats in his freezer," he would tell me, enunciating the number, fifty-one, that he clearly remembered. "He lives at 205 Summer Lane, five blocks away from me. I drove by there this morning to see if he was around, but all I could see was five junk cars lying in his back yard. I'm sure he's in jail by now."

But unable to create a system out of the information he absorbed, he turned his head into a depository of facts, into a junk yard of knowledge that would do nothing to improve his mind. Because he was easily manipulated by what he saw and heard, the information he retained only caused internal friction, driving him to be at war with himself and what lay beyond him. He gave the same amount of attention and weight to John Lennon's lyrics and Rush Limbaugh's propaganda, admiring the words in the song, "Imagine," and in the next breath repeating the talk show host's newly coined phrase, "FemiNazis."

"Lennon was a thorn in the eye of the government because he sang about the power of people," he would proclaim, and then in a moment, he would declare, "I hate those feminists who make women hate men. Rush Limbaugh is right." As I asked him why he thought Rush Limbaugh was right, he would instantly recruit every bit of hate vocabulary in his possession and cry out aloud, frothing in the mouth, “Don’t you know they hate men? They try to persuade heterosexual women to have sex with lesbians because they believe having sex with men is just like being raped.”

As I explained why I was a feminist and why I studied women’s literature, he would listen and immediately modify his statement. He would say, “I don’t mean women like you. I mean women who condemn women who’re not lesbian.”

I would correct him, “If you listen to Rush Limbaugh carefully, he condemns women like me and my friends as well as lesbian women. I’m sure there are some lesbian women who believe heterosexual women sell themselves out for patriarchy, but I’ve never met a lesbian woman in my life who hates me for being heterosexual. As there are men who hate women, there are women who hate men. As there are men who hate men, there are women who hate women. As there are men who are feminist, there are women who are feminist. As there are men who aren’t feminist, there are women who aren’t feminist. Rush Limbaugh picks on a handful of women who hate women and men who’re not like them, and he loves to make careless blanket statements.”

With Lennon and Limbaugh, and then me speaking in his head all at once, Michael would fall into a chaotic pattern of thinking until he sank under a sea of conflicting positions that left him seized by mute anger. He became a man from everywhere and nowhere, torn by a thousand different directions inside, a frustrated, intellectually repressed man whose only weapon was a sudden outburst of violent emotions. To make it worse, his severe, genetic social anxiety left him unable to explain himself to anyone but his immediate family and friends. Sometimes, he couldn’t make even the most casual conversation with anyone with whom he wasn’t entirely familiar. He drank in an attempt to overcome, to reconcile all the crashing thoughts in his head, to get over his fear of people, and to stay sane. He drank because he couldn’t handle the pressure of being alone, because he didn’t have the ability, to use my favorite expression, to endure the silent duels between himself and his environment. Incapable of facing life squarely, of confronting what lay in store for him, he kowtowed to his surroundings. He invited them to win and run over him and then, he resorted to alcohol to forget his shame. He was too weak to master the lifestyle of self-reliance that was the quintessence of the American life.

I mustn’t forget that there are men like Michael in every country. But I believe I may not be entirely wrong when I say that he may represent one of the most serious by-products of the uniquely American lifestyle. Unlike any other country, America is constructed on the concept of creative chaos, a laissez-faire state of existence born of the belief that no control is the best control. Chaos with benefits is what sustains America. But Michael is a prototype of chaos without benefits, a specimen of a man with no sense of direction and an example of intelligence with no guiding principle. He is one of those Americans who epitomize the quintessential American-style loser, endowed with such a huge ability to absorb so much conflicting information, and yet so thoroughly deprived of the training to create a system to process it. Although there are many losers in Korea, I am afraid it would be hard to meet Korean losers with so much knowledge moving in so many crashing directions.

A Korean-American man once said to me, "Even if the United States gives Korea the Grand Canyon, we don't have the land to put it in." He added, "Even if the United States wants to give us all of its smartest and dumbest people, we don't have the land to place them. Dumb people in America are unfathomably dumb, and smart people in America are immeasurably smart. If you're smart and capable, you can rise so high that the sky is the limit, and if you're dumb and incapable, you'll fall to the other end of the earth. For the smart and capable, this country is heaven, but for the dumb and incapable, it is hell. This country is made of a marriage between heaven and hell. The hell is just as deep as the heaven is high."

Because he couldn't afford health insurance and because he knew he could fall fatally sick at any given time from so much hard drinking, Michael was a diet freak.

I heard him complain, "The United States is the only country where the health insurance premium is so expensive. This country is so bad for the poor." Then, I heard him reciting the list of the food he must avoid. He was morbidly worried about what he put into his mouth, reading every tiny letter and number on the label of an item at a grocery store. At one point, he even abstained from drinking milk for a whole year, quoting from a con-dietician who said human beings are the only species who drinks milk as adults. Checking the accuracy of the information didn't occur to him. He was indeed so paranoid about his health that he couldn't afford to question the credibility of the information that merely sounded plausible to his hungry ears.

If there was one positive thing I picked up from hanging out with him, it was a concern about my health. I bought health insurance through the university, one of the few cheap ones available to graduate students making virtually less than minimum wage. It was one of those ridiculous policies that hardly covered anything except the extremely high costs that were incurred in case I got struck by a serious illness, but it eased my constant worries. I no longer had to be one of those numerous graduate students paranoid about their lack of health insurance.

"Don't talk about health insurance," my colleagues would scream from a spasm of anxiety. "I feel sick whenever I'm reminded that I don't have health insurance."

I would sing cynically, "So much for this great country of ours, ha! We'll have to spend two thirds of our monthly salary to buy decent health insurance."

Subconsciously, I probably chose Michael as a lover and then as a friend because he represented and *was* the specimen that could show me a life that was on the hell side of America. By being with him, I had a chance to plunge into the bottomless nadir, to the total opposite of the lives I saw in my professors. Having created a system of their own, all of my professors were on top of their fields, consistently on their way toward a higher place. In terms of knowledge and privileges one could obtain by learning, they were denizens of heaven who saw the sky as the limit of their achievement, the high-minded citizens whose livelihood was producing young scholars who wished to do the same. As one of these young scholars trained by such professors, I worked on the side of heaven, and as a former lover and a current friend of Michael's, I walked on the side of hell. By being with them both, I had chances to traverse the nearly infinite distance between the two realms, to envision myself soaring to the highest point in the big country and to watch myself fall into the lowest place. It was a golden opportunity for me to behold America.

Perhaps, I chose Michael to serve as a vehicle for my egotistic self-exploration. He was the Other in my life, a being to fulfill my longing to be human rather than divine, a presence to embody the hell side of America I desired to see. He brought out the smile in the Cry-Smile in me, the bright color in the drab world of the utopia-painter in me. He aroused the body suppressed under the academic mind I expressed. I thought maybe, I used him to discover myself and America, and I felt guilty. So driven by my ambition to experience everything life could offer me, I objectified a human being and made him in my mind into what I wished him to be.

Chapter 17
Pawns for Heroes

Sometimes, I found hell in the heaven of America, in the very magnanimous attitude that defined what America was to me. In relationships Americans formed with people from other countries, I saw an air of heroism going far beyond a sense of global responsibility, a subtle, but overt sense of superiority born of a savior complex. I had to experience the joy of meeting some very compassionate friends on campus and then the pain of watching these same friends patronize me and my fellow international students who they believed were in need of support. Perceiving themselves as the owners of the country and us as the honored foreigners, they tried to shower patronizing attention on us. They gave us what they thought were gifts for special guests, usually words of comfort coming with simple dinners and cheap wine. These Americans, mostly white males and females born and raised in America, represented and *were* members of the privileged group. They belonged to the side of heaven. But in their conceptions of me and my foreign friends, they became the hell in America, the opposite of how they saw themselves. In a way, the heaven they tried to show me and my lot was darker than the hell Michael showed me. Innocently transparent in his display of the hell, Michael was untouched by a patronizing attitude. But my privileged white male and female friends weren't so transparent. They were deceptive, disguising their sense of superiority—the core of their emotion toward foreigners such as myself—in what seemed to be compassionate humanity. I am in possession of many episodes, but I believe one will suffice.

It is about a white woman named Beatrice. Convinced of her own magnanimous altruism, Beatrice volunteered to befriend a woman she found to be disadvantaged for a successful career in American academia. This woman, Jenny, was a graduate student from an African tribal nation suffering from grave difficulties in her field because of a combination of racism and her own personal circumstances. Having traveled all the way to America from a village without electricity, she was truly remarkable in her courage and intellectual potentials. But culturally, she lived in too distant a past to reach the highly demanding standards of American higher education. She was unable to maintain the degree of academic rigor and speed that was required to sustain her graduate teaching assistantship because she and her husband remained faithful to their tribal custom in Africa and rarely practiced birth control. She became pregnant twice in a row, finding herself in need of the small academic stipend more than ever. Stuck in a mutually hostile situation, she and her department waged psychological warfare, pointing fingers at each other for what was destined to be an unsolvable conflict.

Jenny had a reason to believe her department was unfair. They refused to hire her until she went to the office of Affirmative Action on the campus and filed a complaint, until the head of the office put pressure on them to hire her. But they continued to watch her more closely than any of the other graduate teaching assistants and put her under severe performance anxiety. Her own performance was inadequate as well. Although she was initially as well-qualified as anyone else, she began to slack off. Her frequent absences, many of which were caused by her pregnancy, added to their suspicion. Eventually, she became incapable of confronting herself, and her professors became convinced that she couldn't deliver decent work. They told her that if she didn't improve, they would have to fire her, and she found herself begging them to keep her on the payroll. Although she managed to keep her job, her pride was injured.

To preserve her pride, Jenny entered a state of denial, telling herself that it was their racism, not her poor performance, that was responsible for their decision. She needed someone to agree with her, preferably a very white woman, to tell her that she was a victim of their racist scrutiny and their cultural prejudices. Imagine then, how grateful she must have been to find this very white woman in a trusted friend of hers, in a confidante who had always volunteered to offer an abiding sense of self-justification she thought she was entitled to. As a fellow graduate teaching assistant, Beatrice couldn't do anything for her friend in action. She was in no position to persuade her professors to be more lenient toward her friend or help her change her lifestyle to enhance her performance. All she could do was give her the words that absolved her. But hungry for any support she could get, Jenny welcomed it as a starving person would welcome food from anyone.

"It's not your fault," Beatrice told her. "It's their fault. They're being racist. They're persecuting you because you're not one of them." Beatrice was unaware of how self-serving she was, of how accustomed she was to re-creating a succession of opportunities to stay superior. As a victim of racism, Jenny—the one so beloved to her—was made into a convenient pawn for her own self-styled heroism. She was turned into an object of pity proving her own brave, but narcissistic convictions on justice and equality. She was the one who was there to show what a magnanimous champion she was in defending the rights of the poor victim. In reality, Beatrice needed Jenny as much as Jenny needed her. While the latter craved empathy for her poor performance because of the circumstances that lay beyond her control, the former hungered after the power to be the confessor and absolver, to be the one playing a superior giver over an inferior receiver. If she had seen herself as Jenny's equal, not as her superior, she would have advised her to find a way of both preserving her cultural heritage and adapting to her new country. She would have helped her become a student respected by her professors, a person equal to other graduate teaching assistants, and eventually a successful academician. But she never saw Jenny as her equal, and Jenny very conveniently chose to be seen as less than an equal. They remained locked in a relationship typical of well-intended racism and its eager recipient.

Beatrice and Jenny appeared to have a friendship strong enough to transcend racial boundaries, to be gloriously shielded from the nearly insurmountable cultural barriers. Sharing an abiding sense of moral outrage against the West, which they firmly believed was condescending to the rest of the world, the two women nevertheless reproduced the same giver-receiver dynamic they loved to condemn. I was familiar with their conversation, having participated in it more than once.

"We're looking for science and technology from the West. We don't want handouts," Jenny raged.

"The West wants to maintain its supremacy over you," Beatrice raged back. "It's afraid of you achieving equality."

"If you teach a person how to fish," I injected, "he'll catch a lot more fish."

"The West wants to give us fish, but they don't want to teach us the skills." Jenny complained.

"I see that," I agreed. "But Africans themselves have to be prepared to pick up the skills. To be prepared, they have to clean up the residue of European colonialism and regain their racial self-identity. They have to be ready to achieve equality before the West can grant it to them."

"It would be extremely difficult for them to regain a sense of self-identity after having been colonized by Europeans for centuries," Beatrice observed.

"That's true," I said. "It's nearly impossible for them to be able to tell what is African from what is European, but if they don't wake up from within themselves and construct a solid sense of self, they'll be dependent on the West forever. The West shouldn't just try to give them a sense of self-identity. They should try to help them in ways they can *get it from within*."

"How can they get it from within when their sense of self-identity has been so utterly crushed by European colonialism?" Beatrice insisted.

"As much as I recognize your point," I persisted, "Unless they make the effort to achieve what seems nearly impossible, Africans aren't going to be truly independent. They aren't going to discover who they are and be on their own. Only when they have enough sense of who they are, will they be capable of absorbing advanced science and technology from the West and make it their own."

"Are you sure you aren't asking too much from them?" Beatrice didn't relent. "You're asking them to gain self-confidence when they have nothing of themselves left. That would be just like asking victims to be responsible for the crimes committed against them."

"There's no doubt that they were victims of European colonialism," I kept going, forcing myself to be patient. It wasn't my style to be diplomatic and let go of what I believed was the truth. "But there are only two choices for them. Either, they should de-colonize themselves and be equal to the West or remain an object of pity. I say this because I respect Africans, not because I'm trying to blame the victim."

"Europeans made a mess of Africa and they have to clean it up," Beatrice went on, troubled. I had shifted the focus from Europeans onto Africans and accidentally pointed at the vacuum in her thinking. To Beatrice, who was ingrained in the concept of the white man's burden, my comments came as an intellectual shock. It was beyond her ability to include the colonized as the party with rights and responsibilities. To her, only the colonizers were entitled to exercise the rights and responsibilities and the colonized were little more than victims to be defended.

"It is true that Europeans have a responsibility," I said, suppressing the frown creeping onto my face. "But have you ever seen oppressors clean up their own act? History has shown us time and time again that the oppressed are always stuck with the mess left by their oppressors. What do you think, Jenny?" I turned to Jenny, hoping to get her perspective.

I thought, as an African woman, she should be more eager to talk than the two of us non-African women, but oddly enough, Jenny showed nothing but impassive silence. I gathered that she was too self-conscious to say anything, or maybe even hurt by my comments about Africans being responsible for themselves. Not knowing why she was so silent, I explained to her, "I said what I said because I believe in empowering Africans, because I have faith in their ability to be equal to the West. The West isn't going to take care of them." I kept talking until I felt she understood my true intentions, until I saw a faint smile in her face. I smiled back to her and Beatrice joined reluctantly. In a strict sense, they were both victims of the racism deeply embedded in the global hierarchy, reproducing what they hated in their personal relationship. Beatrice wasn't motivated by a white woman's conscience, but by her carefully camouflaged sense of superiority when she defended Jenny. Jenny sought a patronizing attitude from Beatrice, not a heartfelt desire to help another person. They had a mutually convenient friendship that brought comfort at the cost of the truth.

As everyone is guilty of what they condemn, I am afraid I, too, fell into the trap of being guilty of what I condemned. So hungry for emotional support, I sought some of the same morally corrupt exchanges from both Beatrice and Jenny, making myself into a willing participant in the savior-and-saved discourse. For the two or so years of my so-called friendship with them, I complained about my experience of racism to them as often as they complained to me about the victimization of Jenny. I was glad to be a recipient of the sympathy they doled upon me. Looking back, I could see why I finally turned away from the self-serving exchange with such a severity of emotion. Resolute to avoid the trap of the same false dialogue, I chanted for myself the one simple line that was going to function as a lifebuoy in my professional life, "Against all odds, I'm doing extremely well."

The turning point came when I was preparing for my doctoral coms. Fearful of my slow writing speed, I confided in Beatrice. But instead of telling me what I needed to hear, she told me what she thought I wanted to hear.

She said, "If your professors fail to consider the fact that you're not a native speaker and therefore can't deliver long enough essays, it would be their fault, not yours." I wanted to think I had heard her wrong. It occurred to me that if she was a true friend, she would encourage me by telling me what I should do, by telling me that I should make more efforts than anyone else.

"If I don't fulfill the standards I must fulfill," I returned, "they have the right to fail me. Whether I am a native speaker or not, that is irrelevant. I have to be as good as anyone else." Pausing to give her an opportunity to agree with me, I continued, "If they expect me to master what lies beyond my ability, they'd be unreasonable. They should understand that I can't control the errors I make when I occasionally use a wrong preposition, or get confused between plurals and singulars, or miss articles from time to time. Asian languages don't have any of these things. But I must demonstrate a level of composition to warrant a PhD." Listening to the disagreement in her silence, I made my decision. I was determined to keep a distance from her, to keep her from playing the game she played with Jenny.

Neither one of them knew what happened to me a few years later. After Jenny had gone back to her country, Beatrice was forced to minimize her contact with her, restricted to exchanging only letters over the distant continents. Beatrice also started a family while doing her graduate work, and she couldn't afford to stay in close touch with any of her friends. But under any circumstances, I kept a rigorous emotional distance from Beatrice. I wanted to be able to draw a clear line between my performance and others' racism – and to keep this clear line at all times.

Now, three decades later, I entertain the dream of exchanging an honest, and yet encouraging dialogue with Beatrice and Jenny. I fantasize about us getting together in Lawrence, Kansas for a reunion, where we would sit in Beatrice' living room as we used to as graduate students. I think it may be more than a dream, given how smart and sensitive we were. Although we weren't as honest as we should have been, we were aware enough to be concerned about global injustices and compassionate enough to believe in the rights of the disenfranchised. If I had grown enough to admit that I was a coward hiding what I truly thought, they might have matured enough to see the fallacy in their relationship. I don't think I would be surprised if we embrace each other when we meet again, and I don't think it would be a false hope if I entertain the possibility of sharing a more advanced, honest conversation. I don't have anything but my guesses to support such a possibility, but I hope it is a vision not far from reality. I think it might be true hope when I visualize the three of us together shoulder to shoulder, black, white, and yellow, all of us eager and alert, intent on finding solutions for the problems we used to discuss. As if in a photo, I visualize the three of us standing together, putting arms around each other's shoulders, laughing with trust and faith. In my mind's photo, Jenny is in the middle, the shortest of the three with a round facial contour enveloped by bobby-pinned, shoulder-length hair. Beatrice is on the left, the tallest with her trademark, elliptically shaped, dangly earrings long enough to cover her neck. I am on the right, the second tallest and the fattest with my usual long black hair flowing on my back.

Over five feet, nine inches tall with long, slender legs, Beatrice emanates the Western beauty that short-legged Asian women envy. She has the majestic, sublime physique that tiny Asian women wish they were able to buy. Considerably shorter and a bit more opulent than Beatrice, Jenny exudes the warmth of an earthy mother who envelops everyone around her. I am afraid I am a bit on the sharper side in terms of what my looks show, but I get a sense of comfort, thinking my eyes often shine with the mischief of a curious child examining a cuckoo's nest. I can diffuse the piercing intensity of my eyes with a funny face. With the photo of us three together in my mind, I think I would seek Beatrice and Jenny for advice when I am confronted by racism. Thirty years later, I think they would give me encouraging, but honest words to help me. It is with this faith in who they may be now that I recall an incident that happened to me twenty-eight years ago.

In May 1991, I applied for a teaching position offered by an on-campus program called the Howard Hughes Scholarship for Minority Students, and to my great surprise, I learned that Randy Kane, the Director of the Program, had decided to hire a much less qualified, white female graduate teaching assistant in my department over me.

"He flatters himself by thinking he's a sensitive white male," the Director's secretary said to me. So disturbed by his overt racism, she bothered to call me at home one night after ten o'clock. "I've spent enough time with him in the same office to be able to tell what motivates him. He's driven by heroism. He wishes people to think he's a great guy and uses his minority students as a pawn for his white male savior complex."

To make it worse, Randy used Jane as an excuse. By claiming that it was Jane who had led him to make the decision to turn me down, he attempted to absolve himself.

"When I asked Jane about your qualifications," Randy told me, "she gave me a long silence. She hesitated to give me a resounding yes." As I kept asking him what his specific questions regarding my qualifications were, and as he kept refusing to give me a concrete answer, repeatedly citing the privileged nature of the confidential conversation, he and I arrived at a dead end. He finally said, "She's a well-respected faculty on campus and I'd better go with her opinion."

"What makes you think she knows about my teaching?" I flung back. "She knows me only as a graduate student." I knew Randy was manipulating me by using Jane's supposedly long silence and her skeptical words. I was sure he had created her silence with a question she couldn't answer and the words he most likely put into her mouth, but I was too emotional on the phone to steer the conversation into a direction in which he had to face his own mind game. I was too hurt to confront him. I allowed myself to be led astray.

"If she doesn't know anything about my teaching, she shouldn't have said anything," I said angrily.

"I agree," he cried back in a loud voice, delighted to grab the chance to blame a third person. "Maybe," he suddenly intoned with falsetto sweetness, "she made the mistake of evaluating you as a teacher with her experience of you as a student in her classes."

"If my work wasn't good enough for her," I protested, knowing I was being played by him, "it's because she's too demanding. You have to sacrifice showers and dinners to be any good in her class."

"I heard she's enormously demanding. Is she married?"

"No, she's not. She's single."

"That's why she does nothing but work."

He tried to pin the blame on Jane by defining her as a workaholic single female. His secretary was right. Randy was a master manipulator. To absolve himself, he resorted to the tactic of questioning the emotional health of a single professional female who, according to him, had shown a reservation about my ability to teach. By leading me to the point where I was compelled to say that she knew nothing about me as a teacher and that her long silence about my teaching came from a lack of information, he placed the blame on her and away from himself. He tricked me into saying that Jane was too busy to get to know me as a teacher, being such a demanding workaholic all the time. I was emotionally hijacked by him into an irrelevant place where I found myself criticizing a beloved mentor of mine for an entirely irrelevant reason. I heard myself agreeing with him—so falsely—that a woman without a husband and children must find solace in work alone and that she often ends up misjudging a person because she has very little interaction with human beings. Knowing that Randy wouldn't have asked me such a sexist question about a male faculty, married or single, I went along with his line of conversation.

"I'm in a difficult position," he said. "I have to choose one of two equally qualified candidates."

"You're in a difficult position because you're unable to justify yourself," I flared up, my voice flying through the roof. I shouted to stop the tears gathering in my eyes. "You can tell I have twice as much teaching experience as she does. She studies 19th-century European women writers. She knows nothing of minority literature. I have plenty of background in minority women writers. Any fool can tell I'm much better equipped to teach minority students. Read our resumes."

My firm conclusion—that he was a white male unable to bring himself to practice what he loudly preached—was corroborated by four different individuals on campus, all of whom were known for their professional credibility and integrity.

"Randy Kane is in love with the idea that he's a crusader for justice," the Director of Affirmative Action said as Randy's secretary and I took turns in explaining what we had seen in him.

"Most people on campus think he's a great guy," the Director's assistant remarked, writing down the content of our meeting in stenography. "They don't have a clue who he truly is." She had heard about him from several of his minority students who saw through his lack of sincerity from the beginning.

The fourth person who shared our uniform opinion of him, surprisingly, was an English professor with whom I had worked closely as a graduate student and a teaching assistant. He was a senior faculty member named Joe in my department who also happened to be a jogging buddy of Randy's. Shortly after my meeting with the three university personnel in the Office of Affirmative Action, Joe invited me into his office to apologize.

"I made a stupid mistake," he admitted. "I recommended the other candidate to Randy. I gave him the consent he wanted. I was lazy enough not to think." Watching tears streaming down my face, he handed me a piece of the napkin on his desk and continued, "I hope you can forgive me. And I hope you recognize the difference between a consistent pattern of discriminatory behavior and a one-time error."

He treaded carefully with me, eschewing names of the persons and the specific nature of the incident. Familiar with my experience in the department, he was aware of the emotional chain reaction that could be caused in me by vocabulary such as "racism." By avoiding the word, he was far from trying to justify himself. Motivated by a genuine need to explain himself and hence to differentiate himself from his friend, he never attempted to claim that he had been a victim of anyone's manipulation. Acknowledging his share of wrongdoing, he wished to make it clear that I understood the self-evident fact – that my future had absolutely nothing to do with what Randy had done to me.

"You have just as much chance as a white woman to get a job at a reputable university," he assured me. "You may have to deal with the experience of being treated badly again, and you'll have doubts about the choices you made to live in another country. But I know you. You won't give up. Each time something happens to drag you down, you rebound like a tumbler. One goes down to rise back up. You'll fall to stand back up, and each time you stand back up, you'll be a stronger, more mature person."

Shortly after my pep talk with Joe, Randy left Kansas for a university in another state. From what I heard, he had irreconcilable problems with his minority students. It seemed that they were tired of being used as pawns for his heroism agenda and eventually took the problem to the attention of Affirmative Action. By selecting white male and female candidates for leadership positions in the office over far more qualified minority candidates, he repeatedly ignored his students' wishes to have role models from their own demographic. The white female guidance counselor he picked for his students, for example, didn't have a clue about her students' circumstances. As they came in to confide in her about their siblings who were into drugs, she would throw a pat answer at them such as "Get away from them and move into an apartment of your own." She didn't bother to recognize the fact that none of them could afford to rent an apartment of their own.

On another occasion, she and Randy invited a renowned African-American chemist to the campus to publicize the Howard Hughes Scholarship Program. She then asked one of her students to pick him up and take him out to lunch at the airport. She not only failed to recognize what a large expense this lunch was for this student but also neglected to ask if he had a reliable enough car to carry him out of town. Ever in love with his self-image as that of a heroic crusader for the disenfranchised, Randy kept hiring people like her. To him, whites were the rescuers and the minorities were the rescued. The truth? He had no intention of rescuing the poor minorities. They were to be kept where they were, to be in a place where they fulfilled the function of elevating whites such as himself into a position of supreme leadership. According to his secretary, Randy wanted to start a new career at another university with the same scholarship program he inherited in Kansas. He took the program to another institution where his history as a flawed hero wasn't known.

Let me make it clear that I recognize the good intentions on the part of these white heroes. They *were* magnanimous in their desire to help, in their commitment to human rights and in their dedication to giving to those less fortunate than they. Unique to the richest and the most powerful nation on earth, this generosity of theirs was unfaltering and unreserved. It was a sign of a big mind made possible by self confidence firmly rooted in the position of guaranteed security. When it was, however, bereft of the companionship of honest self-examination, it became a lonely spirit without its best friend, a lost soul without its better half. It turned into a force fulfilling the famous saying, "The road to hell is paved with good intentions." In the process of carrying their good intentions into action, those white heroes lost touch with their initial purpose and grew to harbor the notion that they were superior donors. Instead of being satisfied with the act of giving itself, they sought eulogies and opportunities to aggrandize themselves. No longer committed to helping their receivers achieve equality, they wanted to make them remain in the same place where they could continue to be generous givers from a higher place. Because they didn't analyze themselves, they couldn't go back to the initial purpose. They became mentally corrupt.

In Randy and Beatrice, I indeed saw a pair of large-hearted American citizens whose desire to reach out to those in need was sincere. But unfortunately, this desire was exercised with no self-analysis and was in the end wielded like a double-edged sword. Ultimately, it became the force of a reckless ego. Randy and Beatrice were big and remained big, while their minority students and African friend were small and remained small for the sake of their white benefactors. For them to be big, members of another race had to be small.

I have come to wonder if it is possible to be a white American and be entirely free from this "big American complex," and I have reached the conclusion that it *is* possible, having seen Jane and my professors. They weren't always successful, but they showed me the possibility by making themselves indispensable for my academic success. To help me be their *equal* someday, they sometimes went out of their way. Once, after I had missed an appointment with her, Jane called me at home to find out if I was sick, and as I told her I had forgotten and apologized, she laughed and said I should give her my brother's phone number and address in Korea in case something happened to me. Another time, upon seeing me straggling along the campus from exhaustion, she took me out to dinner to encourage me. She told me to endure. She asked Leo, her best friend in the department who lived close to me, to promise that he would do the same for me whenever he had a chance, and Leo kept his promise. On his way home one day, he came by my apartment to tell me that Professor Hall gave me an extension for the final paper I owed him. Leo had intervened on my behalf and asked Professor Hall to give me more time because I was slower than native speakers. He went beyond the call of duty to look out for me. Jane and Leo were dedicated to my success.

If I claim that these two were never tempted to play the big Americans, I would be denying they were human. I am certain they were just as vulnerable as anyone else, but there is no doubt in my mind that they were highly successful in resisting the temptation. From their behavior, I could tell they never stopped analyzing themselves, that this unceasing self-analysis kept them safe from the mental corruption contaminating so many white Americans. I called them the best Americans because they could be best friends with this ability to analyze themselves.

I don't want to divide white Americans into two groups, one capable of self-analysis and the other incapable. There are many shades between these two opposite ends, and I know how to differentiate them. The differences are in the degrees as some are more capable than others, and I have met many individuals who fought themselves with vigor and honesty. I would like to believe that these individuals were my friends, most of whom I met in the university towns where I studied and taught. Although the desire to be big by making everyone else small never entirely disappeared from their thinking—because it was so deeply rooted in their subconscious—they were courageous enough to admit it and make efforts to change. My friend Melanie was one of them.

"You know the couple who lives next door to you?" I asked her. "I made the mistake of entering their backyard as a shortcut to your house, and they stuck their heads out of the window to yell at me. They could have just told me gently, but they were so defensive and paranoid."

"They're fine people," Melanie cried, suddenly flying into a defensive fit. It shocked me to hear such a high-pitched tone from her.

I remained dumbfounded and she went on relentlessly, "This is the first house they've owned. They're naturally worried. You shouldn't be prejudiced against them."

I understood what she was doing with her loud defense of the couple. Because they were African American, Melanie felt she had to defend them in haste. She surmised that they needed her to rush forward with a cry of support because they were vulnerable to racism in the hands of any non-black person. According to her, the African-American couple had to be helped by open-minded, non-prejudiced white citizens such as herself, being unable to explain themselves in the soft-spoken, civilized manner expected by members of the white middle class group such as herself. I was entirely certain that were they white, she would have never defended them with that much zeal. I knew that she would have laughed with me at their overactive manners and agreed with me for defining them as being "weird." Melanie was being a big person protecting the small couple.

"I didn't say anything about being prejudiced against them or against anyone," I returned. "I just thought they were rather strange. To me, they're just human beings who deserve to be described as they are." I didn't forget to laugh. "You want to prove how unprejudiced you are. If you were truly unprejudiced, you wouldn't have to prove how unprejudiced you are. Are you sure you're not depriving them of their humanity by treating them as citizens dependent on your loud defense? Are you sure you're not reducing them to being a powerless lot who needs your support? You seem to be a hero trying to protect them from being victims of racism. But to me, they're just *people*, period. They're just human beings as weird as I am, just like you and me. They don't need anyone's defense."

I was as straightforward as she in my tone, and from then on, Melanie and I became closer friends. She took my challenge as an opportunity to see herself, and I accepted her as a mirror of myself. I was no longer just her Korean friend as she was no longer just my white American friend. We became eager students and teachers for each other, a pair of individuals who lovingly embraced each other's merits and faults. It was our honesty that enabled us to transcend our national boundaries. Melanie and I formed a relationship that became an example I sought from my peers, a measurement against which I was to compare my so-called friendships with others. Whenever I had to decide who to keep in my life and who to let go, I went back in my mind to the conversation I had shared with Melanie about her neighbor, and those who showed her ability to agree with me became my friends while those who didn't failed to be.

Fortunately, I lived in university towns, where open-minded dialogues were encouraged more than they were in other parts of America. University towns are sanctuaries where *ideas* thrive, where the ugly reality of racism, if not entirely eliminated, is questioned, condemned, and corrected. Now, I live in Murfreesboro, Tennessee, a small town with a large regional university, and I occasionally see men with long ponytails and some openly gay and lesbian students holding hands on the campus. It is in a region where the KKK is active, where the Klan holds its convention semi-regularly, also where my two beloved lesbian friends have been practically married for half a century. Murfreesboro with its university made it possible for this diversity to flourish in the middle of the region that houses the country's darkest corner. As America never stops astonishing me in its ability to practice the extremes in such a short distance from each other, America never stops amazing me in its capacity to show so much good and bad in such a short time. From Murfreesboro, it takes just ten minutes to drive to the village where the Klan holds its conventions, and just fifteen minutes to get to the house where my lesbian friends live.

Kansas wasn't the only state where white heroes thrived on the backs of darker-skinned minorities. It wasn't the only state where there were minorities who tried to justify themselves by blaming whites whom they conveniently categorized as being racist, or where whites were motivated by the heroic desire to speak for minorities whom they defined as being unable to speak for themselves. By the time I had settled in Kansas, I had been to New York and California, where I had chances to witness the same pattern of race hierarchies. In these states, where there was more diversity and therefore less racism, where race relations were undoubtedly more open and progressive, I met people who were engaged in the typical relationship of the generous owner and the persecuted guest in need of the owner's defense. I saw little difference between the Midwestern state and these coastal states in terms of the underlying basis for the interaction between whites and minorities. Although less in numbers, these supposedly more open states weren't at all free of the mind game between the superior defender and the inferior victim. In essence, they were the same as Kansas.

As I portray what happened between Beatrice and Jenny, between Randy and his minority students, and between Melanie and I, I do not intend to single out Kansas. I am using Kansas only as an example. Having lived in the state for over a decade, I had more chances to see the typical race pattern there that was prevalent all over the United States. To be fair, Kansas wasn't better or worse than any other state except that the race pattern was a bit more frequently displayed. Surrounded with a nearly all-white population, Kansans in 1991 probably didn't receive much push from the outside to examine their traditional attitude. As I now go back to the past, I make it clear that it is the *issue* that I am trying to bring up here. I am far from interested in blaming anyone.

Looking now at the progress my alma mater made since I left the school in 1994, I am rather proud. In 2019, Kansas University is an incredibly diverse school with a student body representing many countries of the world, and its staff, faculty, and administrators are just as ethnically varied. In twenty-five years, the university achieved an astonishing degree of progress, a degree of change that would have been impossible without the constant will and enthusiasm on the part of everyone involved. Kansas University proved itself to be an institution embodying the best of the United States, the country second to none in its ability to make fast changes.

It would be a lie to claim that all of my sad memories at KU are gone. Toward the end of my graduate studies there, I started to develop symptoms of chronic fatigue syndrome – the severe illness that put me on disability many years later. Just like the last straw that broke the camel's back, the racism I had to endure became like the last rock that was dropped upon my nearly dead body. As I was sinking under the boulder-heavy weight of the work, I became unable to move. Stuck with the consequences of my experiences in the past, I can't by any means bring myself to say I am free from what happened. As long as my memory isn't free, I am not free – not entirely anyway.

But twenty-five years is a long time, and my feelings aren't as raw and intense as they were before. The cliché that time heals all wounds has carried me to the point at which I can now replace my sad memories with the sense of pride I feel toward my alma mater. As hope is my number one creed—and as my alma mater has given me plenty of reasons to feel an abundant hope—I believe I am honestly motivated to say what I say. I believe I am writing for the purpose of celebrating the progress it has made. As I can be delighted by the distance, I have travelled only by looking back at the starting point, I can be pleasantly surprised by the present my alma mater has reached only by going back to the past.

I would be less than honest if I am not open about my personal reason for such a faith of mine. As a woman who called the United States her husband country, I had to envision a country practicing what it preached. I had no choice. I couldn't go on living in the United States as a married woman couldn't go on living with her husband unless she could give herself the hope that he would eventually grow to fulfill what she saw in him. By working so incessantly hard that I had to watch BBC world news with my eyes closed, I moved my mentors to work hard for me, and by working hard for me, they in turn gave me a good reason to believe in my future. Because I was the good wife proving how worthy I was of my husband, my mentors proved to be the good in-laws ushering me into a firm place in my husband country. For my own survival, I had no choice but to believe in America. For my own sanity, I had no choice but to foster the hope that America would eventually turn out to be the place I had imagined. How could I have lived if I didn't?

For my own emotional wellbeing, I wish to replace my lingering anger and bitterness with optimism. By keeping up a positive outlook about the future of my alma mater and my mentors and friends there, without whom I wouldn't have the niche I now have in my husband country, I can maintain a bright vision for my own life to come. I have more hope for America than I do for any other country on earth exactly because race issues are always so much more serious in this country than they are in any other. If my husband country didn't try to implement racial justice more actively than any other country on earth, it wouldn't be nearly as loud as it has been and as it is now. *The very fact that there is so much more noise about racism here is the very sign that it has more capacity than any other country to house so many different peoples and cultures.* By reinforcing my own personal faith—my own personal faith that tomorrow will be better than today—I try to paint an optimistic picture of my remaining life. With or without evidence, I will keep my hope alive, just as I will brush my teeth tonight even if I know I may die tomorrow morning. With evidence my alma mater has given me so far, I see no reason not to visualize a country in which the shadows of the past ironically have become fertile ground for new possibilities. Descartes said, "I think; therefore I am." I say, "I hope; therefore, I live."

Chapter 18
My Body's Revenge

With my ability to love human beings as intact as ever, I dashed ahead into my dissertation. With Jane's agreement, I chose Asian-American women's autobiography as my topic, of which there were altogether seventeen volumes, including two published by a university press and fifteen by commercial presses in New York. To my great disappointment, I had to exclude Korean-American women's autobiography because there was only one that I respected, and one wasn't enough to offer any information about the tradition established by a group. The other two I discovered were little more than a pair of one-dimensional anti-communist manifestos that Joe McCarthy would have approved. They were written by South Korean women who were known for having pandered to the extreme right-wing dictator handpicked by the United States in 1945. As much as I acknowledged—and respected, believe it or not—that they had the right to promote any ideological beliefs they held, I was severely turned off by the degree of their anti-communism.

Neither of them showed a bit of awareness of how complex history was, why communism and democracy had to fight for hegemony in the Korean Peninsula, and how and why the extreme right-wing dictators used Joe McCarthy-style anti-communism to keep South Koreans united against North Koreans. I would have been as equally repelled by North Korean women, if I had found any, as they would have likely chanted blind anti-South Korean communism perpetuated by the extreme left-wing dictator in North Korea. Lack of knowledge about the historical complexities, by whoever it was shown, failed to engage my interest. So, I was forced to include only Chinese- and Japanese-American women's autobiographies, most of which demonstrated some level of historical awareness. At least none of them displayed the kind of rabid anti-communism or anti-democracy that would have assassinated the essence of literature.

Characteristically, I chose to write about lesser known Asian-American women authors left out of the canon of American literature. Obviously to me, these authors were of more importance than their famous counterparts because, coming from different backgrounds culturally and historically, they created their own narrative contents and forms that were necessary to achieve their own unique literary purposes and goals. Deliberately, they failed to fulfill the critical standards applied by white male and female scholars of American literature. Instead of the typical "me and my environment" narrative consistent with the theme of self-reliance, these lesser-known authors formed a tradition emphasizing a people's journey on the whole. They made themselves into voices not only for themselves but also for their races and their native countries, offering their personal histories as mirrors for the collective histories of their groups. Although my authors did create strong, independent heroes unafraid of challenges, they were more interested in employing these heroes as a medium representing the historical forces facing a people. They were no American heroes, no lone rangers luxuriating in being alone in wildernesses, no solos confronting the vast, hostile environments to be conquered with solitary human willpower. None of them were placed in a hierarchical relationship with the environment, be it nature or civilization. All of them saw themselves as being unique, but not as being special enough to master and conquer anything or anyone other than themselves.

I chose to exclude from my emphasis renowned Chinese-American authors such as Jade Snow Wong and Maxine Hong Kingston, two of the Asian women whose autobiographies were picked out of the many of their group by white audiences, by critics who overtly and sometimes excessively prefer a book about a lone hero's rise above her hostile environment. They were to be discussed by me only briefly, the two together in one short section in the chapter given to second-generation Chinese-American women's autobiographies. While deserving the acclaim they received from the large number of white audiences, Kingston's *The Woman Warrior* and Wong's *Fifth Chinese Daughter* were to be pushed aside to the sidelines because they were made famous partly because of their self-portraits appealing to white audiences. They represented themselves as self-reliant heroes who alone departed the culturally backward multitude and succeeded against all odds to discover themselves. To be fair, I must acknowledge that Kingston's *The Woman Warrior* was much more sophisticated than Wong's *Fifth Chinese Daughter.* A rich narrative tapestry with character and historical complexities and with a range of components making an excellent autobiography – such as dense allusions, powerful metaphors, and myths telling of the human craving to be immortal, *The Woman Warrior* indeed was worthy enough to be called a masterpiece. But exactly because it was a renowned masterpiece, I decided to leave it aside from my focus.

I wanted to explain little known works by little known writers because I wanted to discover another American literature that was little known in the canon. As I habitually sought another America that was within the America that was familiar to me, I always sought another group of Americans who were unsung by the Americans who were familiar to me. I found it infinitely more interesting to talk to a farmer on his tractor in a small town of two-hundred people in Kansas than to talk to the head of agriculture in the state governor's office. The farmer on the tractor, who could tell me about the alliance between American communism, the labor movement, and the farmers' coop, was one of those people who lived in another country that was within the big country. He was one of those who showed me the many Americas – the many Americas for which I was forever searching.

I used my tendency to be on the frontiers, my very American lifestyle, to represent the authors whose narrative goal was exactly the opposite of solitary self-reliance. I used my self-reliant individualism to explain my authors' collective narrative purpose, my lonely independence to describe their commitments to the community as well as the self, and my love of being alone to portray their union with others and themselves. I was thrilled to get lost in the authors unexplained by anyone before, whose tradition was unidentified because they weren't studied by anyone with the intention of illuminating the narrative commonalities established by them. As I liked to wander on the road in my big old clunker, to find myself in the middle of the vast wheat fields of Kansas without an inkling of where I was, and to find my way back somehow by driving around aimlessly, I enjoyed roaming in the wilderness of literary America that was yet to be mapped by critics.

But make no mistake by assuming it was all joy with no pain. Actually, it was far more pain than joy, as anyone who has written a dissertation would eagerly agree. What made it more difficult than—and different from—

anything I had ever done was the loneliness that went into the work. Work for any terminal degree, whether it was an MD, PhD, JD, or any other titles, was hard, but there was nothing that demanded so much war with oneself as a doctoral dissertation. Sitting at the desk alone for several hours every day, staring at the blank computer screen reflecting nothing but one's own face, was an excruciating act of self-oppression that couldn't be matched by any other work. It wasn't comparable to any other labor that required one to watch the faces of others during the process. Medical interns and residents, who had to observe a patient in an emergency for thirty-six hours in a row without a break, seemed to me to have a more endurable job. They had chances to talk to other human beings in their space. Their work was certainly exhausting, but their never-ending hours appeared to be free from the tortuous loneliness that went into facing the mirror of one's own face until it was replaced by words. "They make more money in the end, too," I grumbled. "At the end of all that training, English PhDs make a pittance for those lonely years." I laughed, adding the truth with a hurried sense of humor, "It was my choice to be a poor English professor. I'm a born masochist."

To me, freedom was severe self-discipline that yielded an outcome after what seemed an eternity of unrewarding work. I had always known that. Although freedom and discipline seem to be opposites, it is impossible for the two to exist without each other. I had no right to complain. I was just so unspeakably tired, beginning the final stage of the graduate work that had constantly demanded my sanity. Still slower than most of my peers in terms of my writing speed, I was again faced by a long stretch of time to be filled by hundreds of written pages. Again, I was going to be locked away for another span of time during which I was to spend twice as much time as any of my peers on writing the same amounts. Again, I was going to have to spend a whole half-hour to find a single word. "You have to finish what you started," I preached to the face—my own face—that stared back at me from the blank computer screen. "If you stop now, the tower you've tried so hard to build will crumble overnight."

The sorrow of being stuck with my computer was inextricably linked with the mirth of venturing out into another America within America. I deliberately geared the two emotions up to the highest point in an effort to make them clash against each other. By being immersed in the mirth one moment and plunging into the sorrow the next, I successfully generated a nuclear reactor of intellectual energy inside me that I was highly skilled at creating. As an ABD, I had two things helping me to cope. I had the big old clunker that could carry me out to the road to get lost, and I had a cheap stereo with a pair of used speakers to give me the sounds of the music that embodied the same mirth and sorrow as mine. Mahler was a poor Jew who was forever a Bohemian in Austria, a country well-known for its anti-Semitism. Rachmaninoff, a white Russian forced to leave his homeland by the Communist Revolution, was an eternal vagabond in America, the country to which he fled to continue to make a living as a composer and a pianist. I flattered myself, thinking that Gustav Mahler and Sergei Rachmaninoff were elegant, self-styled exiles whose melodies expressed the same state of existence in which I found myself in another country.

Mahler was my love. In his symphonies, I believed I heard what I liked to call heavenly melodies of the one whose life was defined by the ever-spinning vortex of clashing emotional forces. I thought he had a nuclear reactor in himself that was just like mine, a furnace of intellectual energy traversing the extreme distance between merrymaking and mourning. I hearkened to the inner will in a series of proud strikes against the external forces threatening to engulf him. Just like me, he was on a duel-course with his environment, sad about being so lonely, and yet exhilarated about being so alone in the unknown wilderness. Just like me, he was looking for a country within a country, writing music to seek an Austria that was within the Austria as he knew it. My hungry ears believed that his symphonies were expressions of his wishes for a country that was as good to Jews as it was to Austrians. They were songs of an insider celebrating the country that gave a Jew an opportunity to rise to be the director of Vienna Hofper, but they were also the cries of an outsider grieving the country's demand that he convert to Roman Catholicism from Judaism. Austria was another America to me, a country that forced a competent, eager citizen to negate her cultural heritage and yet refused to treat her as one of their own. "Was and will I ever be treated as one of them by those white Americans who believe in their bones that they are the owners of this country?" I wondered. "Was Mahler ever treated as one of them by those Austrians who believed they were the only true Austrians?" Whenever I found myself looking for a word that didn't come to me, I paid attention to the dissonance in the Jewish Austrian, the lonely artist who embraced the very adversity that made him who he was. He was the one who dedicated himself to the alien turf that made him so sad and happy at once. How I wept at the beginning of the fourth movement of his Symphony Number 5! I felt I could touch the steely streak of the tune's sadness that drilled into my heart, splitting it into two pieces! How I laughed, listening to my fingers on the computer dancing with the beat of the third movement of the same Number 5! Both movements were melodies singing about loneliness, about the journey that created an outcome that was an enlivening joy. They were about the process of dying to live, about my life in America.

As I broke down into a death-like depression, I shouldn't have been surprised. I should have known that I couldn't keep burning up energy with very little gas in the tank. Like a giant car without a drop of oil, I collapsed one night after a trip to the emergency room at Lawrence Memorial Hospital, unable to get out of bed the next morning. I fell into a zombie-like state for days, and instinctively, I knew I was going to live in death for a long time, long enough to make me feel tempted to believe that I would be better off dead than alive. There was no melodramatic hyperbole in my fear and in my diagnosis of my own condition. I knew how severely I had overused my body. For several months in a row, I routinely had forced it to work for thirty hours in a row without a minute of shuteye, to go on starving all day long without a decent meal, and to sit on the cheap wooden chair without any back support for a whole day. My body was saying no more to the cheap hamburgers, to the mountain of junk food I consumed, to the popcorn, the French fries, the potato chips, the baked potatoes, the peanut butter sandwiches, and to the canned beans. It cried for eight hours of sleep per day, for three regular meals with enough grains, vegetables, and fish, for one day off a week, and for a daily hour-long walk.

"Do not abuse me as you have abused your eyes," my body warned me. "Look at what happened to your eyes. You should be grateful they didn't go out on you entirely." Then, it sneered at me, "You still have some of that female vanity left in you. You want to wear contact lenses because glasses make you look like a geek. If you want to look feminine, you'd better treat your eyes better, so that your vision won't get any worse than it is. Even now, your contacts can give you only half of the vision you have with your glasses, and if your eyes get worse, they may not even give you that. You may have to settle with glasses permanently. If the astigmatism on your left eye gets worse, you'll have to say goodbye to contacts forever."

"I do want to continue to wear contact lenses for the rest of my life," I cried back fiercely, entering another one of those lengthy dialogues with myself. "I want to be a *woman* and a *scholar* both! I will not have only one or the other!" I paused to declare to my body, relentless in the silent apartment. I was talking to myself like a pathologically insane woman, "Last night, you saw me drive back alone from the emergency room at Lawrence Memorial Hospital with one of my eyes patched up by a doctor. I bought a toric lens to correct the astigmatic vision of my left eye that scratched the surface to create a scar until I could no longer keep it open. I drove to the emergency room to receive instant treatment. Because I wanted to look feminine with better vision, I bought the toric lens with an irregular surface and I wore it for several days. Although I felt pain in my left eye, I just wanted to think it was in the process of getting used to a new kind of lens. I was being foolish. I refused to admit my eyes were getting angry, overwhelmed by the desire to look like a woman whose beauty was kept intact despite her scholarly endeavors. I was being greedy. I wanted to have beauty and power, beauty of the body and power of the mind. I wanted to live the life of a whole person. What is wrong with that?"

Tired of talking to myself, I plopped down on the couch in the living room. I found myself exploding with anger at what I always believed to be one of the most serious injustices of the world. "What is wrong with women wanting to live as *women* and *scholars*? Men are not only allowed but also encouraged to live as *men* and *scholars* both. Look at the Korean male graduate students at Kansas University. While they study to pursue their terminal degrees, their wives cook well-balanced meals for them, raise their children for them, wash their clothes for them, clean their houses for them, do grocery shopping for them, and type and proofread their papers for them, too. They don't have to abuse their bodies as I do, they don't have to overuse their eyes as I do, and they don't have to make the sacrifices that have to be made by women like me. At the end of their graduate work, they go back home with their wives and children, to be welcomed by colleges and universities that are eager to hire men with PhDs from American universities, to be celebrated as successful career and family men by their loved ones and strangers alike. They don't have to lose anything to have all they want."

I went on, "Korean patriarchy is so grossly unfair. It gives men love and work both without one bit of hesitation. But it gives only one or the other to women. Women have to give up love for work or work for love. We have to put an end to being women to have careers or we have to put an end to our careers to keep the woman in us. Why should I be rebuked for wanting to keep my feminine beauty by wearing contacts? Why should I be punished for wanting to remain a beautiful woman? Why should I be penalized for wanting to preserve my chances to meet a man who'd be impressed by my feminine beauty as well as my scholarly intelligence? Why should I be condemned for being greedy when I want the same thing a man has? Those Korean men who victoriously go back home with their PhDs and their wives and children – they don't have my ability, they don't have half of my competence, will power, and intelligence. None of them ever speak English as well as I do, none of them taught American students as a graduate teaching assistant as I did, and none of them wrote a dissertation as good as mine is going to be. Why should they be given all the privileges that will never be granted to me and women like me?" I kept going back and forth between the rage and the fear of driving back home from the hospital alone. I rambled on in a lost sequence, "I knew driving with one of my eyes patched up was dangerous, but I had no choice. Most of my friends had gone home for the winter holidays, and the couple of friends I had in town were busy trying to prepare for Christmas dinner with their loved ones."

It was on Christmas eve that I checked myself into the emergency room from the burning pain in my left eye, and it was on the same Christmas eve that I was discharged. I felt I had no right to call any of my friends in town to ask them to come and pick me up. I had given none of them a chance to nurture a friendship. Whenever they called, I said I would call them back later and never called them back. I just kept saying we would get together once the semester was over, but I found myself working on my dissertation twelve hours a day seven days a week. I couldn't afford to slow down because the break was the only time during which I could devote myself full time to writing. Because my writing speed was still slower than anyone else's I knew, I had to make the utmost use of every minute available to me. I never returned half of the friendship my friends gave me so kindly. I even had to sacrifice the holidays everyone celebrated. What right did I have to show up at their Christmas dinner?

I paused, thinking of something else. "But I'd be lying if I didn't admit another reason for why I didn't go to any of their Christmas dinners. I didn't want to go because I didn't want to be with my friends' families. One of them,

Connie, invited me to her home where her entire family, including her parents, her two children, her sister and brother-in-law and her second cousin, were going to get together. I knew I'd be reminded of my missing family and would cry all the way home. I didn't want to be reminded of how alone I was. I remember how I cried when I saw a photo of my nephew, Big Brother's son. I had secretly nicknamed him the "Korean cherubim" because he was so absolutely adorable. My father had sent it to me with a letter in which he asked me to buy an extra-thick blanket to stay warm against the brutal Kansas winter. He had also enclosed a photo of the whole family sitting together around the dinner table for a lunar New Year's eve, with all the women and men dressed in colorful traditional Korean costumes to celebrate the time-honored tradition. There in the picture were Mother and Father, Big Sister and her husband, their son and daughter, Big Brother and his wife and their son, the "Korean cherubim," Less Big Brother and his wife and their little girl, and Little Sister, the young spinster living with Mother and Father. I didn't dare to have it framed or display it in my apartment."

I continued without a break, "I was afraid I'd be homesick enough to call them on the phone and break down in tears. So, I placed the family photo in a corner of the closet, next to the three faces of the young bride, to take it out only when I needed to be reminded of the precious truth that there was nothing my family wished for more than my success. I owed success not only to myself but also to my family. I didn't want to jeopardize my young bride's smile, to have the steely stoicism melt down and reveal the easily weeping heart in me. Like the young wife, I had to keep the sorrow hidden behind the mask of joy."

As if in a crazy circle of thought, I went back to the original point, "Driving back alone in the night, on Sixth Street, I lost my sense of direction for a second. Trying to make a left turn, I hopped over a low barricade at the corner and drove on it for a minute or so. Then, I swerved forty-five degrees to get back into the right lane, forcing the car behind me to come to a jolting stop. I thank Mother Nature for the driver's fast action. Had he been a poor driver like me, we would've had a crash on Christmas eve."

In the still of the night, I imagined a scene: I was a Korean male graduate student being driven to and back from the emergency room, with my wife pouring words of loving encouragements to me, "Your hard work won't go unnoticed. Your wife and children appreciate your sacrifices, and I'm sure your future employer will as well. I'm certain your efforts will pay off."

How instantly I went back to cursing my family that I loved and my country that I missed so! My family and my country were the ones who made women such as myself lonely exiles. They were the ones who rewarded men such as the Korean graduate students at Kansas University with the glory of going back home with terminal degrees, flanked by loving wives and charming children even though they demonstrated a fraction of my competence. It was difficult for me to resist the temptation of tearing the family photo into shreds, to abstain from the urges to step on it repeatedly until it eroded into dust. I wanted to keep the picture of the Korean cherubim because he was innocent, having nothing to do with the Korean patriarchy that I hated so. I didn't tear up the family photo because I was afraid I would regret it later. I knew I would look at it again, that I would *need* it again to remember how much they loved me – and how much I loved them.

My body wreaked such vengeance upon me. I wished, over and over again, an armed robber would break into my apartment and shoot me once in the head to put an end to my miserable life. I thought if this happened, it would free my name from the ignominy of suicide. It would make me a eulogized hero, a law-abiding, hard-working citizen innocently gunned down by a callous killer. It would also protect me from being known as a loser who was unable to endure the difficulty of graduate work and loneliness facing an international student. Lastly, it would lessen the pain for my family. Although grief-stricken, they would at least have the comfort of knowing death wasn't my choice. They would be able to preserve positive memories of me. But I knew my body wouldn't be satisfied with such a short revenge. It was bent on making me suffer for as long as it could, determined to receive better treatment from me. I remembered an episode about a man who wished to die. He walked over to a cliff but couldn't throw himself over into the ravine. His body resisted. *That sounds like my body*, I thought. *It will refuse to die unless it's absolutely ready.*

I wrote up a short instruction for myself, "Do not forget to eat," and picked up a thumbtack to put it on the wall in the living room. When I wanted to die, my body wanted to live. When I wished I had no appetite, my body became hungry, and when I lay all day and all night long in bed, my body was ready to move. My body was afraid to fall asleep, fearful of facing the dead woman in my nightmares. It didn't want to see her body stirring in death. I had to find a way of giving my body what it wanted. I had to move.

But I couldn't move. I did fall asleep to see the dead woman in the sumptuous house. I couldn't run from her, screaming for what seemed forever, waking up to the pitch-black darkness of the small, one-bedroom apartment. When I, after several minutes of hard breathing and sweating, managed to stand to turn the lights on in my bedroom, I stared at my bed for a good moment to make sure she wasn't there. Overwhelmed by the terror, I tried sleeping with the ceiling lights on in the bedroom, but unable to fall asleep, I left the lights on in the living room while I slept. Maybe, I hoped, if I slept with a bright space in my apartment, I would be able to summon my dreams of No Name State and beat the nightmares. In my dreams, I thought I would be able to see myself living in a country where I didn't have to die to live, where I didn't have to collapse from depression because of so many years of neck-breaking work. In my dreams of No Name State, I wouldn't have to kill myself over and over again because I was an immigrant and a woman of color. But the dream didn't come, not even once. The nightmare was so crushing that I couldn't have the dream. The depression was so overwhelming that I didn't even have the energy to summon the faintest light.

After a month of continuous lying in bed, during which I saw the dead woman in my nightmares several times, I finally made an appointment with my psychiatrist at the university hospital. I told her Prozac didn't work for me any longer, and she prescribed Zoloft instead and took me off Klonopin for a while. Having dis-enrolled from the dissertation and teaching hours for the spring semester, I was free from the pressure of facing deadlines for a few months and could dispense with the medication for anxiety. But I needed to stay on with an anti-depressant, a new one because the old one had lost its effectiveness after a couple months of daily use.

January of 1992 marked the beginning of a series of severely debilitating and prolonged periods of clinical depression that assaulted me on and off for decades. Having suffered from the amorphous demon since I was a small child, clinical depression was familiar to me. I could even say that it was my lifetime companion through early adulthood and middle age. But my depression in America was wholly another kind. In America, I was alone not only emotionally but also physically, with nothing but Mahler's Symphony Number 5 as a close companion. I had friends, but friendships in a university town, as exciting and inspiring as they were, were transient and fleeting. It was difficult for graduate students to form permanent relationships because most of them were constantly moving to other parts of the country or going back to their native countries from temporary visits. Upon returning to Lawrence, Kansas in July 1989, immediately after my father's death, I was overwhelmed by a sense of being forlorn, learning that five of my friends were gone to other universities and to their home countries. They weren't my best friends, but the campus with all of them gone seemed so empty and desolate, and I felt cursed by the nature of university life. Gathering people from all over the world in a short time, a university could be a magical place, but dispersing them just as fast, it could be fickle with little continuity.

As the new medication kicked in, I started to feel better. Slowly but surely, it began to lift the emotional blackout that had seized me during the month of January, taking away the crying spells one by one. As the dead woman in my nightmare came back to me less often, I found myself eating more, and with less forced appetite. I went out more often, driving my big old clunker around all the more aimlessly than ever. With plenty of apple juice in the trunk of the car, I could always pretend to be Hemingway high on vodka. "He had severe clinical depression," I said, back to the usual pep talk with myself. "But he committed suicide, and I won't. That's the difference between him and I." I laughed that loud laughter of mine, realizing what an egomaniac I was to compare myself to Hemingway. But on second thought, I changed my mind. "I must have the courage to dream," I declared. "I must have the gumption to be an egomaniac."

In the Spring of 1992, my depression set a standard for me. For decades to come, it was to be used as the norm against which all other long-term spells of depression were measured and evaluated. As a person with memories of a near-death experience isn't afraid of facing another brush with death as long as it isn't as serious as the previous one, I was no longer afraid of having another bout of clinical depression so long as it wasn't as severe as the one that hit me that January. It is an experience etched in my mind forever, setting a record of the deepest point to which I could fall. In a way, it helped me be prepared for subsequent bouts during which I found myself falling to an unfathomable depth. Because the abyss where I remained during that brutally cold month in Kansas was so deep, I was fairly certain that I would never find myself in the same place again. As another bout of depression assaulted me in January two years later, and as another one and yet another one took possession of me in the years to come, I could always go back in my memory to that one in January

1992 and find the current one smaller and hence bearable. My nightmares became less of a nightmare from then on.

As my nightmares came less often, my dreams of No Name State came more often. Whenever I found myself in a bout with depression, I saw myself in No Name State, my ability to summon the light growing stronger as the power of the darkness turned more severe. After that fateful January 1992, after I had experienced the sheer terror of succumbing to a total darkness, I learned how not to forget to grab the light. From then on, even in the midst of a vicious depression, I was able to manage to have my dreams of No Name State dashed against the nightmare of the dead woman, to replace her with the living woman in my mind. The living woman was able to cancel out the dead woman whenever the dead woman returned. The two kept coming to me alternately to put me through the two opposing pictures of me, to send me the one I feared and then to give me the one I welcomed. They worked to generate a nuclear reactor in me, to make me live on with the energy rising from the reactor.

Chapter 19
A True Believer

In March of 1992, about a month after I had resumed my habit of aimless driving on the edge of town, I got the news that I was going to be honored at the department banquet that year. The news couldn't have come at a better time because I needed encouragement more at that particular time in my life than I ever had before. I was surprised and honored because as far as I knew, there were many graduate students who seemed more qualified than I was. Kansas University was no Yale or Berkeley, but the English Department at the university had its share of brilliant graduate students who deserved to look forward to obtaining a job at a major institution of higher education in America. Most of the graduate students who had applied for the awards were top candidates in future job markets. They were well-published with plenty of impressive records in attending nationally renowned scholarly conferences and workshops. Some of them had served for many years as editors for the best journals in the Midwest in criticism and creative writing, active in helping talented new writers be published in established literary magazines. Several were effective in their leadership roles for famous professional organizations, well on their way to being prominent representatives for their areas of expertise. They were all native-speakers, all in advanced stages of their work for a terminal degree.

I learned at the banquet that I was distinguished from the rest of these well-qualified graduate students by the uniqueness of my achievement. I had one critical article published in a highly respected journal in Women's Studies, and one on its way to being published in another equally esteemed journal in the same field. Unlike my peers with extensive published accomplishments, I had published in places that were known for being highly selective, for choosing only original manuscripts in the field of Women's Studies. My two articles were definitely original, one of them being about a Korean woman's novella and the other about a comparison and contrast between three Asian-American women authors of East-Asian backgrounds. They both analyzed little known books with ample possibilities to open new frontiers in Women's Studies. In the first one, I explained how the genre of feminist criticism had begun to rise in Korea in the 1980s, and in the second, I illuminated the specific ways in which Asian-American women grapple with multiple priorities of gender, race, culture, and social class in their personal and collective lives. The former was about Korean women facing the unique political problems of a divided nation and at the same time the universal problems of gender concerning all women of the world. The latter was about Asian-American women who fought to extend American democracy not just for women in general, but specifically for women of color. The articles were almost manifestos of my autobiographical goals.

My conference papers were also presented at prestigious conferences, all of which were nationally known to gather experts in related fields. In all of them, I offered new perspectives. One of them was about *Platoon* and *Full Metal Jacket,* two movies about the Vietnam War that ultimately traced the origins of warmongering violence innate to human nature. Neither one of these two movies offered a historical explanation about the war. They were painfully limited to the existential aspect that forces one to consider how a person is forever changed internally after experiencing such horrors as were present in the war. Neither of them asked the question that was more important than any other that could ever be asked about a war: who manufactured the war, why it took place, and what forces convened at that particular historical juncture to shape the size and scope of the war. The individuals who deliberately created and escalated the history of the Vietnam War were entirely left out of the movies, so that they could describe only the emotional and physical repercussions shaping the lives of the soldiers who were there. In one of the papers I presented at the conference, I wrote, "Why doesn't either one of these movies show a Vietnam vet who secretly wants to kill those who are historically responsible, such as Nixon, McNamara, the CIA, the military industrial complex, and everyone else who wanted the war to go on to maximize their personal and political profits? Why do the movies in the end resort to the lame answer, the same old answer of blaming the war—any war—on the warmongering inherent in human beings?"

To me, the movies were a specimen of what I chose to call the American DNA. They reflected the American psyche of seeking answers from within an individual's existence, the American philosophy deeply ingrained in the belief that one is the captain of one's own life. Not knowing this belief is a myth, they remain resolute in insisting that nobody else has the power to run their lives, that whatever happens to them is the outcome of their own personal choices, and that external forces have little to do with events in their emotional lives. In *Platoon* and *Full Metal Jacket,* one sees two of these typical American individuals who in a very American style deliberately limit their messages to what they can and should learn from combat experience personally. These movies show the conventional American taboo against placing the responsibility upon the shoulders of those who consciously made the wrong historical decision and manipulated the public into fighting the war. They absolve the individuals when blaming them is the only right act that can be taken if one is honest enough to tell the truth. The American DNA refuses to confront the truth that often many citizens aren't free enough to be the captains of their own lives. It will very rarely approve citizens who point their fingers at the historically responsible decision-makers because such an act will destroy its firmly held illusion that one is responsible for what happens in one's life. It will reveal the truth that someone else may indeed be responsible for what happens in one's life. The American DNA will not encourage its members to violate this myth about the supremacy of an individual's choice. That is why the Vietnam War is called "this fucking war" so many times in these movies, and why nothing about those who manufactured it is ever mentioned.

At the department banquet, I realized that I had plenty of reasons to have confidence in my writing as well as in my subjects. I had always known that I had a certain vantage point that my colleagues lacked because, being bilingual and bi-cultural, I was able to see what most monolingual and mono-cultural people couldn't. In some ways, this put me on a higher level, equipped with original insights that enabled me to observe the flaws in the American DNA that defined the aforementioned movies on Vietnam. I began to realize that I could apply my original insights as a woman of color in ways highly relevant to mainstream American literature. I began to see opportunities to help the writings by and about women of color be made visible in mainstream academia, to participate in equalizing them with the writings by white male and female authors. I gained renewed confidence in my dissertation.

What surprised me the most was that I received two of the most prestigious awards that could be given to a graduate student in the department. As far as I could remember, everyone else received only one award, for either their research or teaching, but I received one for research and another for a combination of activities in teaching and research. The first one I received was called the Outstanding Graduate Student Award and was for both research and teaching. It was limited to only one recipient and was the single most highly esteemed among them all. The second one, which was for research alone, had another recipient who happened to be a close colleague of mine whose specialty was Shakespeare and the Renaissance.

As several professors and colleagues flocked around me to congratulate me, I heard myself responding with a rather odd confession, "I have such a strong fear of losing. I won because of my fear."

"You took the floor tonight," they said in unison. "Enjoy what you have achieved. You deserve it."

There was no way for them to truly understand what this meant to me as they couldn't see into the darker corners of my life. They didn't know that as I thanked them, I was basically expressing gratitude because this moment in essence saved my life. How could they ever understand that winning for me was tantamount to living and that losing was equal to dying? None of them had ever left their country to go to school, none had ever violated the almighty norms of their country to the degree that they were forced into a form of exile. It was impossible for them to understand the extent to which I was nearly conquered by the fear of failing.

Once again, I saw myself on one end of my journey in America. I was on the side of heaven, at the apex of the country where its greatness was revealed to me one more time. In America, I could criticize the very system that absorbed and nurtured me, and I could even draw praises for such criticism. In terms of accepting and mobilizing new perspectives, there was no other country on earth that could be measured up against America, and I was blessed enough to have the privilege of being one of its citizens. The prospect of being able to create a niche of my own in America, of being able to make myself a valued member of its academia, presented itself to me all the more palpably. I thought I had taken one step closer into the side of the country that was heaven. I thanked my department and my university, my second home and my alma mater, for acknowledging and rewarding me for my ability to criticize the very country that had built them.

But as heaven always comes with hell, I never forgot to keep a caveat for myself. I never allowed myself to be oblivious of the other end of my journey in America, the hell where my disadvantages unrelated to my abilities could raise ungrounded doubts about me. Racism and prejudices were always lurking around me, ready to bring unexpected problems in an effort to claim a chunk of my time and sanity. On my way back from the banquet, I gave myself a warning, replaying in my mind a rather puzzling scene that became a glitch in a perfect evening. It wasn't a particularly harmful scene, nor was it dramatic enough to create a trauma in my emotional life. It was by all means a rather insignificant moment that deserved to disappear from my memory without a trace. But somehow, it created one of those instances that were permanently registered in my memory because in a circuitous way, it reminded me of the very painful first encounter I had with racism in my department. It started with Deborah's apology to Howard, another professor who had served on the awards committee.

"Don't take it personally," Deborah said. Howard was sitting next to me at our banquet table. "Brad and I are moving to another table because we're going to join the committee that selected undergraduate recipients."

"I understand," Howard said, as the couple stood and walked away.

After several rounds of applause for the awardees, graduate and undergraduate, my name was announced for the Outstanding Graduate Student Award, and to my great surprise, I saw Deborah take the stage to give me the certificate in an envelope.

"Congratulations," she said, handing me the award.

"Thank you," I answered. It appeared that we were both sincere in our exchange.

It then seemed to me that she and Brad had moved to another table to avoid feeling awkward with me. Busy applauding the awardees, I pushed into the back of my head the question that inevitably came – why had they felt so awkward about sitting with me? Moving to another table was probably a gesture that they thought was sensitive and considerate, but I couldn't understand for the life of me why they had to think such a gesture was necessary, let alone sensitive. Perhaps, I ventured to think, they didn't know that I no longer harbored any negative feelings. They also didn't know that I no longer cared to recall the less than pleasant emotional interaction that had once made Deborah's attitude toward me less than friendly. All that had happened was in the past, as far as I was concerned, but it seemed that to them, it was still something of the present that continued to linger in their minds.

In the quiet of my apartment later that evening, I recognized the true reason I couldn't erase the couple's action from my memory. It bothered me so much because it reminded me of the same cycle of sin and atonement in which my professors and I had been trapped for so many years and were still trapped. We were put in a place where they, erring in their racism, tried to make atonement by giving me overwhelming support and assistance, and I, being eager to absolve them because I had no choice to do otherwise, returned to them the same extra efforts in achieving excellence. It was the extremely familiar pattern in which they gave me both an illness and the remedy, and after suffering from the illness, I gratefully took their medicine to get well. I must admit that subconsciously, I used the power of their guilt effectively and was successful in playing the creditor gathering from her debtors.

It seemed that by moving to another table, Brad and Deborah tried perhaps to ease their self-conscious feeling about this process of sin and atonement. There was no way for me to find out their true motive, and there was no reason I had to try to find out. Neither one of them had anything to do with my graduate work in the past or the future. As I thought about their gesture, I in the end found myself laughing. Putting myself in their position, I nodded vigorously. *If I were in Brad's shoes*, I said to myself, *I may do the same thing. I'd be embarrassed if I had to give an award to the graduate student I had once so grossly misjudged. Sitting at the same table with her would indeed be uncomfortable*. Not knowing whether he or Deborah was one of the judges who had selected me from among all the graduate students who applied, I thanked him. At least, he agreed with the committee's decision, and there was no reason for me to question the sincerity he agreed with. He knew I was sufficiently qualified. I went as far as to guess that along with the rest of the judges, he probably respected or even admired my strength to rise above the adversities, to achieve something so rare for people from my ethnic background. He was likely motivated by a spectrum of factors, including guilt and atonement, and a desire to give me what he felt he owed me, so he could use it as a chance to make it up to himself. Most of all, it was a sense of fairness that led him to agree to select the most qualified candidate. Whatever his motive was, it didn't matter. He seemed a decent person to me. So did Deborah, who cooperated with him by moving to another table. I decided to be a true believer.

Given the fact that my life was a cycle of soaring to the heaven side of America and then plummeting to its hell, I shouldn't have been surprised to receive another verdict motivated by racism. But I *was* surprised because being a victim of racism was always fresh and traumatic, no matter how accustomed one was to the experience. It was always embittering, just like having a drop of acid poured into a huge, raw gash caused by a sharp, deep-reaching knife. Even at the height of my achievement as a graduate student, I had to worry about what may come next, about what may be waiting for me in my mailbox.

This time, it was a letter of rejection signed by two editors as a nationally renowned journal in Women's Studies. I was surprised because it was for one of the two articles that had given me the research award and because I had followed the editors' suggestions for revision to a tee. Instantly, I knew the editors' decision stemmed from racism because their letter explicitly mentioned that they rejected mine to accept a different manuscript written by another Asian-American woman. They said they couldn't publish two articles by Asian-American women in the same issue. As I tracked the editors down on the phone and confronted them, I learned that there were two women involved in making the decision. One of whom, Sarah, actually admitted to me that she and the other woman had chosen the other Asian-American woman's article over mine because she was a renowned scholar in American literature, a tenured professor at a university in California. The other woman, Susan, with whom I also had a chance to talk, confessed to me how guilty she felt after making the decision.

"You can't be a feminist and a racist at the same time," I protested when I confronted her. "You wouldn't have accepted one and rejected the other if they were both written by white women. You'd have been glad to publish both in one issue."

"I can help you to find a journal that might be interested in your article," Susan offered. "I'll give you a list."

"You sabotaged me," I flared up. "Every editor has their own subjective ideas and every one of them is going to give me a set of suggestions to revise. I spent so much time accommodating your suggestions, and then you reject me. I can't even submit it to more than one journal at once because it's against the rules. Who knows how long I'll have to wait for a decision from one journal before I can try another?"

"I know. You get a bad reputation if you submit it to more than one place at a time."

"I'm under a time-sensitive situation. My department is pressuring me to be published. My career is at stake. They keep asking me, 'Where's your article?'"

I lied to her, pretending to be a tenure-track hopeful in a dire need to publish. I knew that until she and Sarah recognized the magnitude of their wrongdoing—that they had gravely damaged my opportunity for tenure—they wouldn't wake up enough to face the consequences of their actions and actually try to do something to help me. If they found out that I was just a graduate student trying to enhance my resume by being published, they weren't going to be serious about finding options for me to take. I didn't feel bad about lying to them. In light of their wrong, mine seemed small and even necessary.

"Why can't you publish mine in a later issue?" I asked the same question I had asked Sarah, predicting the answer.

"We can't. We already signed off." She sighed.

As I predicted, I received two more rejections from nationally recognized journals in Women's Studies, along with suggestions for drastic revisions. There was no way I could fulfill them in the near future. I couldn't afford to take time off as I was severely pressed to make progress for the dissertation.

The editor from one of the journals who sent me a rejection seemed out of her mind. She was a scholar specializing in a literary theory called "deconstruction." There was and is a consensus among many scholars that deconstruction is an expensive, worthless toy that only those with plenty of intellectual leisure play with. Its excellence is found in its total lack of value to human society. To those who study literature with a passion to emphasize its relevance to human lives, it is virtually a joke. Some scholars call it a literary tool for mental masturbation, a short cut into an intellectual luxury with no function for the true purpose of literature. All that one needs to understand deconstruction is that it claims the words on a page are an illusion and therefore can't be believed. It also claims that there is no true meaning in a book. "It's hogwash," my colleagues in Murfreesboro say and laugh unanimously. "Deconstruction is de-composition or de-compost. It's what critics invented at the end of their rope. Luckily, we don't have a deconstructionist in our department. We're smart enough to have one in every area except that."

Deconstructionists are also convinced that a literary text is a product of human alienation, that alienation is a human condition one can't overcome, and that the only recourse for a human being is to live within this human condition and to even further this human condition to maximize the narcissistic solace one can find in it.

The theory of deconstruction completely lacks the true purpose of literature, the purpose of serving as a voice for invisible people such as myself. Nothing could be more removed from the reasons I study literature. I study literature to research and write about books such as Harriet Beecher Stowe's *Uncle Tom's Cabin,* Rebecca Harding Davis' *Life in the Iron Mills,* and Upton Sinclair's *The Jungle,* books that serve as generators for humanity and social change. Deconstruction is a bastard of American academia, a product of the attitude that sees higher education as a sheer ivory tower with no connection with the rest of the world. It is a sign of how far some academicians would go in an attempt to pursue what is purely theoretical.

As I read my peer reviewer's letter, in which she accused me of having misread a passage in one of the books I discussed, claiming that written pages are nothing but an illusion, I roared with laughter and tossed the letter into a trash can. The single-spaced five pages were nothing but complaints about the points I made that she found disagreeable. To her deconstructionist mind, they shouldn't even exist. I laughed at myself for having been fascinated with deconstruction for one brief semester while working on my master's degree, and I hoped that my reviewer would reach the same conclusion eventually.

What made me furious wasn't the feedback I received from my peer reviewer. It was the reaction Susan gave me as I called her to share the very "laughable" experience with her.

"Now I know why I rejected your article. She saw the same thing I should have seen," she blurted out. She cleverly latched on to the ungrounded review and even added another reason to whitewash her wrong. "Books are based on an illusion, and the books you discussed in the article are even less reliable because they are memoirs and fictions about the authors' past lives. When the authors write about their own lives, they become the least reliable."

"What?" I protested, struggling to contain my voice. "You're siding with deconstructionist theory to justify yourself? You think you can retroactively absolve yourself by agreeing with an absurd review?"

"I don't know how to help you," she returned in a cutting monotone.

"This all happened because you sabotaged me."

"I'd better go," she said with a tone of finality. "My daughter is crying."

Had she been in my presence, I wouldn't have been able to contain myself. She was smugly twisting her way out of a place of blame, agreeing with a peer's poorly grounded review.

It was in November of 2003, over a decade later, that I happened to read a report about Sarah, one of the two editors who had made the decision about my article, in a Korean women's weekly paper called *The Women's News*. A large photo of her was on the front page where she talked about the global network she was trying to build for Women's Studies. She was impassioned about the possibility of constructing an organization for women of the world, from both first and third world countries. It seemed that she had made efforts to broaden her race-consciousness, to transcend national boundaries in pursuit of justice for women, and I was glad. I hoped she had evolved beyond the narrow scope of feminism she had once shown me by refusing to publish two different articles by Asian-American women in the same issue. "I hope she finishes what she started," I briefly prayed for her. "I hope she's not just making a heroic gesture." Having never found out about the outcome of her efforts or how long they lasted, I don't know how to tell the degree of her sincerity. But while reading the report, I got the impression that she was eager and well on her way toward a very important feminist goal, bringing women in the world together in an effort to solve global women's issues. I hoped she would become one of those women who could help worldwide sisterhood, divided by racism, to be whole again. Almost smiling, I pictured her being delighted to accept two or three or even four articles by the same group of women, be they white, black, yellow, brown, or whichever color.

I continued to write my dissertation, sometimes for thirty hours in a row, sometimes for thirteen hours without stopping, and sometimes for nine hours successively. I was back to the same old feverish cycle, well aware that another bout of depression may strike me at any given time. But I had no choice. Having lost a whole semester to recuperate from the lethal depression, I was behind enough to have to face the possibility of having to extend the time limit for graduate work one more time. I barely had time to eat. When a colleague of mine, the one who had received the research award with me, told me he took two hours off every working day to go out with his buddy to enjoy a beer, I let out a sigh of intense envy. Such a luxury sounded like a dream to me. Because I was always so frantic and my sleep cycle became totally erratic, I couldn't make any plans ahead of time, let alone go out for a simple break for a beer. I was developing the symptoms of chronic fatigue syndrome that followed me like a demon for decades.

Chapter 20
The Banality of Racism

What broke my peace of mind during that academic year wasn't the overwhelming fatigue coming from writing the dissertation and teaching two classes at the same time. It was an incident involving two professors of mine, one of whom was Jane and the other was her best friend in the department named Professor Johnson. It was one of those incidents that felt like deja vu, which functioned to remind me of what I wished I could forget more than anything else in my life – the condition of being singled out for being different. One more time, I was forced to face the painful fact that I stood out like a word in red ink on a page full of black lines. Once again, I found myself wasting time and energy on recuperating from an entirely unnecessary trauma. It started with a phone conversation I had with Professor Johnson one night.

"How dare you call a professor after ten o'clock at night?" She shrilled. Her voice was so high-pitched that I was afraid her vocal cords would break. It made my hair stand up on end.

"I just hoped you could help me with something," I said in a low, frightened voice. "I tried to call you earlier, but you didn't pick up the phone. You gave me permission to call you at home a while ago, and I thought it still stood. But if you don't have time to talk right now, I can talk to you some other time."

"I've been sick with bronchitis for ten days," she screeched, frustrated that she couldn't be any louder. Her raging soprano was indeed so piercing that it sounded ready to burst out of her tiny mouth and bust her small face into a thousand pieces. "Let's get it over with. What's bothering you?"

I told her what Sarah and Susan had done to me and sought her advice as to where I could send my article.

"How long did it take you to revise the article?"

"It took me over two semesters, but that has nothing to do with their decision."

"You should've revised it faster," she bombarded on. "If you're slow, someone else may submit another manuscript in your field and put yours in the shadows."

"But in this case, that has nothing to do with the result," I repeated in what Koreans call a "mosquito voice" because it was so low and timid.

"If you don't want to listen to me, why did you call?" Her volcanic anger continued to erupt, strong enough to threaten to cause the phone to shatter.

When I hung up, I placed my hand on my heart to slow down its palpitation. I could barely stand up from the shock. For the first time in decades, I realized how powerful a human being's voice could be. It could even destroy one's sense of worth, worse than anything else that could be used to break down human dignity. Physical violence can kill a person physically, but a voice used to punish can make one mentally sick and cause an emotional death. Professor Johnson's voice was such indeed. I was so amazed to see that her tiny body could generate a voice huge enough to force me to stop moving for nearly an hour! She was reminiscent of a small-sized troll with too many overcharged batteries to be contained in her body. She had to find ways of shedding the overwhelming excess energy. On the phone with me in that evening, she found a way of draining some of her extra batteries by yelling at me.

Barely four feet, ten inches tall, Professor Johnson was better known by her nickname, the Midget, on campus. One glance revealed that her raging insecurities came from her inadequate physical size. If, however, it wasn't for the extremely unpleasant pattern of behavior she had developed in an attempt to overcompensate, nobody would have called her by such a demoralizing nickname. None of the people who called her that name behind her back were motivated by anything undesirable such jealousy, contempt, or hate. None of them were thoughtless enough to judge a person by their appearance. Most of these people were fair-minded individuals who were mature enough to observe a person's personality before forming an opinion about them. If anything, they were eager to show more respect toward a person with a physical handicap of any kind because they understood that handicapped people deserve more deference.

Professor Johnson was known among her students to be incapable of being human with anyone. A career woman with nothing but work in her life, she lived with a dog whom she called her baby. As far as I knew, she had a couple friends in the department, but she very rarely shared any of the intimate details of her private life with anyone. In contrast with other professors in the department who often made themselves accessible to their students and cared to exchange a personal conversation with them, she almost never did, not even with the graduate students working closely with her. She never established a relationship with anyone she worked with, particularly hesitant to make any sort of human connections with the students whom she perceived as being subjugated to her. It seemed that she was so afraid of losing her sense of authority over her students that she defined her interaction with them as being nothing but strictly professional. Unlike most professors of the department who preferred to be called by their first names, she never allowed herself to be called by anything other than Professor Johnson.

And yet, I saw a warm human being shining through her rigid demeanor. I knew that she put on the troll-like pattern of behavior to keep her students from taking advantage of her, to hide a caring person in her out of the fear of seeming vulnerable. But the mask, as necessary as it might have been, was so iron-clad that it became nearly impossible to see her true face. Whenever I felt frightened by the cold militancy of her mask, I tried to remember the real person I thought I had seen. I wanted to believe I knew her true face. I repeatedly recalled one of the conversations I had had with her.

"This is the list of the journals you want to send your article to," she said, handing the typed list to me. I had written an article about a Korean woman's novella as the final paper in her class, and recognizing its originality, she suggested that I try to get it published in a Women's Studies journal. She kindly put extra time into finding the journals that might be interested in it, and I was grateful.

"Can I send the article to more than one journal at once?" I asked. Since it was the first article I was submitting to a journal, I didn't know the rules.

"No, you can't," she answered, her sharp eyes diffusing into shimmers of affection. She was being a benign tutor instructing an amateur. "If you send it to more than one journal, you get a bad reputation."

"No matter how long it takes, I should wait until one journal makes its decision before I send it to another," I said.

"Yes," she said, "the journal that accepts it would give you guidelines for a revision, and if you fulfill them, you'll be most likely published."

“I know you’re incredibly busy,” I said cautiously, “but if I have the good luck of revising it for the journal that wants it, can I bring the revision to you, so that you can see if it’s ready to be re-submitted?”

“Yes, you can,” she said resoundingly. “I’ll be happy to read it with an editor’s careful attention to details.” Glowing with the loving pride a teacher bestows upon a dear student, she summarized, “It’s very good to have an article published when you’re a graduate student.”

When I finally received an acceptance letter from the journal that was satisfied with my revision, I wanted to thank Professor Johnson first. I wanted to surprise her by giving her one of the two free copies the journal gave to an author. But I was forced to wait because the editors postponed the publication of my article for a whole year, burdened with a backlog to be published immediately. To surprise her, instead of leaving a thank you note in her mailbox, I decided to wait until the issue with my article came out. Even if I had to wait for a year, I thought that a surprise gift would be a better sign of gratitude than a thank you note. To me, a thank you note seemed a bit of a cliché, but a surprise gift was refreshing. Until she yelled at me on the phone in that shocking night, I didn’t realize that she saw my lack of a thank you note as a sign of an ungrateful attitude. She felt betrayed by me after having gone out of her way to help me, and she reacted in a frightful manner, her mask rushing back to steel her into a hard person. It backfired on me because I called her late at night, but its force was all the more virulent because my voice brought out of her what she feared the most – being taken advantage of by a student.

There was a scared child in Professor Johnson, a child thickly covered with an adult’s mannerisms, with a machine-style behavior pattern. She was a child paranoid about being found out, a child who was very small mentally as well as physically and was heavily cloaked in a mature woman’s clothes. Although she was highly fashionable with a strikingly unique sense of style, she wasn’t a glamorous woman. Once, I saw her dressed in a long black coat with a tale tapered down to touch the ground in a stylish way, but it failed to bring a look of splendor to her. Always intent on being heard, she wore high heels that made distinct sounds on the floors of the buildings, so that one could tell she was coming from a mile away. Because she was so bent on being noticed, people hardly noticed her except in negative ways.

Whenever I saw her iron-clad mask, I deliberately tried to think positively of her. In my relationship with her, I was always on a pendulum, swinging from compassion to pity, from respect to contempt, and from anger to forgiveness. I tried hard to keep in mind the smile peeking through the cracks of her steely mask, cherishing the glimmers of warmth that managed to emanate from her eyes. I thought I saw a sense of humor in her when I heard a singsong voice from her at a party in her house.

"I need a strong man to move this table to the living room," she sang, pointing at a small table in the kitchen. "I'd appreciate it if one of you men can move it for me. You know what a fragile female I am!" She burst out laughing and the guests, too, roared into laughter.

"It'll be my pleasure," a male graduate student sang back. He picked up the table, curtsying to her.

"I shall be much obliged to you," she said, laughing.

Over thirty people, including some faculty and graduate students, gathered in her house, and I thought that if this many people liked her well enough to come to her party, she must be a socially well-balanced person. At the party, she played the funny, entertaining host, drinking wine and laughing with the rest. Seeing her without the mask of a cold professional, the guests were pleasantly surprised, relaxed to the point of starting a joke line.

"Most people can be categorized in two groups, one in the dog group and the other in the cat group," a male faculty started. "I'd prefer to be in the cat group because cats don't have to do anything to be loved. All a cat has to do is sit there and be fed and patted." He then turned to Professor Johnson and asked, "What group would you like to belong to?"

"I'd like to belong to the cat group," she said. "But I probably belong to the dog group. I am too loud and vocal to have a cat's sly advantages."

Everyone burst into laughter and she added, "Most people who're like dogs prefer to be like cats, and most people who're like cats prefer to remain like cats. Cats are definitely blessed with more."

Her guests cherished these brief moments because they knew that on the following day, she would go back to wearing the mask closed to all feelings. They wanted to fill their minds with the rare pictures of her pleasant face, so that they could stay reminded that the cold, rigid face was only a mask.

Professor Johnson was by no means ugly. I even thought there was a peculiar charm in her face. In those rare moments when she could bring herself to smile fully, she looked attractive, her narrow jaws opening into a wide shape to broaden the lower side of her face and make it nearly even with the upper side. She had a short face with the contour of a reverse triangle, a sharply cubic nose slightly on the aquiline side, and large, round eyes lustrous with an ebony glow. It reminded me of the face of a cute prodigy feverishly focused on finding an answer for a question, or a brilliant child whose pleasantly large forehead indicated an original mind set upon a course for new discoveries. She had an unusual face that could be fostered into a fascinating one by some effort. Were she endowed with a bit more sense of humor and self-confidence, she could have channeled her small face and body into a large asset exuding the energy of an engaging mind.

I was bent on finding a good, warm human being in her because I identified with her. Just like her, I was a raging feminist, and just like her, I was set on indicting inequalities and injustices against women in my writing. Just like her, I was always in pursuit of the ways in which I could participate in helping the disenfranchised become franchised. I spent much time on thinking about her good and bad qualities, just as I spent much time on thinking about my good and bad ones. I wished she would take off her mask more often because I wished I could take off my mask more often. Although mine was the mask of a merry bride, I thought it was hardly different from hers. Ours were the masks of lonely women in whose lives work without love created nothing but an overweening professionalism. I thought that even my walking style resembled hers. Professor Johnson was always in a hurry, and she took a penguin's fast steps as I did, unable to cover much with numerous short strides. Although I was much taller than she, my gait resembled hers so closely that I had to laugh aloud to dispel the comic sadness. Without the merry bride's mask, I would have been Professor Johnson. I would have made myself into a caricature of a woman that the others in the department swore they would never be. Although I was eventually well-known for the quality of my work, I wouldn't have been admired by those who knew me. I might have been renowned for being impeccably honest and fair-minded, but I would have rarely been praised for such virtues. I would have failed to engage people.

Professor Johnson and I were a pair of women who, so unselfishly devoted to the work of seeking a just world in printed words, became selfish in our personal relationships. Wishing to help our fellow human beings by constructing a more compassionate, loving society on paper, we failed to help them in our daily lives. Hoping to leave visions of a kinder, gentler nation for our academic posterity, we practiced unkind, harsh behaviors toward our colleagues and students. So warm in our pursuit of humanity, we turned cold. Although my doctoral coms were over and I remembered my decision to do more giving and less taking, I still was a cold academician who failed to show concern for my loved ones. So bent on finishing a doctoral dissertation about the America in my mind, the America that included and welcomed women of color as its first-class citizens, I forgot to call my mother in Korea for two months in a row, causing her to be frantic with worry. As Professor Johnson, so dedicated to printing words necessary to promote humanity, left only half an hour a week as her office hours, forcing her students to chase her in a desperate hurry, I made my family try to find me until my phone nearly broke from ringing. So warm and cold, so passionate and indifferent, and so selfish and unselfish, Professor Johnson and I were two of a kind.

Because I could hide my cold face under the merry mask of a bride, I could fool people exceptionally well. I could succeed in giving people the impression that I was who I wasn't in my personal life. Seeing only the warm person that I was in my professional life, they missed that in my personal interactions, I could be a lot like Professor Johnson. "There's a little bit of Professor Johnson in all of us," everyone who knew her would agree in unison. "But none of us behave like her." Because Professor Johnson couldn't hide the coldness she cultivated to protect her warm devotion to work, she failed to fool people.

Over the eight years as a graduate student, during which I worked hard to make my merry bride's mask hide my cold face, I came to realize that if I pretended to be who I wasn't well enough, I would eventually become who I pretended to be. I saw myself trying little by little to be the warm, caring person capable of making connections with the people I worked with, to be the merry bride I wanted to be. In my personal relationships, I made conscious efforts to replace the iciness in me with warmth, however phony this warmth might be, and I deliberately made attempts to offer more than a passing, monosyllabic reply when my colleagues and students asked me how I was doing. When they asked me about my cat, my most frequent topic of conversation, I would sing, "He's fine. He's going out less because he's getting old."

Although I have now been practicing the art of the merry bride for twenty-five years as a full-time faculty member, I still have a long way to go. Many times, the mask falls off my face to show the ruthless person in me, and I have to catch myself quickly. I am so busy creating a blueprint for a kinder, gentler world in my printed words, I fail to be kinder and gentler with the people around me. My merry mask isn't yet the face I show in my written words. Laughing to encourage myself, I think how infinitely better it is to have the merry bride's mask than not. If I wear the mask of a cold person to hide the warm humanity I show in my printed pages, I may indeed become what I pretend to be, a cold person. But if I wear the mask of a warm person, I may indeed become what I pretend to be, a warm person. I may in the end become a person in touch with her emotions in both work and personal relationships. Because I chose the merry bride's mask as mine, I could eventually try to make my mask the same as my face. Although I am far from successful in making these two entirely consistent with each other, I am in the process.

How, even today, I wish Professor Johnson had put on the mask of a caring human being instead of that of a rigid machine! With all that emotional liveliness I saw in her, with all that passion she put into her work, she could have made herself into a remarkable combination of rigor and compassion, an extraordinary blend of scholarly logic and human affection. She could have made her mask embody the warm humanity she put into her written pages. But because she adhered to the mask of an icy-cold person for so long, she unfortunately became the person on her mask. She failed to be the person she was in her written words. Although she was full of humanity in her work, she became a person lacking humanity in her daily life.

"I also erred many times," I pondered after my phone conversation with her that disastrous night. "I've yelled at my students. One time I insulted a whole class." Remembering the insecurities that had controlled my classroom behavior during the first year or so of my teaching, I tried to understand Professor Johnson. I believed I could forgive her only by forgiving myself, and because I believed laughing was the fastest way to forgiving, I tried to laugh off the whole incident on the phone. I let it go.

It wasn't until a month or so later that I learned it was far from over. In fact, I learned it had been snowballing for a month when Jane called me in to her office one day.

"Professor Johnson asked me to talk with you," Jane started in a low voice, her pale blue eyes glittering with ire behind her glasses. So intense and sharp, her gaze seemed ready to dart out of her eyes and carve a scar on my face. I instantly knew this was about Professor Johnson.

"I was wrong to call her at home after 10:00 pm," I began, struggling to clamp down the strong emotion rising in me. It wasn't even anger or contempt that threatened to take away my control, it was the realization of how absurd the whole thing was. Professor Johnson had made a mountain out of a molehill, carrying the matter to my mentor in hopes of changing my outrageously "disrespectful" behavior. "Because she only has half an hour a week for her office hours, I hardly have a chance to speak with her," I continued with a subdued face, my voice trembling. I knew that I mustn't forget Jane was my dissertation adviser, that she was the one who had the power to make or break my career. The last thing I wanted to do was to make her angrier by being as stirred up as she was. "So, I called her at home and as she didn't pick up the phone, I continued to try until after ten o'clock. I thought she wouldn't mind because she allows her students to call her at home."

"Oh!" escaped her mouth, faint but clearly audible. "Well," Jane resumed, "we can learn from this experience. You can learn how to say things in a more professional manner."

I stared at her, wide-eyed, lost as to why she suddenly changed the subject.

She continued, "When you leave notes for a professor to ask them for a favor such as writing letters of recommendation, you may use expressions such as 'I'd appreciate it if you could.'" Embarrassed to learn that she had heard only her friend's side of the story, she was trying to change the subject.

"You mean I should be more respectful when I ask a professor for a favor?" I asked.

"Native speakers use expressions such as, 'We'd be grateful if you…' It's time for you to pick up subtleties of the English language like that," she suggested.

"I'm not the only person who forgets to use those niceties," I said. I heard my voice slightly rising because my control mechanism was threatening to fall apart. She was picking on my English to find a way of sustaining the awkward conversation, targeting my weakness to find blame for what had transpired. Suddenly, I heard myself bursting into a silent scream, reliving the comments written by my students in their evaluations of my teaching: "I'm failing in this class because my English teacher is a foreigner. I can't understand her English," "She speaks broken English," "She doesn't speak English, but she teaches it," and "She shouldn't teach English at all."

Fighting my silent scream, I managed to float a smooth look over what I thought was a severely contorted face. I spoke rapidly, "So many people speak bluntly. Some people in our department talk with such directness that they nearly sound insensitive. It's not because English is a second language to me. If you hear me speak in Korean, you'd hear the same lack of so-called politeness. It has nothing to do with one's nationality. Look at New Yorkers. They say what they think without mincing words, and they're Americans and native speakers. And yet, as far as I know, neither you nor Professor Johnson ever accused them of being disrespectful. Nobody in the department ever did."

"When you're asking a professor for help, you need to show gratitude. Gratitude is all you have when you're a graduate student."

"Doing things for their students such as writing letters of recommendation – isn't it part of their job?" My voice was reaching toward the height of the limited volume I struggled to maintain.

"Yes, it is, but they help you succeed."

"As much as I appreciate their help, I don't have to be so subserviently grateful. I refuse to be grateful to a professor who abuses me as a human being."

For the first time in my several years of professional—and personal—relationship with Jane, I took off the mask of the merry bride to show my unrestrained anger. More accurately, the mask fell off in spite of itself, pressured by the overwhelming emotional force damned up under my true face. Probably, it instinctively fled from my face out of the fear of being broken into pieces. A mask requires a break just like any real face made of flesh and blood. If overworked, it is bound to be damaged, to be worthless in the end and to bring its own demise. I so very often saw daughters-in-law crack up under the smiling mask of the merry bride. They lost themselves when they reached the point where they couldn't handle their relationships with their mothers-in-law anymore. Because they were so relentlessly and constantly forced to wear the mask, they deprived it of sufficient room to breathe and move about, eventually causing it to be crushed under the weight of its own burden. I saw so many daughters-in-law and mothers-in-law falling out and turning into sworn enemies against each other as a result. Instinctively, the merry bride left me to live. She left it up to me to handle my relationship with my mother-in-law, the woman who was supposed to guide me into a successful marriage with my husband country.

I told Jane all about Professor Johnson, about what everyone said behind her back. I even told her that she was unanimously called the "bitch of the department" by graduate students.

"Why is she so incapable of being human?" I asked the same question asked by everyone in the department. "With her achievement and stature, why is she so insecure?" Swept into a torrent of words, I kept on going without giving Jane a chance to respond. "I'm not an idiot. I know we work in academia, a place as hierarchical as anywhere else. When it comes to work, I absolutely and unequivocally follow you. Your wish is my command. You know I work like a demon to fulfill your or anyone else's standards. But I refuse to be denigrated as a human being. Just because she has authority over me professionally, that doesn't mean she's above me as a person."

I didn't know what Jane and Professor Johnson had discussed about me, but I could tell that the two women together had made me into an ugly person who was used to taking advantage of people. Jane wouldn't show that much ire without some seriously damaging information about me. But what made me feel sickened was that they blamed my English for Professor Johnson's paranoia. If Jane had tried to gently teach me about the subtleties of the English language, I would have been grateful to learn. Being a relentless learner, I was eager to grab any chance to improve my English. But her condescending attitude seemed to indicate to me nothing but borderline racism. I knew that she wouldn't have made the same effort to teach the same thing to a graduate student from New York who spoke with the same blunt style as mine. She wouldn't have made the same attempt to teach a European student whose English might be worse than mine.

"How many beatings should I take from them?" I cried in the lonely silence of my apartment. "When they questioned my ability to teach the most rudimentary English, they were being overtly racist. Now, they are being subtly racist. When will they stop treating me as a second-class citizen? When will they put an end to punishing me more brutally when I make the same mistake anyone else makes? How many more beatings will I have to take?"

Unbelievably, it took only a few days to hear myself saying something different. It would be a lie for me to say that it took me only that long to forgive them, but in the sense that I began to exercise my imagination and place myself in Professor Johnson's position, I wasn't too far from forgiving her and Jane, too. "If I understand what happened to Professor Johnson in the past, particularly when she was a vulnerable child," I pondered with the same guesses again, "her behavior would be explained. She can't be absolved or excused just because of what happened to her, but unless I know everything about her experience, I've no right to pass judgment on her, as she has no right to pass judgment on me before she knows everything about my experience." Entering another stage of my meditation, I thought the same thing I had always thought, "I see a lot of good in her, so much compassion and kindness. She's just scared. She'll come back to herself."

I took a deep breath and went on, "Like many Americans, she's used to hearing thank you and sorry immediately. From what I've seen, Americans are extremely eager when it comes to claiming the credit they deserve. Unless they hear words of gratitude and apology instantly, they think of it as a sign of ingratitude or callousness. I was mistaken when I made Professor Johnson wait, wanting to surprise her with one of the free copies of the journal. Unlike American students, many Korean students wait until they can go home and find thoughtful gifts for their professors or invite them to dinner for a home-cooked meal. There's a lot of Korean graduate students at Kansas University, and I know most of them choose to take the trouble of bringing sincere tokens of appreciation to their professors. Americans rarely do anything in action, they use words to show appreciation to those who helped them, but Koreans use small acts of kindness. Actions take time and many times are more precious than words."

I stopped as I went into the next step in my monologue, in the debate with myself that was by now a daily routine in my life, "No wonder relationships in this country are so shallow, built so quickly and gone just as fast. People in this country prefer to spend money on buying material possessions because they're afraid of being hurt, because they don't know when their loved ones will move away. This country is all about grabbing opportunities to achieve success, so people move whenever and to wherever as they find better opportunities for themselves. They feel it's wiser to buy brand new cars that'll carry them to new places instead of investing in people who can't be carried around like material possessions. What a lonely country!"

Perhaps presumptuously, I came to feel sorry for these professors of mine who had enraged me so. Given what I knew about them, I could tell that they, too, were suffering. I could picture them feeling terribly guilty and contemplating ways of making it up to me. I knew who they were. Typical of highly sophisticated and conscientious intellectuals, they were brutally honest with their self-analysis, fast in righting their wrongs and speedy in delivering the work expected of them. I had seen how fast they were to help me get the graduate teaching assistantship. In a week or so, Jane had taken the trouble of persuading everyone on the committee to positively consider my candidacy, while Professor Johnson had instantly delivered a glowing letter of recommendation for me. They were hit in the face by the very knowledge that they dreaded the most, the realization that they were committing the sin they so condemned – the woeful act of discriminating against a human being because of their accent and skin color. As a result, they moved with a sense of urgency touched by compassion and respect. I could tell with certainty that they were ready to move on with the same voluntary kindness as before. I could tell they would be happy to do anything they could for me in the future. I knew that Jane would do whatever was in her ability to help me write the best dissertation possible, seeing me though the process until the very last line. I knew that Professor Johnson would also help me if I needed her.

I would be a liar if I didn't admit that for my own good, I wanted to retain a good relationship with both women. I couldn't finish my dissertation without Jane, and I was going to need Professor Johnson's letter of recommendation when I started to apply for a job. I couldn't afford not to forgive them. But honestly, my self-interest was only a fraction of the reasons why, without anyone's intervention or persuasion, I changed my perspective on what had happened. I realized that all of us were spinsters with cats and a dog or at least with plans to have a cat in the near future. Jane had two long-haired black cats climbing all over her shoulders, Professor Johnson had a dog, a large malamute that jumped on her lap, and I dreamed of having a long-haired tuxedo cat crouching on my computer desk. We were all women who gave up marriage and family to pursue careers, who sought happiness in our work and animals. It was our choice to trade a life with a man for a life with animals, and none of us were unhappy with our choices. Jane was as happy as any married or unmarried man or woman I had ever seen. Professor Johnson wasn't exactly unhappy although she was so notoriously machine-like. Nor was I miserable about being alone. As angry as I was at the Korean patriarchy that rewarded men far more than women, I never regretted the tradeoff I had made to opt for work.

“Most of the male faculty in our department, particularly of the same generation with Jane and Professor Johnson, have their wives to lighten their burdens,” I observed. “But most women faculty, even some of the younger ones, don’t have anyone to go home to. As stress is accumulated for a long time, it deprives them of the emotional leisure to sit back and take it easy. Anything that even slightly goes wrong at work becomes a big deal in their lives. Even the smallest incidents become snowballed and take over their entire routines until they turn into monstrously important issues, and some of them end up developing a persecution complex. This is partly what happened to Professor Johnson. Of course, even if she was married with a family, she may not be entirely different. Her personality is her personality, but I’ve no doubt that decades of going back to an empty home has reinforced the way she is.” I let out a sigh of commiseration. “American women suffer from patriarchy too, not just Korean women. Women are automatically expected to sacrifice love for work. Women should be kind to each other and fight together to make progress for women. Jane and Professor Johnson and I must be united in our fights. I know how lonely they are as they know how lonely I must be. Didn’t I tell them more than once how those Korean feminists, most of them single, have to endure so much alienation and sorrow? In America, it’s hardly different.”

I wrote a short letter for Jane and delivered it personally to her house. Not surprisingly, she called me back immediately to say she was grateful.

A month or so later, I received the two free copies from *Frontiers: A Journal of Women Studies,* and I left one of them in Professor Johnson’s mailbox, along with a short letter explaining that I had waited to get the free copies to thank her. And as I read her notes thanking me for having faith in her, I smiled. I kept it safely in the pile of letters from my father, wrapped in the silk wrapping cloth I had brought from home.

I am writing about what happened to the three of us for one reason—for one reason only. I am writing because I am burning with a wish to tell the truth I witnessed for over sixty years of my life—that it is impossible for human beings to be entirely free from preconceptions and prejudices that one group of human beings is bound to harbor toward another group of human beings. No matter how extraordinary some individuals may be, they are still human beings, and all human beings are vulnerable to the same flaws, whoever and wherever they may be. By all means, Jane and Professor Johnson were two of the most advanced individuals in terms of their sense of justice. To this day, I haven't seen individuals who could surpass them in their ability to carry out their dedication to justice for all women, including women of color. I can proudly say how positively influenced I am by them. As they tried to make amends with me, I tried to make amends with them. I continued to work until I felt as if my eyes were bleeding, knowing nothing would make them as happy as my success. I continued to respect Professor Johnson because I came to understand her as a human being—a human being just like myself—and because I retained love for her as I retained love for human beings.

It is easy to condemn racism. It is a fashion in the 21st century to condemn racism and whatever consequences it may bring. But racism isn't a nefarious evil as we may be inclined to believe. It is a ubiquitous element in human beings, as common and universal as the air we breathe, a virus that invades everyone. Those of us who are lucky enough to have a strong immune system will overcome the virus, while those of us who are unfortunate enough to have a weak immune system will suffer from the virus. This is why even an individual such as FDR, one of the greatest leaders who ever shaped the history of the world as we know it, was a racist. He not only believed the Japanese were an inferior race but also interred 110,000 Japanese Americans behind barbed wires during World War II.

I don't condone racism. But I am firmly convinced that racism isn't a matter of an individual, that it is a universal evil shared by human beings, an impulse that is found everywhere. Once we understand and accept this nature of racism, I believe we can accomplish the American dream that brought me and so many of my friends to this country faster and more effectively. It will help us to examine ourselves more concretely and honestly before we rush ahead into condemning "racism out there," as if it were "out there" and not "here in ourselves." It will also help us if we can learn how to tell the differences between the degrees of racism that are shown by different individuals. We can cultivate more hope for a true democracy if we can see the variations between individuals such as Jane and Professor Johnson who are smart enough to see and change what lies inside themselves and those who are not – between individuals who carry their thoughts into action and those who choose to turn a blind eye to what is in themselves.

I will echo Hannah Arendt who coined the term, the "banality of evil," to explain that evil isn't a creation of a few particular individuals, that evil is inherent to human nature. After Arendt, I will coin the term, the "banality of racism," to disprove the common notion that if one is a racist, one is automatically a bad person. I will go as far as to say, "Even if one is a racist, one may be a good person," because the banality of racism is such that any human being, even you and me, is vulnerable to it. As banal as racism is, individual human beings have the choice to make it less or more commonplace.

As much as I understood the nature of racism, I never stopped fearing it. Rather, because I understood the nature of racism, I feared it even more. I knew that it wasn't a monopoly of the KKK or organizations with self-professed hate. It could come from anyone I trusted, from anyone dedicated to pursuing justice and equality for all human beings. For the past thirty-nine years of my life in America, in the country I embraced as my husband, I have constantly feared racism, always aware that even the most sensitive and conscientious people could turn on me, perceiving me as an easy target. Even as a tenure-track faculty and then as a tenured faculty, I was forced to endure all kinds of racism, blatant and subtle, conscious and subconscious, from both my students and colleagues who didn't know they were being racist. For the past thirty-nine years of my life in America, I never stopped asking, "Is it entirely possible for members of the same group to treat members of another group as equals?" and my answer has always been a rather sad no. Sadly, I rather observe a transparent gap between theory and practice, between the loud rhetoric of racial equality and the silently persistent racism that is being secretly practiced by the most unlikely individuals. *Racism has gone underground, harder to detect and more difficult to prove.*

But four things have kept me from falling out of love with America, my husband country. One was that there was a strong condemnation against racism and that a proven case of racism was expected to be investigated and punished. Second, there were extraordinary leaders, such as Abraham Lincoln, Martin Luther King, Malcolm X, and Robert Kennedy, who weren't afraid to die for their belief in racial equality. Third, there were highly sophisticated, conscientious individuals such as Jane and Professor Johnson who made it their lifetime purpose to spread the gospel of humanity they inherited from these leaders, and fourth, there were immigrants such as myself who were dedicated to expanding American democracy for women of color. Most other countries in the world didn't have even one of these features that made America unique.

Partly because of this uniqueness in America, I didn't live my life in fear *entirely*. I always feared racism, but I didn't let this fear dictate my life. Although I knew racism could strike me anytime, anywhere, I never hesitated to speak my mind, never stopped in fear of the consequences. Even when I knew I may have to pay a grave price, I went ahead and reported on the wrong I saw. From my experience, I had reasons to entertain hope that the very system that betrayed me would come around to rescue me. Although it took what seemed an eternity to wait for the system to come down on my side, and the injustice and agony sometimes ruined my physical and emotional health, I refused to stop hoping because I believed I would be eventually heard.

I never forget to remember the factor that makes me more vulnerable than anyone else from another country – that I teach English as a non-native speaker. I am one of those rare breeds who invade the main turf that is almost exclusively owned by native-speakers of the English language. I am not in math or sciences that are represented well by international students and faculty.

Chapter 21
A Peanut of Privilege

As I was dedicated to writing my dissertation, Jane was dedicated to reading it. Together, we moved as fast as we could, and by the summer of 1993, we were finished with the first draft. Once the draft was ready, Jane graciously took a chunk of her precious summer break to re-read it and make all the detailed, painstaking comments to help me improve the content and tighten the prose. Then, it was handed over to the second reader on my dissertation committee, a professor by the name of Aaron who was a nationally renowned scholar in the genre of autobiography. He read it one more time to put finishing touches on it. Had it not been for the third reader, a woman in another department in the liberal arts college, the whole process, including writing, reading, and defense, would have been accomplished much faster. I had contemplated the option of placing a faculty member from outside the department on the dissertation committee, having heard it was a good idea from a peer of mine who had defended his dissertation recently. The chair of the graduate committee in the English Department confirmed that it was a great idea. He said having such a diverse committee would show the scope and depth of my dissertation.

I chose someone named Amy in the History Department, a specialist in East-Asian history, only to learn shortly afterward that she was better known on the campus by the name of the "bogeyman." She was notorious for being un-cooperative, for being dogmatic and stubborn, and for being ignorant of her subjects. I soon had chances to find out from my own experience. When she couldn't understand certain parts of my dissertation, she blamed me. When she found it difficult to follow my metaphors, she reproached me. When she couldn't grasp the complexities of my issues, she reprehended me. And when she couldn't appreciate the complexity of my sentence structure, she criticized me. She would change my perfectly clear, well-composed sentences into short, simple lines, killing not only the meaning but also the fluent style that was approved and respected by the first and second reader of the dissertation, both of whom were two of the most respected scholars on the campus. A phrase such as "historical waves," deliberately chosen by me to emphasize the unexplainable nature of history, was changed by her into "historical developments." According to her, "waves" was supposed to be used exclusively for events in the natural world. She nitpicked everything, wasting weeks of my time when I was faced by a rapidly advancing deadline.

"You can get some good tips from a native speaker," Amy said. "I can help you with idiomatic subtleties you may not be aware of."

In my head, I was able to bite back, "I know the subtleties of the English language far better than you, and my writing is ten times better than yours. You will never be able to write as well as I do in your life. How dare you claim you can teach me anything about writing at all!" She was wielding two different weapons over me, one of which was the fact that she was a native speaker of the English language and the other was that she was a faculty member with authority over me. Lacking competence—the only true authority anyone could exercise over anyone else—she had to resort to her *positional* superiority over me, using an advantage that had nothing to do with her achievement. In terms of her English, she reminded me of my freshman students who didn't know how to compose the simplest sentence. And yet, she felt entitled to correct my composition simply because she was a native speaker. She was abusing her authority. "Is being a non-native speaker a crime?" I yelled internally. "How long am I going to be punished for something that shouldn't even be considered an offence, let alone a crime?"

In October 1993, while I was under the prospect of finishing my dissertation in the following Spring, I had my dossier prepared with my graduate transcripts and five letters of recommendation to be sent out to colleges and universities that were searching for faculty with my specialties. Having learned from my experience the previous year, I took the trouble of making extra certain that there was nothing in any of the letters of recommendation that could potentially hurt my candidacy. The year before, I made the mistake of sending out a dossier that was one-year old with year-old letters of recommendation. I also discovered that a letter from Aaron had played a role in having me perceived less than positively by the search committee at one of the universities. In his letter of recommendation, he happened to write a clause that, if scrutinized, could call for doubts about the quality of my dissertation. He used an honest expression that could be misunderstood because it read, "Although it is not as cogent as it needs to be, it will be a useful dissertation when finished." A woman who served on the search committee at one of the universities I had sent my dossier to informed me of the expression, along with two members of search committees at other universities. To verify it with my own eyes, I asked a woman working at the University Placement Center if she could forward me all the letters of recommendation, and she eagerly complied.

I believed what Jane told me after talking with Aaron. I knew Aaron had written everything in an effort to be honest.

"As much as I appreciate his honesty," I said to Jane, "when I'm competing with three-hundred candidates, honesty may hurt." As Jane agreed with me and encouraged me to continue to work with him, I eagerly returned, "Yes, I do want to continue to work with him. I'm glad to have an opportunity to work with someone so astute and rigorous. He helps me a lot." There was no cynicism in my response. I *was* glad to work with him. There was nothing I wished more than to improve my writing and join the circles of the English professors who, despite their flaws, represented the best of America, the conscience and hope of the country I called my husband. I believed Aaron was one of them.

Candidly, Aaron could be a pain. Being a perfectionist, he was well-known for the habit of making a "gruff" comment at the end of a piece he very much enjoyed. After profuse praises, he would write a sentence or so to raise a question in an attempt to deny the perfectness of the very perfection he had eagerly approved, as if he were afraid of spoiling a child by giving away the whole package. After reading Chapter One of my dissertation, which I had revised as thoroughly as I could to accommodate his suggestions, he raised a question in his memo sheet about something so minor that it was nearly irrelevant. He wrote, "Doesn't 'history' mean 'public history' anyway? Why do you feel the need to specify 'public history?'" He understood that the reason for the separation was crystal clear. I laughed and didn't bother to respond to him, knowing it was his style. In his letter of recommendation for me, I knew he had written the "lethal" clause for the same perfectionism that was one of his academic trademarks. Because my dissertation was in progress waiting to be revised, he believed it wasn't entirely cogent, and yet he had to say so.

It's the fault of the system, I thought. "If the system encourages professors to evaluate their graduate students' merits and faults honestly instead of dispensing routine praise, it would follow that Aaron's honesty be considered invaluable. It would not only help with the process of fair selection but also contribute to a positive outcome. It would even work on a candidate's behalf because it would enable the search committee to make a highly informed decision and to understand the candidate as a human being with shortcomings. But the whole process of applying for a job won't allow for such honesty. The system has to change, so that it could allow for honesty. But will it change when there are three-hundred candidates to choose one from?"

In October 1993, I was certain that Aaron abstained from such an honesty of his. Without one look at my dossier, I could tell that in all the letters, including Professor Johnson's, they were nothing but positive about my qualifications. I was hoping for a few MLA (Modern Language Association) interviews. These were the initial interviews that screened the handful of candidates chosen in paper by the search committees at colleges and universities, and I was prepared. December was the month during which the candidates were chosen for MLA interviews and were contacted on the phone. When the month arrived, I braced myself and checked the messages on my answering machine almost every hour. But as the month wore on, not one phone call came, and I found myself facing Christmas break alone again.

Instead of crying, I laughed maniacally. I grumbled incoherently as if I were insane, "Who said I'll get more interviews than any of the white male or female PhD candidates in the department because I'm an Asian female, a member of a protected group? My peers say that because they don't know what they're talking about. If being a woman of color gives me privileges like they so smugly predict, why am I not getting any news at all? If being a white male or female is such a disadvantage, why are they getting interviews, not me? The privilege they believe I have is a peanut, compared to the handicaps I suffer from. If they ever had a chance to experience all that racism I've endured, they'd never want to be in my shoes." Having heard that the English departments in America were desperate to fill the quotas for minority women, I couldn't believe what was happening to me. What I heard about minority women's privileges seemed like an ungrounded rumor, having never applied to me. It never gave me anything that could be remotely construed as special treatment.

And yet, several of my white male and female colleagues assumed that I was the one to get preference in hiring and that they were the ones to be pushed out by women such as myself. If I was ever hired by a school, they were going to instantly presume that it was thanks to my gender and race.

A white male peer of mine had told me, "I hate Affirmative Action when I'm a victim of it. I can't get a job because women and minorities are getting all the jobs I should be getting."

"Then, you've just started to feel how I've been feeling for the past three or four decades," I replied.

As he was hired for a tenure-track position several months earlier than I was, he never repeated his complaints about Affirmative Action to me again. I wondered if he had realized how mistaken he was about his prediction that I would be hired before he was. I wanted to ask every white male or female who entertained the notion that my gender and race was going to give me an upper hand in being hired, "Did your dissertation adviser ever tell you that he or she was going to nominate you for a Joan Davis Dissertation Award?" The Joan Davis Dissertation Award was given to a PhD recipient who wrote an outstanding dissertation. From what I understood, it wasn't given each year. It was given only once in several years because it was only awarded to truly phenomenal dissertations. Jane told me that she was going to nominate me for the award and that it would be given to me if I was selected during the summer graduation in August. "If I don't have a job by then," I said, "I'd be happy to attend the graduation ceremony to receive it. But if I have a job before the end of the summer, you won't need to bother. I wouldn't need the award because it wouldn't make any difference any more. Besides, I'll be moving and wouldn't be able to attend the summer commencement." For many months to come, I rewound this conversation in my mind to savor the glory of being mentioned for such an honor.

As the third week of December ended without a phone call, I gave up. I preferred to call it a kind resignation, wishing to be kind to myself for being rejected by so many schools. I didn't make the decision to put a permanent end to the job search, but it was time to stop my hopes of getting a job interview before the end of the year. I had to wait to look for job advertisements in the next year's MLA Job Bulletin or the Chronicle of Higher Education. On

December 22, just two days before Christmas, I emptied my suitcase and went to a video store to rent several movies at once. All of them were trashy Hollywood movies about sex and violence because I wanted to watch stupid stories with corny plots to be lost in stupor, to avoid having to think – and suffer. Surprisingly, a phone call came as if to prove the saying, "When you stop looking, it shows up." I got a phone call from a college in New Jersey that wanted to interview me in Toronto, Canada, where that year's MLA convention was being held. I could tell I wasn't a top candidate, being chosen as late as I was. But I couldn't afford not to go. I decided to take the chance and began to re-pack my suitcase.

It wasn't until I arrived at Newark Airport to change planes that I realized I had left my passport in my apartment. Initially, I had put it in my suitcase, but I had taken it out as I started to unpack, out of a fear of keeping it in the wrong place and losing it. It was a US passport because I was a naturalized US citizen, and I knew that once I lost it, it would take an inordinate amount of bureaucratic process to have it re-issued. I also knew that while waiting for a new passport to arrive for me, it would be difficult to prove my citizenship without a passport in my hand.

There are no words that can describe how I felt when I was told by the airline agent that I wasn't allowed to fly to Toronto. I was afraid I was going to have a heart attack, plopping down on one of those stark-looking black chairs in front of the gate.

"Toronto immigration inspects Asians with more scrutiny," the agent told me, bringing me a glass of water, "because there's a lot of illegal aliens from China."

"Now, Mother Nature is punishing me for being an Asian immigrant," I murmured, placing my hand over my mouth. I didn't want to be heard by anyone because I didn't want to be perceived as a crazy woman talking to herself, even though I *was* a crazy woman talking to herself. I had been a crazy woman for all those years in America, but nobody else except myself had seen it.

"Try to relax," the agent attempted to comfort me across the hall. "This isn't the end of your life. You'll have another job interview sooner than you'll ever know." I felt as if all the blood had been drained out of my body, and I thought she saw it.

Two hours after I was told I wasn't allowed to fly to Toronto, I managed to get a hold of the phone number of a friend and her husband who had moved a few years before to New York City from Lawrence, Kansas. After staying the night at a hotel near the airport, I called the couple to ask if I could stay in their apartment for a day or so, to which they responded with an eager yes. Then, upon arriving at their apartment, I called the manager of my apartment building in Lawrence to ask if he could enter my apartment and pick up my passport. I told him where it was and what pages to send to my friends' fax number, hoping to receive the pages with my photo and the information concerning my citizenship in an hour or so. But I learned on the following day that the faxed pages weren't going to work.

"Anyone can fake this sort of document," one of the airline agents said flatly. "You need your real passport." Again, I felt the familiar feeling of blood flowing out of my body. I couldn't even walk toward one of those ugly black chairs. I fell on the cold tile floor at the airport, making a thumping sound with my suitcase.

I will make the rest of the story as short as possible. I will say that I still pursued the possibility for an interview with the college with the focus of a cat chasing a mouse. First, I got hold of the phone number of the hotel in Toronto where Beverly, one of the search committee members who had initially called me for an interview, was staying, waiting to interview the other chosen candidates. Then, I successfully persuaded her to arrange an on-campus interview for me and the rest of the search committee on one of the days immediately after they got back from Toronto. And then, I called a friend in New Jersey to ask if I could stay in her house for a few days until the interview was over. Being within ten minutes of driving distance from the college, her house was a lot closer than my friend's apartment in New York. Finally, I invited Beverly out to lunch at a restaurant a couple days before the on-campus interview was scheduled to take place. I wanted to thank her for taking the trouble of arranging it for me.

Why I totally ruined my hard-earned chance at the interview remains an unsolved mystery to me to this day. After going through all that unbelievable trouble to have it arranged, I made a series of mistakes that can't be explained by anything within the realm of common sense. It was all the more uncanny, given the advantages Beverly graciously volunteered to offer me. During our lunch, she had given me invaluable information, including the questions that she thought were likely to be asked by the search committee, brief personal and professional profiles of the faculty who were to interview me, and the particular quirks of each faculty that might be helpful for me to keep in mind. The interview went so poorly that I didn't remember what their questions were at all when it was over. Nor did I remember what my answers were. All I could remember was the dreadful fact that I kept saying, "It's in my file," whenever I was unable to recall specific information about their questions. It was the worst kind of answer one could give at an interview, an answer telling of the candidate's incompetence and laziness. I knew perfectly well that when I didn't remember enough concrete facts, I should at least make the effort of gathering some speculation that could suggest possible answers. I also knew that no candidate could answer all the questions with all the specific data because nobody could or was expected to memorize everything concerning a subject. All that a candidate was required to do during an interview was to put together as much information as they could remember and then try to create a context in which this information was connected to reveal a consistent narrative continuity. And yet, I failed to do such. Instead of trying to create a context instantly, in which I was known to be an expert, I kept skipping from one point to another, missing the bridges between these points. My repeated confession about the information that escaped my memory, "It's in my file," failed to serve as these bridges. My presentation was like a big tapestry of facts that were loosely put together with frequent holes here and there. It wasn't a whole piece.

I knew I ruined my chance because my dream told me. In my dream that night, I was standing outside a house, a huge house of gables with multiple units and yards. It was a traditional Korean house during the Chosun Dynasty, a castle rather with one layer of low, round stone walls on the outside encompassing all the smaller houses on the inside. Separated without walls, the smaller houses inside were divided from one another by the yards with short pine trees and flower gardens, and some of these smaller houses were clustered together more closely to form a unit away from the others. It was the kind of house inhabited by a powerful noble clan that was often reproduced in Korean calendars, a house called by common folks as the "back of a whale" because it was so majestic. I was standing outside because I wasn't invited in.

I had another breakdown in January 1994. It lasted for a whole semester because, although I functioned enough to teach, I was seized by crying spells that assaulted me without warning anytime, anywhere. I cried at the sight of a young woman with a hat, I cried at the sight of a boy on a bicycle, and I cried at the sight of an old woman driving a car. Still, I refused to increase my dosage of the anti-depressants. With one pill of Zoloft and Klonopin each day, I wasn't yet at the very maximum, but I was afraid that if I increased the dosage each time my depression became worse, I might have to increase it again at another time. I was worried that in the near future, I might find myself totally dependent on the pills. What I wanted was help, not dependency.

I refused to increase my dosage because whether I admitted it to myself or not, I still had hope. I still felt I had reasons to be optimistic because someone somewhere would see my application and be impressed. I kept working. I kept revising the dissertation until it became as good as a dissertation could be, and finally succeeded in defending it in front of the five members of the dissertation defense committee, including the three who had participated in advising the writing and revising and the two who were selected ad hoc to read it and ask questions. From my memory, every one of us six individuals enjoyed it, engaged in a lively, provocative dialogue without any animosity. Having heard about some highly unpleasant dissertation defenses from some colleagues of mine, one of whom had actually told me that two members of her dissertation defense committee waged a prolonged fistfight of words during her defense, I was a bit worried. But nothing of that magnitude happened.

Even as I called the welfare office in town to find out if I was qualified to receive food stamps after my employment as a graduate teaching assistant was over, I wasn't without a streak of optimism. I was terribly distressed, as depressed as ever, but a ray of hope cut through the darkness to sever it in two, to help me fill the chasm with laughter. As April, the month of my dissertation defense, passed into May to finish the spring semester of 1994, I put a sign on the wall in my living room, "Stop waiting," hoping the wisdom of such advice would inspire me. "When you let it go, it comes" was the familiar wisdom I had heard all my life.

"Can I speak to Jid Lee, please?" It was a woman from Middle Tennessee State University, the last place one would think would be interested in a woman of color specializing in Asian-American women's literature.

"You're one of the few selected for a potential on-campus interview," she said as I confirmed I was the woman she was looking for. "I hope you get hired because I'm your Number One fan."

In a few days, another woman on the same search committee called to set up a date for my on-campus interview. But as the phone rang, I was in the bathroom, listening to her voice on my answering machine. I darted out of the bathroom to pick up the phone to say, "I'm sorry I was sitting on the pot."

As I heard loud laughter on the other end, I said again, "I'm sorry."

"Sorry for sitting on the pot?" she said, still laughing.

"Yes!" I said, laughing.

Apologizing for being on the toilet when she called was telling of my sense of humor, which was already common knowledge among the search committee. I could tell it was going to work to my advantage because it gave the committee members a chance to form a positive opinion about me, to think I was easy and fearless with strangers. I was as afraid as anyone of meeting new people and being misunderstood by them, but I was good at disguising this fear with a sense of humor.

I could relax because I knew I was going to get the job. Father told me on one of the nights following the phone call from the second person on the search committee. In my dream, he drove a jeep toward a burnt building, making that loud laughter of his, his eyes puckered with long wrinkles reaching down to his cheeks. He showed me a burnt building topped with soaring black smoke to tell me that the game was over, that the job was mine. Fire is a symbol of prosperity in Korean dream interpretation. The building was already burnt out before he started to drive toward it because the outcome was a done deal.

Determined to avoid the mistake I had made at the college in New Jersey, I was somewhat over-prepared for the interview. I not only answered the questions from the search committee with specific, detailed information but also offered concrete suggestions to enrich the curriculum of the English Department and Women's Studies. As my presentation came to the point where I had to explain the roles of the civil rights and women's movement for some of my authors, I deliberately cracked a joke, "As a feminist, I don't want to engage in male-bashing, but it helps," to cause a ripple of hearty laughter among the audience. Knowing the power of humor, I set my joke directly against the very serious points I had been building up. At the end of the interview, I emphasized that I didn't want to be hired because I was a woman of color. I said I wanted to join my prospective colleagues because they believed I was the one with the best qualifications. Then, I added an essential point – that I thought I could help the university to achieve more diversity because what I taught and researched came from my firsthand experience, not from my secondhand knowledge.

In mid-June, the chair of the department called me. He told me that making a job offer to a candidate was his favorite thing to do. Just like misery, joy loves company, and I received another phone call from a friend in the English Department at KU, who asked if I was, for the month of July, willing to teach pre-college English for minority students who were going to attend schools in the health professions. I responded with an eager yes, as I was ready to file my dissertation away after correcting a few minor errors.

If there ever was an extended period of *being* in my life of thirty-eight years, it was in the month and a half during which I taught English to the minority students while putting a finishing touch on the dissertation. I was moving as fast as ever, having to finish everything on time and preparing to move, but I was free from the rushing sense of having to *become*, from the imminent threat of successive deadlines and being constantly evaluated by everyone. For the first time in decades, I felt I owned my life instead of having it owned by those with the power to decide my professional fate. Routines with hard work no longer seemed to be challenges against adversities. They seemed to be merely days going by to keep me in the plateaued cycle of habits. Driving through the vast wheat fields of Kansas in my brand new Honda civic, I wasn't looking for a reprieve from the breakneck work schedule. I was looking for an open space to breathe deep and feel how big the world was outside my home. I wanted to smell the grass. I knew I had bought a brand new car to help me to *live and work,* not just to work.

I loaded the car with my books. Being a hatch back, the small car could hold a lot more than it seemed capable of. Although I had never kept a whole lot of books in my stacks, they added up to be a carload because I decided to throw out everything except the Korean titles I couldn't purchase in America. Even the ones with my handwritten notes were going to be dumped because I had always believed that the knowledge in my head was sufficient for a knowledgeable life. English was my Bohemian because I was a bohemian at heart, and Bohemian was my only language. Every book I had read and was going to read was to have a temporary stay in my mind.

Perhaps, I didn't even need the knowledge in my head. All that I needed, I thought, was the innate wisdom, no matter how little, that I was born with. At thirty-eight, after all the studying that had nearly made my eyes go out on me, it occurred to me that nothing of what I had learned from books was going to be of any use to me. I found myself wishing to be a disciple of Wonhyo, the greatest—yes, the greatest—Buddhist monk who has ever lived in the five-thousand-year history of Korea. An avid reader and a prolific writer on Buddhism, Wonhyo, one day suddenly, forsook all the learnings he had accumulated in schools to follow the path that was shown to him purely by an accident. On his way to China one night in the year of 661, he collapsed under a low dirt hut during a severe rainstorm, utterly exhausted. He managed to grab a round bowl that felt like a gourd in the pitch dark, and he placed it flat on the ground to gather the rainwater to quench his thirst. Upon waking in the morning, however, he saw that the container he had thought was a gourd was a human skull, shocked to realize that he had drunk the water in the head of an old corpse. The water, the sweetest thing that his mouth had ever tasted, was in fact the ugliest thing that his eyes had ever seen. He was enlightened as if struck by thunder.

Everything is in my mind, he said to himself, turning to go back home. *I was in a grave, but I thought I was in a hut. I was in a hut.*

He no longer felt the need to study in China, having discovered the secret to wise living. He revolutionized the Buddhism that was popular in Shilla, his tribal kingdom of the 7th-century, and made Buddhism available to people from all walks of life, including the uneducated masses from the lowest social classes. Buddhism in Shilla back then was the privilege of the nobility, closed to common citizens who couldn't read the scriptures because they were accessible only to the elite few. Travelling all over the country, Wonhyo communicated with the illiterate, with slaves and servants, with the lowly and the poor, and with the abandoned and the outcasts. In easy language, he explained the scriptures to them, exchanged dialogues with them about how to walk on the road to enlightenment. They were his equal. They were him. Wonhyo spread the gist of Buddhism into every corner of his country, the concept that made Buddhism the most democratic religion that has ever been created by humankind – the concept, the truth that there was no *distinction* between human beings of any kind. *Because he no longer felt it was necessary to read books, he read so many books*, I thought. *Because he no longer felt it was necessary to write books, he wrote numerous books.*

I drove the car to Clinton Lake, where I used to go to take a break from work, to dump all the books into the water. I wanted to have them drowned out by the vast depths and make them sink into the bottom where they would dissolve away, becoming part of the dirt upholding the water. It was the least I could do for the lake that had given me so much by being so indispensable. Taking ginger steps on the nearly flat levy of rocks, dragging a sack loaded with books, I realized I would miss the lake more than anything else in Kansas. It was a place where I routinely came to crave a sense of being nothing and everything, where I wanted to feel how infinitesimal I was and how infinite the universe was. As I parked on the wide-open spot right beside the state highway and lay on top of my big old clunker to watch the stars in the night, I felt strangely fearless. I knew I could be robbed or raped or even killed because the area surrounding the lake was pitch black with no lights. But as long as I was in a zen state of mind, I felt nothing could hurt me.

I recited the zen koan made famous by a Korean Buddhist monk, "A mountain is a mountain and water is water," trying to chant my interpretation of its meanings until they became nearly memorized. "A mountain is huge, made of a million various elements," I sang, "and all these elements are incredibly small. They're rocks of many sizes, soils of numerous kinds, trees of numberless heights, waters of innumerable components, and stones of countless shapes. Against the whole mountain, each of these elements is so small that it's nearly non-existent, but the mountain can't be there if anyone of them was missing. Each of these elements is significant enough to make the whole although it's insignificant enough to be only a tiny segment of the whole. And against an endless ocean, buckets of water are invisible, but an endless ocean itself is made of invisible, trivial ounces of water. If a cup is missing, and if another cup is missing, and if the missing of these cups continues, the ocean will be dried up eventually. And every drop of this water contains all the ingredients of the ocean." Arriving at my summation, I said, "The earth is made of soil and water. Soil is separate from the earth, and the earth is separate from the soil. But together, they make a whole. Without one or the other, the whole can't exist."

Watching the sky in the night, I created my own zen koan in imitation of the one given by the famous Korean Buddhist monk, "The sky is the sky and a star is a star." Compared to the sky of which the beginning and the end were unknowable, the stars were merely a minute cog of the wheel that was instantly knowable. But every one of those stars took part in making the sky, unimportant but indispensable at once. With even one of the innumerable stars gone, the sky wouldn't be the same as it was. Or, even if only one of the stars was gone, the sky would be in trouble because of the orbits made awry by what was lost. "I'm one of the stars," I said. "I'm enormously important because the sky wouldn't be the same without me, but I'm hugely invisible because I'm only the smallest component of the sky."

I went on, meditating about my work, "I've given everything I've got, except my soul, to my work. What a staggering achievement it is because without it, the academe would be without one of the most uniquely qualified individuals who can bring a fresh breath to her colleagues and students! And yet, what a trivial success it is because without it, higher education would lose no more than one from among fifty-thousand PhDs! It would lose one who can be replaced by another chosen from ten-thousand English PhDs. My work is invaluable because the academe won't be able to find anyone exactly like me, but it's of little value because it'll have few problems finding someone with the same areas of specialization. I mean everything and nothing at once to the world."

The books I dropped into the lake floated on the water. Riding on the waves, they rushed leisurely toward the other end of the shore, and I envisioned them eventually sinking down to the bottom to become part of the soil. But most likely, they would float on until all the pages became torn, eaten by the water, and the colorful covers were faded by the raw sunlight to become thin rags of paper. Perhaps, they would reach the other end of the lake, and someone would pick them up and read my handwritten notes in the margins. Or possibly, a lone duck, isolated from the rest of the crowd, would look at them and wonder what they were. The books would keep him company.

By the beginning of August, I was ready to file my dissertation away, but Jane put a break on it. Knowing I was under severe time pressure to finish everything before leaving, she insisted that I modify one of the mechanic formats of the dissertation to make it look visually pleasant. Because the footnotes were at the bottom of the pages and the computer had to make adjustments to make room for the footnotes, some of the pages had a large blank space between the main content and the footnotes while most pages didn't have nearly as much blank space. This resulted in printing some odd-looking pages that looked ugly to her, and to get rid of these pages, she told me to gather all the footnotes at the end section of the book. After trying in vain to persuade her to spare me from the time-consuming computer chore because it was only a matter of appearance, I yielded. She believed the dissertation was as much her baby as it was mine and wanted to make it as good-looking as it was good reading. I had to devote a full week of the two weeks I had left to give it the face lift she desired.

Over the next few months, I came to laugh at how foolish her request was, but I also came to realize how much of her expensive time she must have spent on reading and commenting on my writing. I was in fact flattered that she felt the dissertation was as much hers as it was mine. I believed she deserved far more from me than a mere thank you. I took down one of the prized masks on the wall of my apartment in Murfreesboro, Tennessee, carefully packed it, and mailed it to her home with a short note reading, "When I give someone something I've cherished for a long time, it means I want to give them a piece of my energy. This mask is a part of me."

It was the face of a character named Clever Servant, one of those delightful characters in Korean mask plays who, as members of a severely disempowered group, learned to master the skills of operating underground and pulling tricks on the highly empowered ones. Aware of his master's every secret, the Clever Servant exercises a mysterious power over him, and can manipulate him to the point where the master has to do whatever he wants him to do in order to preserve his face and appearance. Furtive and subservient, yet innocent and proud, the Clever Servant himself is as two-faced as the master. But certainly, he is the more intelligent of the two, endowed with marvelously surreptitious wisdom that can instantly read unspoken dynamics between individuals. He smiles like a fool, but he perceives like a genius. When he laughs, everything in his face laughs – except his clever, observant eyes. Jane was going to love the mask and my explanation of the character.

As I developed the same perfectionism with which she had steered my work for several years, I became very much like her. Over these years, I grew to foster the same high standards with which she had taught her students in her classrooms, and the same attitude that suggested a belief that literature has the power to change the world because it shows the complexities of human nature. As far as I could tell, none of her numerous students and disciples, graduate and undergraduate alike, were afraid to call her at home, and few of them showed any hesitation in seeking her help. I myself called her at home whenever I needed her, and she was never less than glad to hear from me. She was known for never saying no to anyone, no matter how many people wanted to work with her. Jane was one of those selfless women who gave a piece of herself to everyone who asked for it.

I went one step further in emulating her. I adopted two cats and delighted in watching them crouching on my desk, flanking both sides of my laptop. I pictured her with her two cats competing to jump on top of her computer. As she probably was, I was made aware of my body by my cats. By touching me with so much love and trust, they put me in touch with the importance of cherishing the physicality of my being. Touching my cats' backs, I could also return to a state of simplicity in which I was grateful to be alive and be able to feel in my hands the shining silky fur, the perfect beauty created by no more than food and water. Mentally, I had a chance to be back to the world of the cats in which the very basics sustaining my body were enough to make me feel alive.

But I wasn't nearly as dedicated to my students as Jane was, far from as giving as she was with my energy and time. Ruthlessly efficient in screening candidates for my friendship—for what little I had in my heart for another human being—I refused to grant an entrance into my life to anyone who couldn't offer me anything new to learn. Having made myself into a selfish monster in an effort to be an unselfish votary devoted to seeking the magic of words, I eventually put an end to the process of investing myself in individuals who became demanding of my emotional energy for nothing fulfilling in return. To this day, I'm afraid I never will be a desired carbon copy of my former mentor in terms of the ability to give.

More vain than Jane, I face the mirror more often than she probably does. I crave to look both sexual and feminine, always letting my hair down to cover half of my back, wearing a skirt baring part of my calves. I admit I am exceedingly proud of the shape of my legs, and I want to show them off to whoever I can. Didn't Jane used to put on nice skirts revealing her long, slender legs? I never forget to apply some makeup before I go to my classes, as she rarely forgot when she came to campus for work. With my makeup, I try to create some cubic impression in my rather flat Asian face, as she probably tried to make the angular features of her white face look less cubic. We both did the same thing, I believe, trying to accentuate the beauty in our very different faces by emphasizing the pleasant contours.

It took a while to give away what little I owned in my apartment in Lawrence, Kansas. "When you want to get rid of what you have," I grumbled, laughing, "you suddenly find out you have a lot more than you thought you did." I wasn't selective at all about whom I gave my furniture to. There wasn't much and what I had was cheap. But I was picky about who I let have my plants. All dozen or so in the living room and the bedroom were so marvelous as to earn my utmost admiration during the nine years of my graduate studies. Alive and well, breathing deep and soaring high, they grew such rich foliage with so little given to them. I often flattered myself by thinking that it was my classical music, particularly Mahler's Symphony Number 1, that gave them the inspiration to flourish under the care of such a poor, negligent graduate student. I wanted to give them to someone who would behold them with the same astonishment, and I found one such person shortly before leaving.

There were two things I left in Lawrence, Kansas. One of them was the pot of morning glories on the balcony of my apartment. I didn't dare to remove it because I would have had to cut its stem loose from the bars on the edge of the balcony, along with the flowers and leaves tightly entangled around them. I couldn't bring myself to kill the living thing that kept climbing up the metal bars in order to rise to a higher place, the energy in the little tree-like life that strove to greet the morning sun by making flowers. I took out an index card from my stack to write a note for the next tenant, "Please water this friend," and used a piece of scotch tape to attach it on a spot right above the pot on the metal bars.

The second thing I left in town was by mistake. Or maybe, it wasn't a mistake. It was entirely possible that I secretly wanted to leave it where I left it, longing, in spite of myself, to leave a trace of me for someone to see. It was a box of miscellaneous items containing a batch of my students' theme papers, a few Christmas cards from some colleagues of mine, a memo pad or so with handwritten to-do-lists, a couple pieces of napkin from the campus cafeteria, and a prized photo of my niece that I had attached on the wall in front of my desk. All of these were in the office I had shared with two other graduate teaching assistants, and they had to be taken out before another one moved in to take my desk. I gathered them in a cardboard box and placed them beside my desk. I planned to take them home to decide which to keep and which to throw out, but I forgot. I suppose I was taken by the same longing that takes some of those mountain climbers who stop on their way to carve their names on the trees. Longing to leave something of me behind, I perhaps gathered my things in the box and deliberately forgot to remove it. I wanted to be seen by someone who was totally unknown to me and who never knew anything of me.

Chapter 22
The House of My Future

With only a carload to carry, I expected a painless drive. Having moved my futon into the hatchback, I spread my sleeping bag on the floor and fell asleep comfortably. As most Koreans do, I preferred to sleep on a hard surface. I was certain that no matter how long I lived in America, I was going to choose to sleep on a futon or on the floor that was separated from my body by no more than a thin blanket. In motels where I found the bed too soft for my comfort, I made my own bed on the floor. I placed the sheet on the carpet to serve as a mattress. "What a shabby way of sleeping!" a friend of mine once told me jokingly, and I responded as jokingly, "I'm a peasant from Korea. I'm not a civilized American like you."

I would have told her that even in my dreams, I was a humble Korean woman who slept on the floor and lived in a shanty house. As if to remind me, I was indeed back to being this humble Korean woman in my dreams the night before my move to Tennessee, in the very few hours before I was to start a glorious new life in the civilized country with a civilized American PhD. It wasn't the spacy, sumptuous house with fancy furniture where I saw myself watching my own dead body. It was a shack, wide and long without a window, with nobody dead or alive, with no furniture except a wooden desk upon which was placed a pair of ugly, thick glasses with a black plastic frame. I wasn't exactly terrified, but I was nearly conquered by a feeling of emptiness splitting my stomach into two pieces, unable to move. The only thing that seemed to be of me in the house was the eyeglasses, but they were nothing of me because they were un-wearable with one of their temples missing. I let out a smothered scream at the dark gray walls, hearing the silent echoes reverberating through the snow-white ceiling that was so high that it made the big house look even more hollow and barren.

Waking up, I shuddered. Instinctively, I knew the dream was about what was going to be my life in the new place awaiting me. It was the house of my future. In the part of me buried under the layers of my thick masks, I could tell I was going to find myself in the same old cycle—the everlasting repetition of being hurt by the same old racism, of forgiving, of being the receiver of the sinners' efforts to make an atonement, and of growing more fully human in the process. *I was going to be treated as a Korean English professor, not as an English professor*. I was going to be surprised over and over again by what had stopped surprising me many years before—by the painful fact that anyone, even the most enlightened individual in whom I placed total trust, was capable of turning on me with the weapon of racism they didn't know they possessed. For as long as I could see, in the eyes of those around me, I was going to be that peasant Korean woman living in a shack.

Or maybe, the dream was about who I was to my own people at home, about a woman who had no choice but to make a shabby home in an alien country. I wasn't one of those men returning home with the glory of an achievement, with a PhD that was going to be eagerly embraced by an institution in Korea and to open doors of prestige for him and his family. I was one of those women because I was certain that there was more than one woman such as myself somewhere in the world, in whose life an anti-depressant was a necessity and chronic fatigue was a daily occurrence.

It was a man, a Korean man, who once said to me, "Why can't you be the one sacrificed on the cross? Why do these women, these independent women so to speak, complain about inequalities? If they aren't happy with their choices, why do they live with them?" I felt an impulse to stab him with my tongue, the occasional sharpness of which was notorious among the ones who were unfortunate enough to be its recipients.

But astonishingly, I found myself returning with the smile of a wise old woman, "If you could say the same thing to the men who're brave and happy enough to stay married to those independent women, you may be not only justified but also entitled to say so. If you were one of these brave and happy men, I'd praise you for putting yourself on the cross along with your wife, for living with your choice well enough."

As the anti-depressant I had taken in the morning put me into the usual spell of afternoon drowsiness, I pulled the car over onto the shoulder and stopped. To erase the whizzing sounds of the cars cruising by, I cranked up the volume of the CD player as high as it would go, registering the marvels of the allegro second movement of Mahler's Symphony Number 5. *Loneliness has its privileges*, I thought. Because I am a woman, I believed I was happy to abstain from the temptation of wielding the sharp side of my tongue upon the self-righteous Korean man and could instead use its soft, loving side.

With the help of the anti-depressant, I was able to steer my thoughts until I could bring them to the emotional plateau I wanted to construct. My life after all was made of routines of seeing the other side. I started to count one by one the beautiful end results of the loneliness I had endured during my fourteen years in America. I thought I now had in my possession the skills with which I could try to deliver beautiful prose. Although far from the level I envisioned, my composition had begun to pass from being correct into being lyrical. Being able to command a spectrum of nuanced shades between words of the same meanings, I was ready to embody the complex concepts jammed in my head in clear, effective language. As an adult would look back at her childhood and laugh, I reminisced over how I used to write. "Henry James and Edith Wharton," I recited from my memory, "were friends united by their common desire to find a land where they could discover who they were, enjoy their writing lives, and experiment with words and artistic lifestyles, and where they could avoid the vulgar materialism of their native country that was defined by money and commercialism and therefore made them flee…" I heard Mahler's symphonics for a reason. I heard them because I thought that if I could transpose his sounds into words on printed pages, I could render the most complicated expressions of a soul in the most sophisticated language. Now, I was prepared to go on the journey toward this language. I was ready to go through another spell of nightmares to make my dreams possible. The nightmares, so heavy that they had made my glasses lose one of their temples, were going to carry me toward the final destination where this language was waiting for me.

Getting back onto I-70, somewhere in the middle of Missouri, I seemed to have forgotten what I had decided to think. I muttered in a spasm of fury, "I'm deluding myself. I convince myself of the privileges of loneliness because loneliness is all I've got. The joy of solitude, or what I think as such, is nothing but the work of the happy drug in my brain." Back to the usual cycle of what was bitter reality and what I was to make of this bitter reality, I went on with my relentless self-mockery, "You comfort yourself by believing you have more than those men to whom much more is given. You're just like a poor person who chooses to feel she has a better life than a rich person because she doesn't have much to spend and so she has simpler wants. Look squarely at your life in America. You're the one who got hurt in the process of you and your friends and mentors growing more fully human. They were the ones with the weapon of racism and you were the one on the receiving end. They suffered as well, from their guilt and efforts they made to make it up to you, but it's you who have earned chronic fatigue syndrome, you who have to bear with the clinical depression that got worse over the years. And yet, you're happy to issue a pardon for them in your mind because you know they had good intentions. You absolve them because you believe they were victims of their own prejudices."

I retorted to myself, "Don't accuse me of being a hypocrite. I'm truly grateful to those friends and mentors who helped me to achieve my life goals. Without them, I wouldn't be where I am. No words could be more sincere than the two in the 'Thank you' that I offer to them." As a matter of truth, no words in the world could be more sincere than the pair that made this simple sentence. In a way, my mentors and friends at KU weren't so dissimilar to my family. Just as my family loved me very much but still followed the ways of brutal Korean patriarchy, my mentors and friends at KU cared very much about me but still followed the ways of brutal American racism. As my family were the ones who gave me the weapons with which I could criticize their sexism, my mentors and friends at KU were the ones who equipped me with the weapons with which I could criticize their racism. I loved them all. As my family were the angels and the devils sitting on my shoulders forever, my mentors and friends were to be the angels and the devils with whom I was destined to grapple for an eternity. The angels on one side of my shoulder would win the war eventually, but the devils on the other side would continue to surge, and I would be perpetually ready to fight.

Passing through the heavy traffic by St. Louis was a challenge. Lost in another debate with myself, I was afraid I may cause an accident. So many times, I had failed to pay attention and provoked another driver's fury by suddenly turning into the right lane to avoid missing an exit. Gripping the wheel with deadly firmness, I almost microscopically measured the distance between me and all the other cars around me. I scrutinized every little and big sign on the road as if I were trying to spot the tiniest germs stuck on it.

Swearing to the gods that I will not ever repeat the habit of the wheel-monologue, I found myself again in the throes of my ancient woe. "Driving will never be an instinctive part of life for me like it is for most Americans. It'll always be a challenge for me. It'll forever remind me that I'm not from this country."

I heard myself letting out the listless laugh I had heard before, a laugh like the sound of a large, hissing plastic ball that had been punctured. It was the sound escaping me at the end of a powerful frustration over which I was to remain powerless. I said, "Driving is only one of those things that'll remind you, one of those small things compared to many other big things. Something much larger will always try to remind you that you're not from here. Something much bigger indeed – didn't it actually take place recently?"

Something much bigger did take place right before I left Kansas. Dr. Hayward, the Dean of the Liberal Arts College at Kansas University, paid me only two thirds of the salary I was initially scheduled to receive for teaching English to pre-college students headed for the health professions. Had it not been for the friend who had offered me the job and later told me about it, I wouldn't have known how he had cheated me so blind.

"I can't believe how racist Dr. Hayward is," she said. "He gave more money to the graduate teaching assistant in math, to the white woman who taught math to the same students you taught this summer for the same amount of hours. She was far from finishing her PhD, but you'd already finished yours. Your qualifications were far superior, but he arbitrarily changed the amounts to give her more – to give you less, rather. I don't know why, but I can tell he was motivated by personal reasons, one of which was racism."

My instant response was laughter—the rage under the mask—and I said, "He may have a vendetta against me. He might've heard from someone that I wasn't terribly fond of William Faulkner, his idol, or he might've picked up a negative opinion of me from an acquaintance. Or he may even feel guilty because once, he promised to write a letter of recommendation for me and never kept his word. In fact, he lied to me twice, which I found out from the woman gathering applications for the dissertation fellowship I applied for. She said she'd never received a letter for me from him even after she'd sent me a card to remind me that one of the three letters I was supposed to have included in my application package was missing – even after I'd told him about her card and asked him to resend his letter. He lied to me for the first time when he initially agreed to send his letter, and he lied to me for the second time when he said he'll resend it. I wouldn't be surprised if he'd tried to turn his own guilt on me and resented me for having asked him. You never know about people. But no matter what his feelings were toward me, he had no right to be so unfair."

As I was leaving Missouri for Tennessee, I was fuming with indignation. I was bracing for the series of unfair treatments that I could foretell would beleaguer me at my new campus in Tennessee. As clearly as I could see the road signs ahead of me, I could see what lay in store for me. All that was in my past was merely a harbinger of all that was to be in my future. I knew I was going to be on the same everlasting journey during which I, finding myself under the gun of racism, was made to persevere, to denounce when my turn came, and to issue a pardon eventually because those who had turned on me with the weapon of racism were in fact my colleagues, friends, and my students whom I couldn't bring myself to hate, some of whom I couldn't even stop loving. In the process, I could tell I was going to be nearly murdered by my chronic fatigue and clinical depression.

But I was going to endure and continue to look for the America that was mine, to listen to the sounds of my America that were made of the laughter and tears of immigrants in search of the same America I had come to. I was on my way toward No Name State, the country that was still alive in the minds of my fellow Americans. I was going to tell my fellow Americans how to get there, and to tell them how to get there, I would see again and again the dead woman in my nightmares and the living woman in my dreams. Weren't my dreams made possible by my nightmares?